FREE DVD   **FREE**   **FREE DVD**

CMA Exam DVD from Trivium Test Prep!

Dear Customer,

Thank you for purchasing from Trivium Test Prep! We're honored to help you prepare for your exam.

To show our appreciation, we're offering a **FREE *CMA Essential Test Tips* DVD by Trivium Test Prep**. Our DVD includes 35 test preparation strategies that will make you successful on you exam. All we ask is that you email us your feedback and describe your experience with our product. Amazing, awful, or just so-so: we want to hear what you have to say!

To receive your **FREE *CMA Essential Test Tips* DVD**, please email us at 5star@triviumtestprep.com. Include "Free 5 Star" in the subject line and the following information in your email:

1. The title of the product you purchased.
2. Your rating from 1 – 5 (with 5 being the best).
3. Your feedback about the product, including how our materials helped you meet your goals and ways in which we can improve our products.
4. Your full name and shipping address so we can send your **FREE *CMA Essential Test Tips* DVD**.

If you have any questions or concerns please feel free to contact us directly at 5star@triviumtestprep.com. Thank you!

- Trivium Test Prep Team

CMA Exam Preparation Study Guide 2019 – 2020

CMA Exam Prep Review and Practice Questions for the Certified Medical Assistant Exam

Copyright © 2018 by Trivium Test Prep

ALL RIGHTS RESERVED. By purchase of this book, you have been licensed one copy for personal use only. No part of this work may be reproduced, redistributed, or used in any form or by any means without prior written permission of the publisher and copyright owner.

American Association of Medical Assistants was not involved in the creation or production of this product, is not in any way affiliated with Trivium Test Prep, and does not sponsor or endorse this product. All test names (and their acronyms) are trademarks of their respective owners. This study guide is for general information and does not claim endorsement by any third party.

TABLE OF CONTENTS

I. ANATOMY AND PHYSIOLOGY

Anatomy and Physiology - - - - - - 7
The Integumentary System - - - - - - 11
The Musculoskeletal System - - - - - - 17
The Respiratory System - - - - - - 29
The Cardiovascular System - - - - - 35
The Female Reproductive System - - - - - 43
The Male Reproductive System - - - - - 51
The Urinary System - - - - - - - 57
The Digestive System - - - - - - 63
The Hemic and Lymphatic Systems - - - - 69
The Endocrine System - - - - - - 75
The Nervous System - - - - - - - 81
The Senses - - - - - - - - 87

II. PSYCHOLOGY

General Concepts - - - - - - - - 95
Behavioral Theories - - - - - - - 97
Death and Dying - - - - - - - - 101

III. PROFESSIONALISM

General Concepts - - - - - - - - 107
Job Readiness and Seeking Employment - - - - 111

IV. COMMUNICATIONS, LAWS AND PRIVACY

General Communications Concepts	115
Legal Requirements and Guidelines	121
Medical Records and Privacy	127
Responsibilities, Rights and Ethics	131

V. ADMINISTRATIVE CONCEPTS

General Computer Concepts	135
Records Management	139
Mail Administration and Scheduling Appointments	143
Resource Information and Community Services	147
Office Policies, Procedures and Protocols	149
Financial Management	153
Coding	161
Accounting and Banking Procedures	169

VI. CLINICAL CONCEPTS

Infection Control	173
Environmental Safety	181
The Treatment Area	185
Patient Preparation and Assisting the Physician	193
Preparing and Administering Medications	209
Emergencies	215
Nutrition and Oral Hydration	223
VII. PRACTICE QUESTIONS	227
VII. EXCLUSIVE TEST TIPS	282

Exclusive Trivium Test Prep Test Tips and Study Strategies

Here at Trivium Test Prep, we strive to offer you the exemplary test tools that help you pass your exam the first time. This book includes an overview of important concepts, example questions throughout the text, and practice test questions. But we know that learning how to successfully take a test can be just as important as learning the content being tested. In addition to excelling on the CMA Exam we want to give you the solutions you need to be successful every time you take a test. Our study strategies, preparation pointers, and test tips will help you succeed as you take the CMA Exam and any test in the future!

Study Strategies

1. Spread out your studying. By taking the time to study a little bit every day, you strengthen your understanding of the testing material, so it's easier to recall that information on the day of the test. Our study guides make this easy by breaking up the concepts into sections with example practice questions, so you can test your knowledge as you read.

2. Create a study calendar. The sections of our book make it easy to review and practice with example questions on a schedule. Decide to read a specific number of pages or complete a number of practice questions every day. Breaking up all of the information in this way can make studying less overwhelming and more manageable.

3. Set measurable goals and motivational rewards. Follow your study calendar and reward yourself for completing reading, example questions, and practice problems and tests. You could take yourself out after a productive week of studying or watch a favorite show after reading a chapter. Treating yourself to rewards is a great way to stay motivated.

4. Use your current knowledge to understand new, unfamiliar concepts. When you learn something new, think about how it relates to something you know really well. Making connections between new ideas and your existing understanding can simplify the learning process and make the new information easier to remember.

5. Make learning interesting! If one aspect of a topic is interesting to you, it can make an entire concept easier to remember. Stay engaged and think about how concepts covered on the exam can affect the things you're interested in. The sidebars throughout the text offer additional information that could make ideas easier to recall.

6. Find a study environment that works for you. For some people, absolute silence in a library results in the most effective study session, while others need the background noise of a coffee shop to fuel productive studying. There are many websites that generate white noise and recreate the sounds of different environments for studying. Figure out what distracts you and what engages you and plan accordingly.

7. Take practice tests in an environment that reflects the exam setting. While it's important to be as comfortable as possible when you study, practicing taking the test exactly as you'll take it on test day will make you more prepared for the actual exam. If your test starts on a Saturday morning, take your practice test on a Saturday morning. If you have access, try to find an empty classroom that has desks like the desks at testing center. The more closely you can mimic the testing center, the more prepared you'll feel on test day.

8. Study hard for the test in the days before the exam, but take it easy the night before and do something relaxing rather than studying and cramming. This will help decrease anxiety, allow you to get a better night's sleep, and be more mentally fresh during the big exam. Watch a light-hearted movie, read a favorite book, or take a walk, for example.

Preparation Pointers

1. Preparation is key! Don't wait until the day of your exam to gather your pencils, calculator, identification materials, or admission tickets. Check the requirements of the exam as soon as possible. Some tests require materials that may take more time to obtain, such as a passport-style photo, so be sure that you have plenty of time to collect everything. The night before the exam, lay out everything you'll need, so it's all ready to go on test day! We recommend at least two forms of ID, your admission ticket or confirmation, pencils, a high protein, compact snack, bottled water, and any necessary medications. Some testing centers will require you to put all of your supplies in a clear plastic bag. If you're prepared, you will be less stressed the morning of, and less likely to forget anything important.

2. If you're taking a pencil-and-paper exam, test your erasers on paper. Some erasers leave big, dark stains on paper instead of rubbing out pencil marks. Make sure your erasers work for you and the pencils you plan to use.

3. Make sure you give yourself your usual amount of sleep, preferably at least 7 – 8 hours. You may find you need even more sleep. Pay attention to how much you sleep in the days before the exam, and how many hours it takes for you to feel refreshed. This will allow you to be as sharp as possible during the test and make fewer simple mistakes.

4. Make sure to make transportation arrangements ahead of time, and have a backup plan in case your ride falls through. You don't want to be stressing about how you're going to get to the testing center the morning of the exam.

5. Many testing locations keep their air conditioners on high. You want to remember to bring a sweater or jacket in case the test center is too cold, as you never know how hot or cold the testing location could be. Remember, while you can always adjust for heat by removing layers, if you're cold, you're cold.

Test Tips

1. Go with your gut when choosing an answer. Statistically, the answer that comes to mind first is often the right one. This is assuming you studied the material, of course, which we hope you have done if you've read through one of our books!

2. For true or false questions: if you genuinely don't know the answer, mark it true. In most tests, there are typically more true answers than false answers.

3. For multiple-choice questions, read ALL the answer choices before marking an answer, even if you think you know the answer when you come across it. You may find your original "right" answer isn't necessarily the best option.

4. Look for key words: in multiple choice exams, particularly those that require you to read through a text, the questions typically contain key words. These key words can help the test taker choose the correct answer or confuse you if you don't recognize them. Common keywords are: *most*, *during*, *after*, *initially*, and *first*. Be sure you identify them before you read the available answers. Identifying the key words makes a huge difference in your chances of passing the test.

5. Narrow answers down by using the process of elimination: after you understand the question, read each answer. If you don't know the answer right away, use the process of elimination to narrow down the answer choices. It is easy to identify at least one answer that isn't correct. Continue to narrow down the choices before choosing the answer you believe best fits the question. By following this process, you increase your chances of selecting the correct answer.

6. Don't worry if others finish before or after you. Go at your own pace, and focus on the test in front of you.

7. Relax. With our help, we know you'll be ready to conquer the CMA Exam. You've studied and worked hard!

Keep in mind that every individual takes tests differently, so strategies that might work for you may not work for someone else. You know yourself best and are the best person to determine which of these tips and strategies will benefit your studying and test taking. Best of luck as you study, test, and work toward your future!

I. ANATOMY AND PHYSIOLOGY

GENERAL CONCEPTS

Anatomy and Physiology are the studies of body parts and body systems. This section will cover all necessary medical terms, word parts and terminology, as well as the anatomy and physiology of each body system.

Directional Terms

- Superior - Toward the head, or toward the upper body region
- Inferior - Toward the lower body region
- Anterior (Ventral) - On the belly or front side of the body
- Posterior (Dorsal) - On the buttocks or back side of the body
- Proximal - Near the trunk or middle part of the body
- Distal - Furthest away from the point of reference
- Medial - Close to the midline of the body
- Lateral - Away from the midline of the body

Word Parts

A medical term often has three parts: the prefix, the root, and suffix.

- Prefix - Begins the word, modifies the root, and not a part of all medical terms.
  Example: hyperactive; hyper- modifies the word active.

- Root - Center part of the word, holds meaning, and is often referred to as the "body" of the word.
  Example: Tonsillectomy; tonsil is the root word.

- Suffix - Ends the word, modifies the root, refers to a procedure, action, or condition, and is not part of all medical terms.
  Example: Vasectomy; -ectomy modifies the root word vas.

Prefixes

- epi-   on/upon
- hyper-   over
- hypo-   under
- intra-   within
- para-   beside
- per-   through
- peri-   surrounding
- sub-   under

Suffixes

- -coccus   spherical bacterium
- -ia   condition
- -ectomy   removal
- -malacia   softening
- -tome   an instrument to cut
- -tomy   to cut
- -rrhea   discharge
- -plasty   surgical repair
- -opsy   view of

Combining Forms

- aden/o   in relationship to a gland
- adip/o   fat
- albin/o   white
- aut/o   self
- cauter/o   burn
- crypt/o   hidden
- derm/o   skin
- diaphor/o   sweating
- erythem/o   red
- ichthy/o   dry/scaly
- kerat/o   hard
- jaund/o   yellow
- melan/o   black
- necr/o   death
- onych/o   nail
- pil/o   hair
- py/o   pus
- seb/o   sebum/oil
- trich/o   hair
- ungu/o   nail
- xer/o   dry

Body Cavities

- Cranial cavity - Contains the brain
- Spinal cavity - Contains the spinal cord, and extends from the brainstem in the cranial cavity to the end of the spinal cord
- Thoracic cavity - Contains the lungs, heart, and large blood vessels, and is separated from the abdomen by the diaphragm

- Abdominal cavity - Contains the stomach, intestines, liver, gallbladder, pancreas, spleen, and kidneys, and is separated from the thoracic cavity by the diaphragm
- Pelvic cavity - Contains the urinary bladder, urinary structures, and reproductive organs

Cell Division and Movement

Cells vary in shape, size, and function, but they all contain similar components. The cell membrane is the thin outer layer of the cells, which regulates what leaves and/or enters. The cytoplasm is a colloidal substance in the cell that holds structures in place. The nucleus is the center of the cell that contains DNA. The nucleolus is a small structure inside the nucleus that contains RNA and ribosomes. Centrioles are rod-shaped material in the cytoplasm. Cilia are hair-like processes on the cell surface. Flagella are whip-like processes on the cell surface that allow movement. Cell division is a process where one cell splits into two identical cells. This occurs in phases:

- Interphase - The DNA duplicates and chromosomes double.
- Mitosis - Four phases of cell division.
- Prophase - Centrioles move to opposite ends of the cells, and form two poles.
    - Metaphase - Chromosomes line up along a central line along centriole filaments
    - Anaphase - Chromosomes separate and each move toward opposite centrioles
    - Telophase - The nucleus divides in the center and forms two cells

The movement of nutrients and waste products in and out of the cell is required for the maintenance of homeostasis and fluid balance. This movement occurs at the cell membrane. The types of movement include:

- Diffusion - Movement of molecules from an area of high concentration to an area of low concentration.
- Osmosis - Water diffusion through a semipermeable membrane.
- Filtration - Movement of water and materials through one side of a membrane.
- Active transport - movement of molecules from are of low concentration to high concentration.
- Phagocytosis - Ingestion and digestion of bacteria

INTEGUMENTARY SYSTEM

The integument is the skin, which makes up around 18% of the body's weight. Skin is necessary to protect a person from the invasion of microorganisms, as well as to regulate body temperature and manufacture vitamins. The skin and accessory structures (glands, nails, and hair) make up the integumentary system. The three layers of the skin are the epidermis, the dermis, and the subcutaneous tissue (hypodermis)

Anatomy

- Epidermis - The epidermis is the outermost layer, and contains four sections called stratum. The stratum basale is the deepest section.
- Dermis - The second skin layer is the dermis, which contains two sections: papillare and reticular. The dermis also contains\ nerves, blood vessels, nails, glands, hair, and connective tissue.
- Hypodermis - The subcutaneous tissue contains connective tissue and fat tissue. The hypodermis connects the skin to underlying muscle.
- Nails - These are the keratin plates that cover each finger and toe. The lunula is the white growth area at the base of the nail plate, the eponychium is the cuticle, a narrow band at the sides and base of the nail, and the paronychium is the soft tissue around the nail border.
- Sebaceous (Oil) Glands - These glands are in the dermis, and they secrete oil (sebum) that lubricates the skin and hair.
- Sudoriferous (Sweat) Glands - These glands are in the dermis, and they secrete salty water to cool the body.

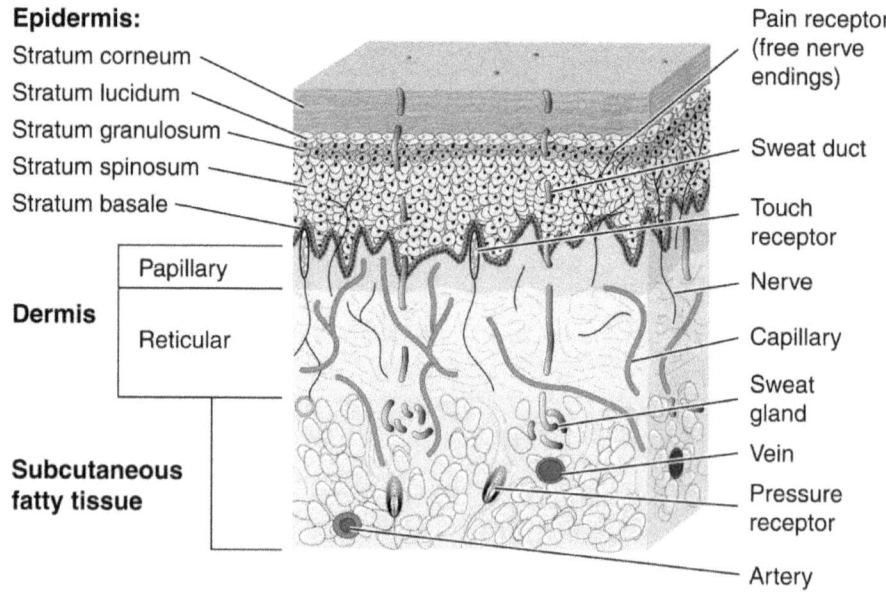

Terminology

- Adipose - Fat or fatty.
- Allograft - Same species graft (homograft)
- Alopecia - Condition associated with hair loss
- Anhidrosis - Lack of or decreased sweat
- Autograft – A graft with skin taken from and applied to the same person
- Biopsy - Removal of a small section of tissue
- Debridement - Removing dead skin tissue
- Electrocautery - Cauterization with a heated instrument
- Epithelium - Structure that covers various body organs
- Erythema - Skin redness
- Fissure - Groove or cleft.
- Furuncle - Skin nodule caused by bacteria entering a hair follicle.
- Hematoma - A localized collection of blood
- Hyperhidrosis – Too much of or increased sweat.
- Ichthyosis - Condition associated with scaling of the skin.
- Incise - To cut into
- Leukoplakia - White patch on mucous membrane
- Lipoma - Fatty tissue tumor
- Melanin - Pigment of the skin
- Melanoma - Malignant tumor of the skin
- Mohs surgery - Procedure to remove skin cancer in layers
- Pilosebaceous - Pertains to sebaceous glands and hair follicles
- Seborrhea - Condition associated with excessive sebum (oil) secretion
- Steatoma - Fatty mass of the sebaceous gland
- Stratified - Layered
- Subungual - Beneath the nail
- Xanthoma - Tumor that contains yellow lipid material
- Xenograft - Different species graft
- Xeroderma - Condition associated with scaly, dry, and discolored skin

Pathophysiology

Lesions, Growths, and Ulcers

- Macule - Flat skin mole or freckle
- Papule - Solid, elevated 1.0 cm skin lesion, such as a wart, mole, or lichen planus
- Nodule - Solid, elevated 1- 2 cm skin lesion, such as a lipoma, lymph node, erythema nodosum
- Pustule - Elevated fluid-filled skin lesion, such as a pimple, impetigo, or abscess
- Tumor - Solid, uncontrolled, and progressive growth of cells, such as a neoplasm, lipoma, or hemangioma
- Plaque - Flat, elevated 1.0 cm or greater skin lesion, such as psoriasis or seborrheic keratosis
- Wheal -Temporary, localized skin elevation, such as an insect bite or allergic reaction

- Vesicle - Small blister that is less than 1 cm, such as shingles (herpes zoster) or chickenpox (varicella)
- Bulla - Large blister that is greater than 1 cm in diameter
- Fissure - Skin cracks, such as athlete's foot or cracks in the corners of the mouth
- Crust - Dried skin exudate (scab)
- Scales - Flakes on dry skin
- Erosion - Loss of the epidermis from blisters or necrosis
- Scar - Skin lesion from excess collagen production, which is caused by trauma or surgery
- Atrophy - Loss of a portion of the skin, which is a physiologic response to aging
- Ulcer - Skin destruction of the epidermis, such as decubitus ulcer, bedsore, or pressure sore
- Keloids - Irregular-shaped, elevated scars that occur from excessive collagen in the corneum during tissue repair
- Cicatrix - Normal scar that occurs with wound healing

Inflammatory Conditions

- Atopic Dermatitis (Eczema)
  - Cause - Irritants or allergens that activate mast cells, eosinophils, T lymphocytes, and monocytes
  - Risk Factors - Occurs in those with a family history of the condition, as well as those with asthma and allergies. It is more common in infants and children
  - Symptoms - Dry, flaky, itchy, erythematous skin

- Contact Dermatitis (Allergic Dermatitis)
  - Cause - Hypersensitivity to drugs, microorganisms, allergens, latex, chemicals, metals, and plants
  - Risk Factors – People with occupations involving chemicals and being outdoors. It is more common in children
  - Symptoms - Vesicular lesions, scaling, erythema, edema, and itching

- Stasis Dermatitis
  - Cause - Associated with phlebitis, varicosities, and vascular trauma
  - Risk Factors – Aging, long periods of standing, and injuries
  - Symptoms - Begins with pruritus and erythema and progresses to hyperpigmentation, scaling, petechia, and ulcerated lesions

- Seborrheic Dermatitis (Dandruff and Cradle Cap)
  - Cause - Chronic inflammation of the sebaceous glands
  - Symptoms - Scaly, white, itchy flaking on the scalp, eyebrows, eyelids, nose, axillae, chest, and/or groin

- Psoriasis

- Cause - Unknown, but thought to be caused from immunologic disorder, a triggering agent, or biochemical alterations
- Risk Factors – Usually occurs in patients under twenty years old
- Symptoms - Well-demarcated plaques and scaly, flaky, and inflamed skin

- Pityriasis Rosea
  - Cause - Unknown
  - Risk Factors - Occurs more in young adults
  - Symptoms - Primary lesion is called "herald patch," which is a salmon-colored, circular 3 to 4 cm lesion. Secondary lesions are oval, reddened, and itchy, occurring around days 14 to 21

- Lichen Planus
  - Cause - Unknown autoimmune inflammatory condition
  - Risk Factors - Occurs between ages 30 to 70
  - Symptoms - Lesions are pink or violet pruritic papules that are 2-10 mm

- Acne Vulgaris
  - Cause - Unknown, but thought to be due to sebum accumulation and pore inflammation
  - Risk Factors - Occurs between ages 12 to 25
  - Symptoms - Whiteheads, blackheads, pustules, cysts, and papules

- Diaper Dermatitis
  - Cause - Exposure to feces, urine, and diaper materials, as well as Candida albicans infection
  - Risk Factors – Excessive exposure to feces and urine
  - Symptoms - Reddened skin on the genital area

Benign Skin Tumors

- Seborrheic Keratosis - Dark colored lesion that results from proliferation of basal cells
- Actinic Keratosis - Scaly pigmented premalignant patch caused by sun exposure.
- Keratoacanthoma - Scaly pigmented patch that occurs in hair follicles.

Malignant Skin Tumors

- Squamous Cell Carcinoma - Scaly cancerous lesion that occurs in the squamous epithelium
- Basal Cell Carcinoma - Shiny, reddened cancerous lesion that grows slowly in deep skin layers and basal cells
- Melanoma - Malignant lesion that originates in the melanocytes
- Kaposi's Sarcoma - Rare form of vascular skin cancer associated with HIV/AIDS

Bacterial Skin Infections

- Impetigo - Highly contagious pyoderma caused by Staphylococcus
- Cellulitis - Infection caused by Staphylococcus, usually as a result of injury
- Folliculitis - Infection of hair follicles, resulting in erythema and pustules
- Erysipelas - Bright red, warm itching, tender lesions caused by A beta-hemolytic Streptococcus
- Furuncles (Boils) - Infected hair follicles usually caused by Staphylococcus

Viral Skin Infections

- Herpes Simplex (Cold Sores) - Red blisters near the lips and mouth (type 1 HSV-1) or genital area (type 2 HSV-2)
- Herpes Zoster (Shingles) - Red blisters that burn and sting and occur on an area of skin innervated by one of the cranial nerves
- Veruccae (Warts) - Growths caused by the human papillomavirus (HPV) that spreads by contact

Fungal Skin Infections

- Tinea - Capitis (scalp), Corporis (ringworm), Pedis (Feet), Manis (hand), and Unguium (nail)
- Candidiasis - Red rash on skin and white patches on mucous membranes caused by Candida albicans

THE MUSCULOSKELETAL SYSTEM

The musculoskeletal system is comprised of the bony skeleton, skeletal muscles, cardiac muscles, and smooth muscles. There also are 206 bones, as well as cartilage and ligaments. The muscular system protects the organs, produces heat, assists with movement, and forms body shape.

Prefixes

- inter-   between
- supra-   above
- sym-   together
- syn-   together

Suffixes

- -asthenia   weakness
- -blast   embryonic
- -clast   break
- -desis   bind together
- -physis   to grow
- -porosis   passage
- -schisis   split
- -stenosis   narrowing

Combining Forms

- ankl/o   bent or fused
- arthr/o   joint
- articul/o   joint
- calc/o   calcium
- calcane/o   heel
- chondr/o   cartilage
- cost/o   ribs
- crani/o   cranium
- disc/o   vertebral disc
- humer/o   humerus
- ischi/o   ischium (pelvic)
- kinesi/o   movement
- lamin/o   lamina
- lumb/o   lower back
- myel/o   bone marrow
- my/o   muscle
- olecran/o   olecranon
- orth/o   straight

- osteo/o   bone
- pelv/i   pelvis
- radi/o   radius
- scapul/o   scapula
- synovi/o   synovial joint
- tend/o   tendon
- vertebr/o   vertebra

Anatomy

Types of Bones

- Long Bones - Tubular (femur, tibia, fibula, humerus, ulna, and radius)
- Short Bones - Cuboidal (carpals and tarsals)
- Flat Bones - Thin and flat (scapula, sternum, and skull)
- Irregular Bones - Varied shapes (zygoma and vertebrae)
- Sesamoid - Rounded (patella)

Axial Skeleton

The axial skeleton includes the skull, hyoid bone, vertebral column, sacrum, ribs, and sternum.

- Skull Bones - Frontal (forehead), parietal (sides), temporal (lower sides), occipital (posterior), sphenoid (floor), ethmoid (between eye orbits and nasal cavity) styloid process (below ear), and zygomatic process (cheek).
- Middle Ear Bones - Malleus (hammer, incus,)anvil), and stapes (stirrup).
- Facial Bones - maxilla (upper jaw), nasal (bridge of nose), zygomatic (cheekbone), mandible (jaw), lacrimal (near eye orbits), vomer (nasal septum), palate (between oral and nasal cavities), and nasal conchae (turbinates)
- Hyoid Bone - U-shaped bone that supports the tongue
- Spine - 33 vertebrae (7 cranial, 12 thoracic, 5 lumbar, 5 sacrum, and 4 coccyx)
- Thorax Bones - 12 pairs of ribs and the sternum

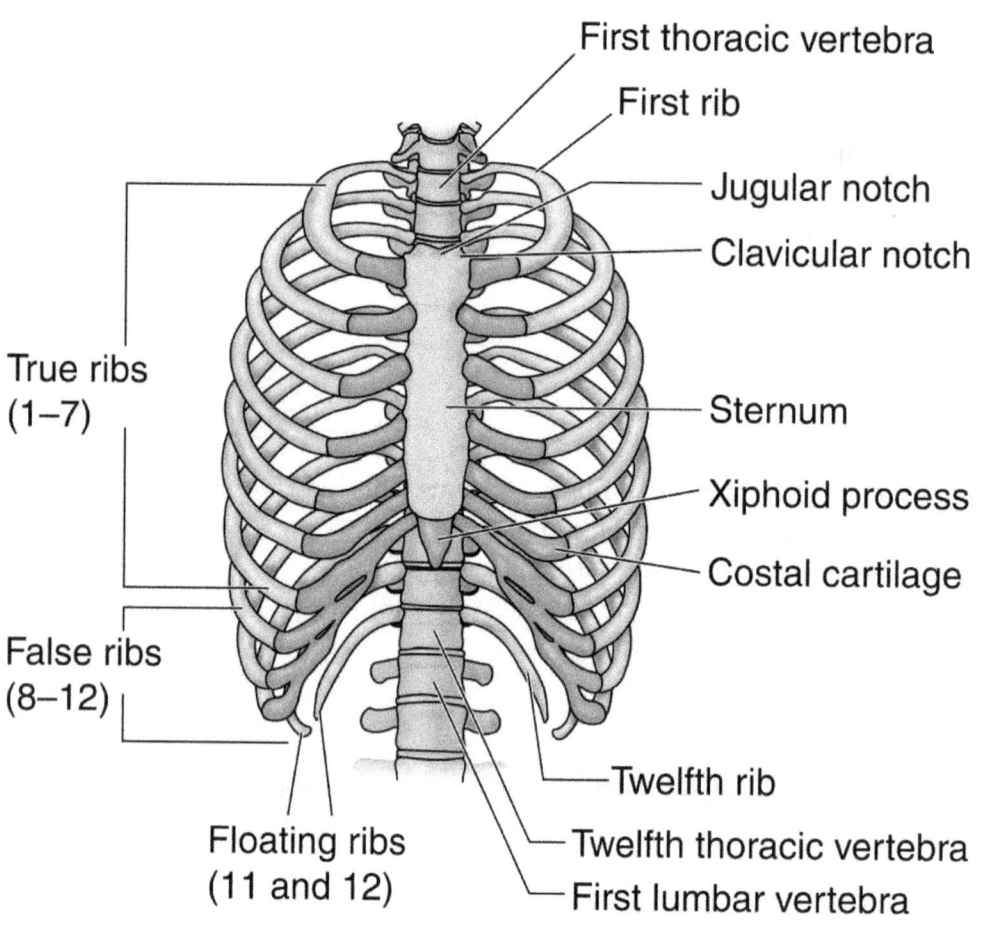

VERTEBRAL COLUMN

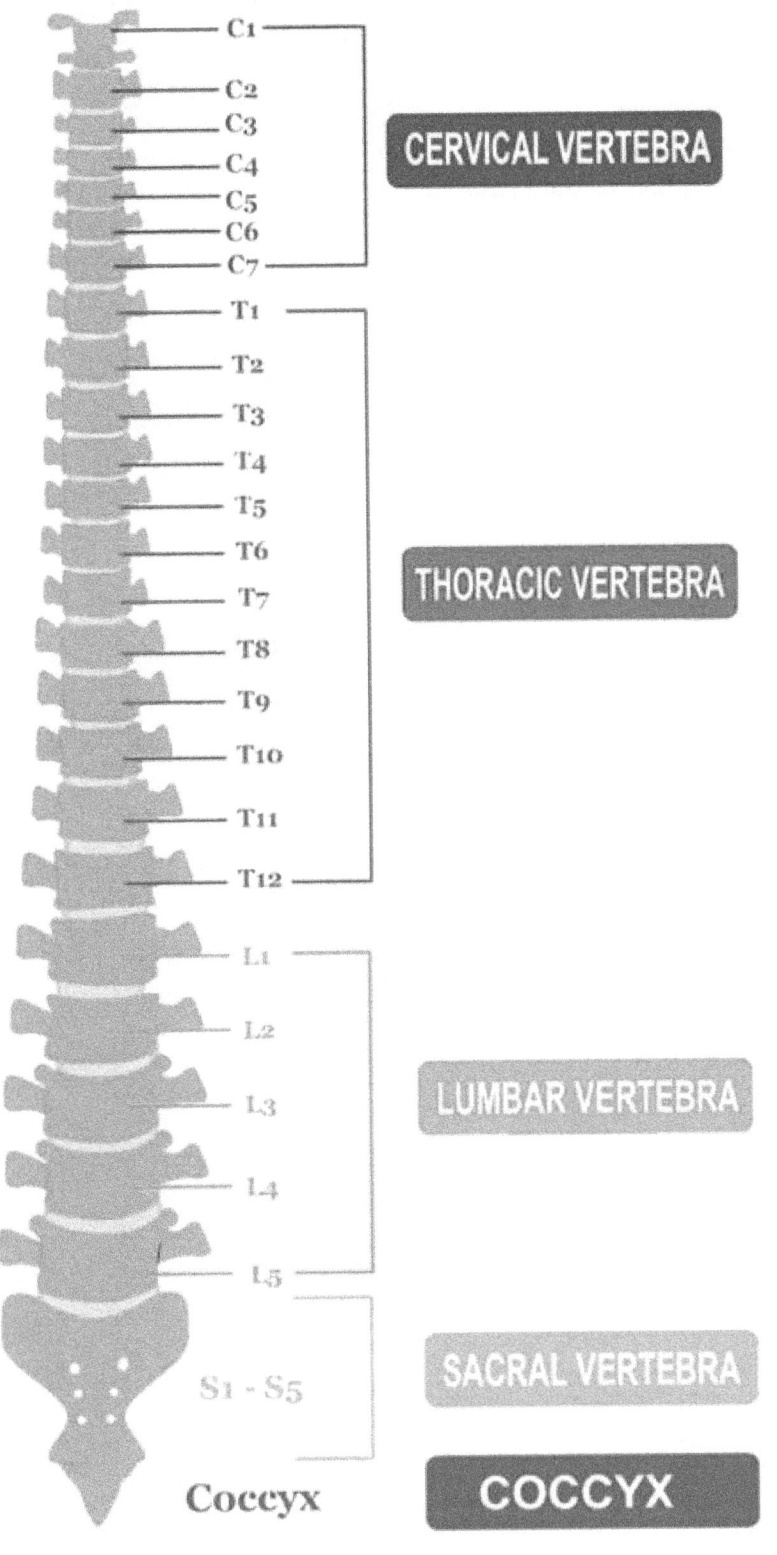

Appendicular Skeleton

- Pelvis - Contains the ilium (upper part), ischium (posterior part), pubis (anterior part), and pubis symphysis (cartilage of the pubic bones)
- Femur - Thigh bone
- Patella - Kneecap
- Tibia - Shin bone
- Fibula - Smaller, lateral lower leg
- Talus - Ankle
- Calcaneus - Heel
- Metatarsals - Foot instep
- Phalanges - Toes
- Clavicle - Collarbone
- Scapula - Shoulder blade
- Humerus - Upper arm
- Radius - Forearm
- Ulna - Smaller arm bone
- Olecranon - Elbow
- Carpals - Wrist
- Metacarpals - Hand
- Phalanges – Fingers

BONES OF THE UPPER EXTREMITY

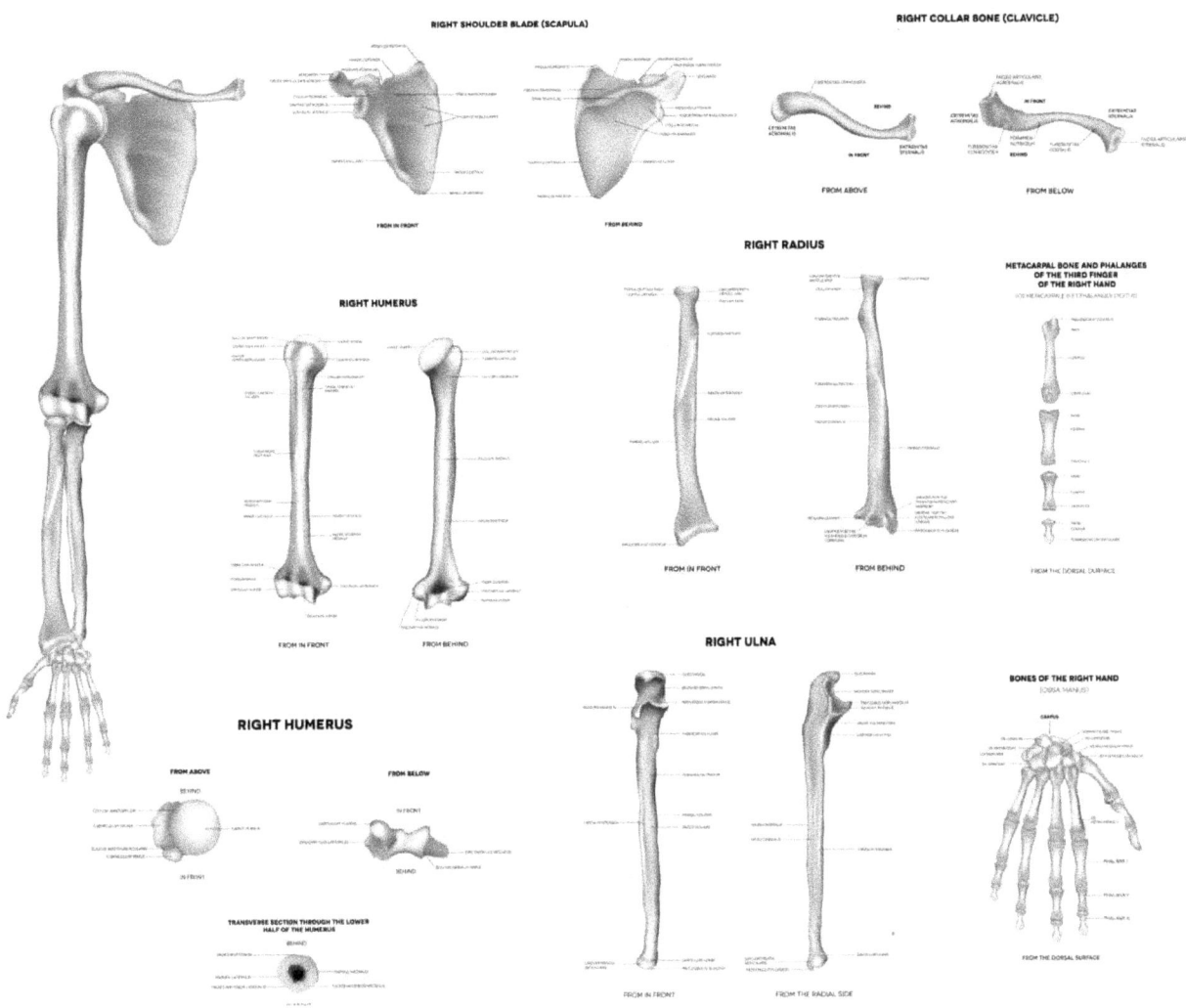

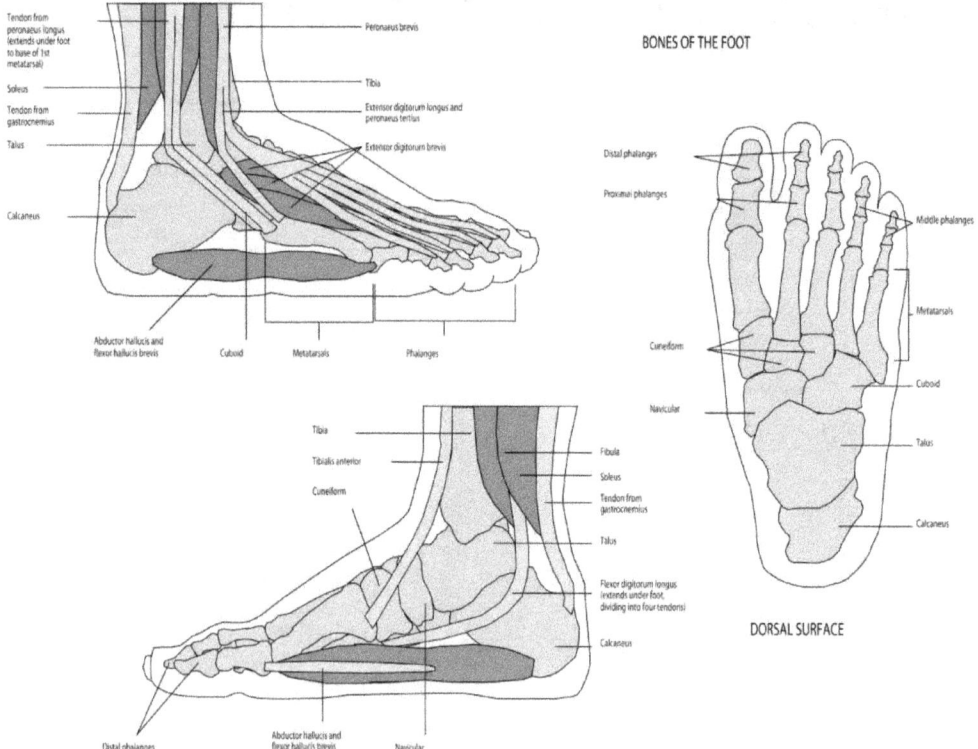

Types of Tissue

- Skeletal Tissue - Striated tissue that attaches to bones
- Cardiac Tissue - Heart muscle that is both striated and smooth
- Visceral Tissue - Smooth tissue that lines the bowel, blood vessels, and urethra
- Tendons - Fibrous structures that anchor muscle to bone
- Ligaments - Fibrous structures that anchor bones to bones

Muscle Names

- Masseter - Used to chew
- Temporalis - Closes the jaw
- Pterygoids - Grates teeth
- Sternocleidomastoid - Flexes head
- Trapezius - Extends head
- Biceps - Flexes elbow
- Triceps - Extends elbow
- Deltoid - Abducts upper arm
- Pectoralis major - Flexes upper arm
- Rectus abdominis - Flexes trunk
- Diaphragm - Enlarges thorax during inspiration
- Intercostals - Raise and depress ribs
- Gluteus group - Includes maximus, medius, and minimus
- Rectus femoris - Flexes thigh

- Gastrocnemius - Calf
- Achilles tendon - Behind heel

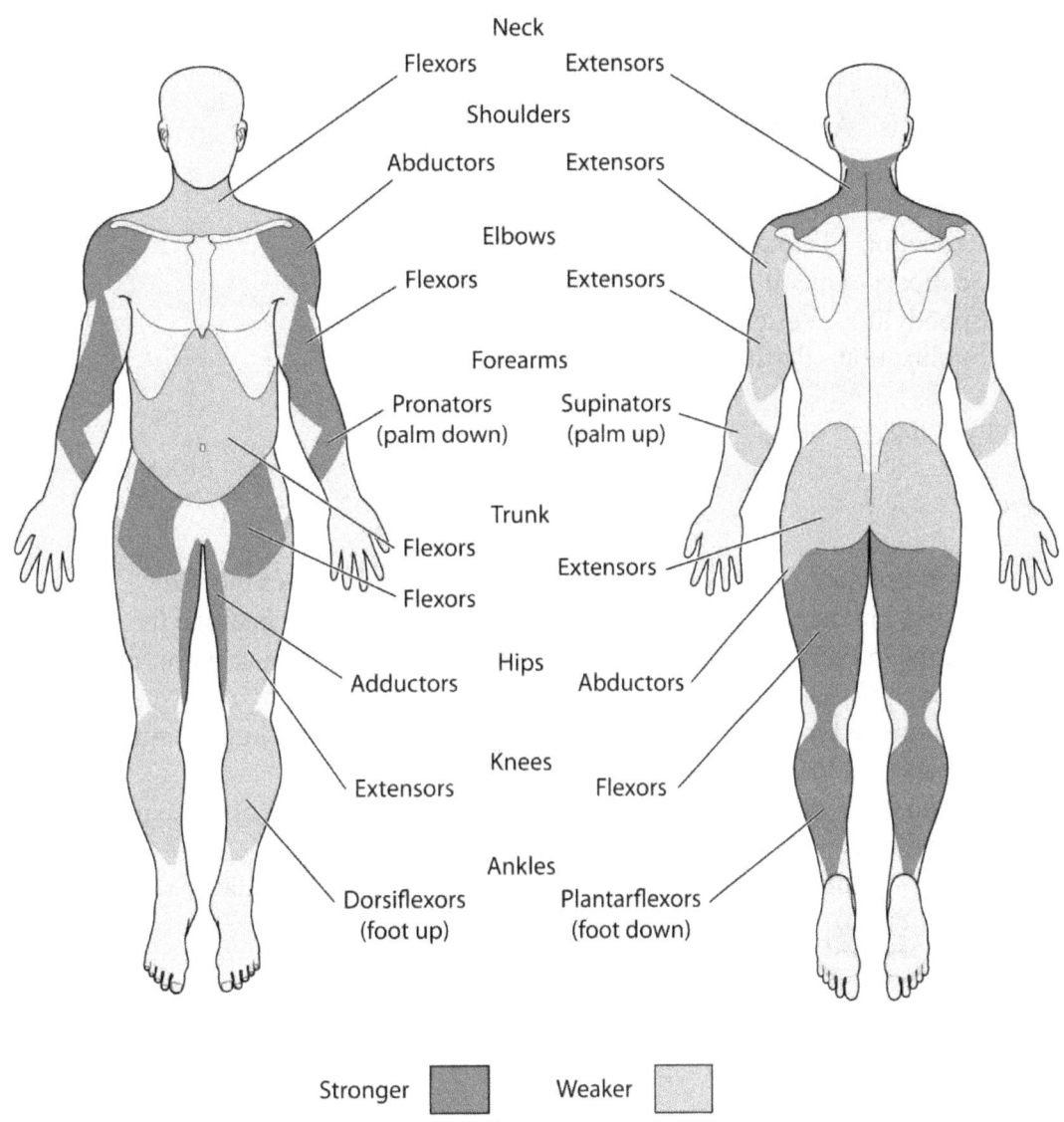

Terminology

- Arthrocentesis - Injection and aspiration of a joint
- Arthrodesis - Surgical immobilization of a joint
- Arthroscopy - Use of scope to view inside a joint

- Articular - Pertains to a joint
- Aspiration - Use of a needle/syringe to withdraw fluid
- Atrophy - Muscle, skin, or structure wasting
- Bursitis - Bursa (joint sac) inflammation
- Chondral - Pertaining to cartilage
- Colles' fracture - Fracture of the lower portion of the radius
- Dislocation - Moved out of original location
- Ganglion - Knot-like mass or cyst
- Kyphosis - Humpback
- Lordosis - Anterior spinal curve
- Osteoarthritis - Degenerative joint condition
- Percutaneous - Through the skin
- Reduction - To put back in normal position or alignment
- Scoliosis - Lateral spinal curve
- Spondylitis - Vertebral inflammation
- Subluxation - Partial dislocation

Pathophysiology

Injuries

- Open Fracture - Compound break were the bone penetrates the skin
- Closed Fracture - Simple break where the bone does not penetrate the skin
- Complete Fracture - Break where the bone is in two pieces or more (oblique, spiral, linear, and transverse)
- Incomplete Fracture - Break where the bone is not broken in two or more pieces (greenstick, torus, stress, and bowing)
- Sprain - Soft tissue damage from overuse or overextension of some part of the musculature
- Strain - Damage to the tendon and/or ligament caused by trauma

Types of Bone Fractures

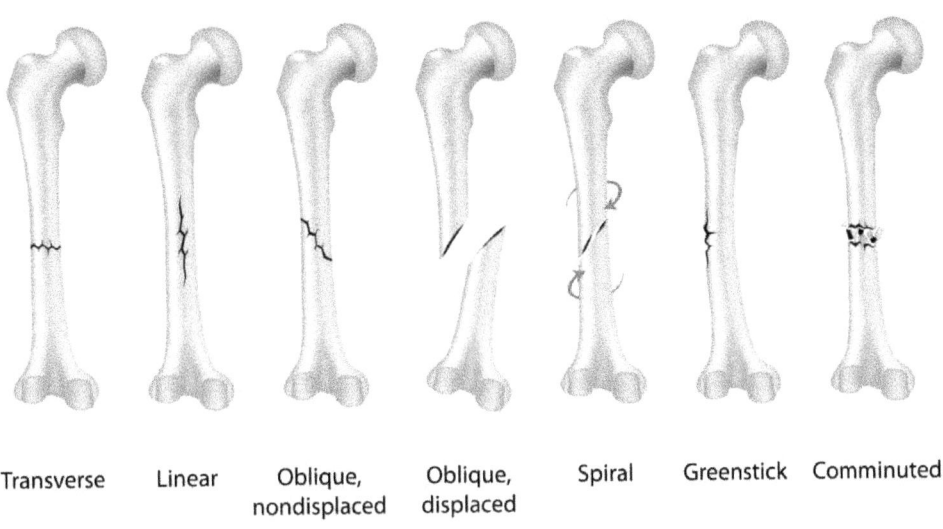

Transverse   Linear   Oblique, nondisplaced   Oblique, displaced   Spiral   Greenstick   Comminuted

Bone Disorders

- Osteomyelitis - Bone infection caused by bacteria
- Osteoporosis - Decreased bone mass and density that occurs due to malabsorption of calcium and other substances
- Osteomalacia - Softening of adult bones
- Spina Bifida - Congenital abnormality where vertebrae do not close around the spinal cord

Joint Disorders

- Osteoarthritis - Degeneration and inflammation of the joint
- Rheumatoid Arthritis - Progressive autoimmune disease that affects connective tissues and joints
- Septic Arthritis - Infectious process that generally affects a single joint
- Gouty Arthritis - Caused by excessive uric acid in the joints
- Ankylosing Spondylosis - Progressive inflammatory disease that affects vertebral joints

Structure Disorders

- Muscular Dystrophy - A progressive degenerative muscle disorder with a genetic predisposition
- Fibromyalgia - Generalized pain and aching that often affects middle-aged women
- Polymyositis - Generalized muscle inflammation that causes weakness

Bone Tumors

- Osteoma - Benign outgrowth of bone
- Chondroblastoma – Rare, benign growth
- Osteosarcoma - Malignant tumor of the long bones
- Multiple Myeloma - Malignant cells in the soft tissue and skeleton
- Rhabdomyosarcoma - Rare, aggressive, and invasive malignant carcinoma

THE RESPIRATORY SYSTEM

The upper respiratory tract includes the nose, sinuses, turbinates, pharynx, and larynx. The lower respiratory tract involves the trachea, bronchial tree, and lungs. These structures supply oxygen and rid the body of carbon dioxide.

Prefixes

- an-   not
- endo-   within
- eu-   good
- dys-   difficult
- pan-   all
- poly-   many

Suffixes

- -algia   pain
- -ar   pertaining to
- -capnia   carbon dioxide
- -centesis   puncture to remove
- -eal   pertaining to
- -ectasia   stretching
- -emia   blood
- -gram   record
- -itis   inflammation
- -meter   measurement instrument
- -osmia   smell
- -oxia   oxygen
- -phonia   sound
- -pnea   breathing
- -ptysis   spitting
- -rrhage   excessive flow
- -spasm   muscle contraction
- -sphyxia   pulse
- -thorax   chest

Combining Forms

- alveol/o   alveolus
- atel/o   incomplete
- bronch/o   bronchus
- capn/o   carbon dioxide
- epiglott/o   epiglottis
- laryng/o   larynx

- lob/o — lobe
- muc/o — mucus
- nas/o — nose
- ox/o — oxygen
- pector/o — chest
- phon/o — voice
- phren/o — diaphragm
- pleur/o — pleura
- pneum/o — lung
- py/o — pus
- rhin/o — nose
- sept/o — septum
- spir/o — breath
- thorac/o — thorax

<u>Anatomy</u>

- Nose - Nasal septum divides interior
- Sinuses - Includes frontal, ethmoid, maxillary, and sphenoid
- Turbinates (Conchae) - Bones of the nose that can be inferior, middle, or superior
- Pharynx - Throat passageway for air and food
- Larynx – Voice box that contains vocal cords and cartilage
- Trachea - The windpipe; has C-shaped cartilage
- Bronchi - Two bronchus that derive from the trachea and go into the lungs
- Lungs - Cone-shaped organs that are covered by pleura

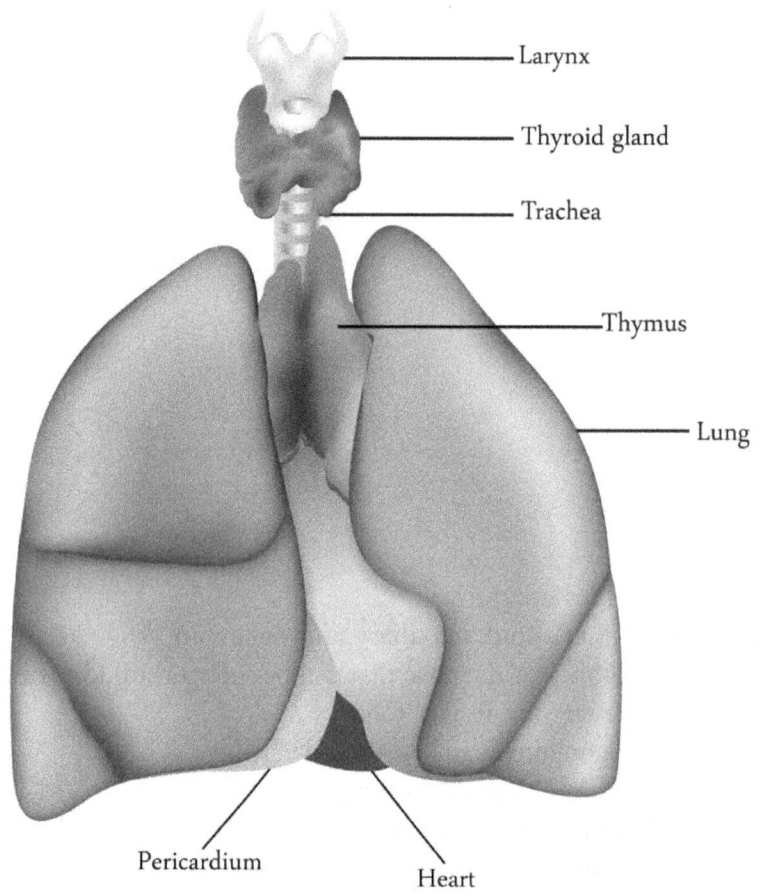

Terminology

- Apnea - When breathing stops
- Asphyxia - Lack of oxygen
- Atelectasis - Incomplete lung expansion
- Auscultation - Listening to lung sounds
- Bronchiole - Small division of the bronchial tree
- Bronchoscopy - Use of a bronchoscope to inspect the bronchial tree
- Cyanosis - Bluish discoloration of the skin or lips
- Dyspnea - Shortness of breath
- Epistaxis - Nose bleed
- Hemoptysis - Coughing up blood
- Hypoxia - Reduced oxygenation of the tissue
- Intubation - Insertion of a tube
- Lavage - Washing out
- Orthopnea - Shortness of breath when laying down
- Pleura - Lining that covers the lungs

- Pleuritis - Inflammation of the pleura
- Rhinorrhea - Drainage from the nose
- Spirometry - Measure of breathing capacity
- Tachypnea - Rapid respiratory rate

Pathophysiology

Pulmonary Disorders

- Hypercapnia - Increased carbon dioxide in the arterial blood caused by poor alveoli ventilation
- Hypoxemia - Reduced oxygenation of the arterial blood
- Acute Respiratory Failure - Condition of inadequate gas exchange, which results in hypoxemia
- Adult Respiratory Distress Syndrome (ARDS) – An acute injury to the alveolocapillary membrane, which results in atelectasis and edema
- Bronchiectasis - Chronic dilation of the bronchi that can be cylindrical, varicose, cystic, or saccular
- Respiratory Acidosis - Excess retention of carbon dioxide leads to low pH levels
- Bronchiolitis - Obstruction of the bronchioles caused by inflammation from a viral pathogen, such as RSV
- Pneumothorax - A condition where air collects in the pleural cavity
- Pneumoconiosis - Chronic condition of the lung where coal, asbestos, or fiberglass particles invade the tissue
- Empyema - Infectious pleura effusion where there is pus in the pleural space
- Pulmonary Embolism (PE) - Occlusion due to air, blood clot, or tissue that lodges in a pulmonary artery
- Pleurisy (Pleuritis) - Inflammation of the pleura due to an upper respiratory infection

Pulmonary Infections

- Pneumonia - Inflammation of the lungs due to aspiration, bacteria, protozoa, viruses, fungi, or chlamydia
- Chronic Obstructive Pulmonary Disease (COPD) - Chronic, irreversible obstruction of the lungs that decreases expiration
- Chronic Bronchitis - A form of COPD that causes dyspnea, wheezing, and productive cough
- Emphysema - A form of COPD that causes enlargement of alveoli and loss of lung elasticity

Notes
intentionally left blank

Notes
intentionally left blank

THE CARDIOVASCULAR SYSTEM

The cardiovascular system consists of the heart, blood, and blood vessels. The vessels carry blood throughout the body, the heart pumps the blood and allows for oxygen-carbon dioxide exchange, and the blood transports nutrients and hormones.

Prefixes

- bi-   two
- brady-   slow
- de-   lack of
- dys-   difficult
- hyper-   over
- hypo-   under
- meta-   change
- peri -   surrounding
- tachy-   fast

Suffixes

- -dilation   widening
- -emia   blood
- -lysis   separation
- -megaly   enlargement
- -oma   tumor
- -osis   condition
- -sclerosis hardening
- -stenosis   blockage

Combining Forms

- angi/o   vessel
- aort/o   aorta
- ather/o   yellow plaque
- arteri/o   artery
- brachi/o   arm
- cardi/o   heart
- coron/o   heart
- cyan/o   bluish
- myx/o   mucous
- ox/o   oxygen
- phleb/o   vein
- sthe/o   chest
- thromb/o   clot
- valv/o   valve

- vascul/o   vessel

<u>Anatomy</u>

Blood

- Function - To maintain a constant environment, carry oxygen and nutrients to cells, deliver waste and carbon dioxide to and from organs, and transport hormones from the endocrine system
- Liquid part - Plasma is extracellular with 91% water
- Cellular part - Contains leukocytes (white blood cells WBCs), erythrocytes (red blood cells or RBCs), and thrombocytes (platelets)

Vessels

- Function - To transport blood and carry away cellular waste and carbon dioxide
- Arteries - Lead away from the heart and branch into arterioles
- Veins - Lead to the heart and branch into venules
- Capillaries - Connect between arterioles and venules

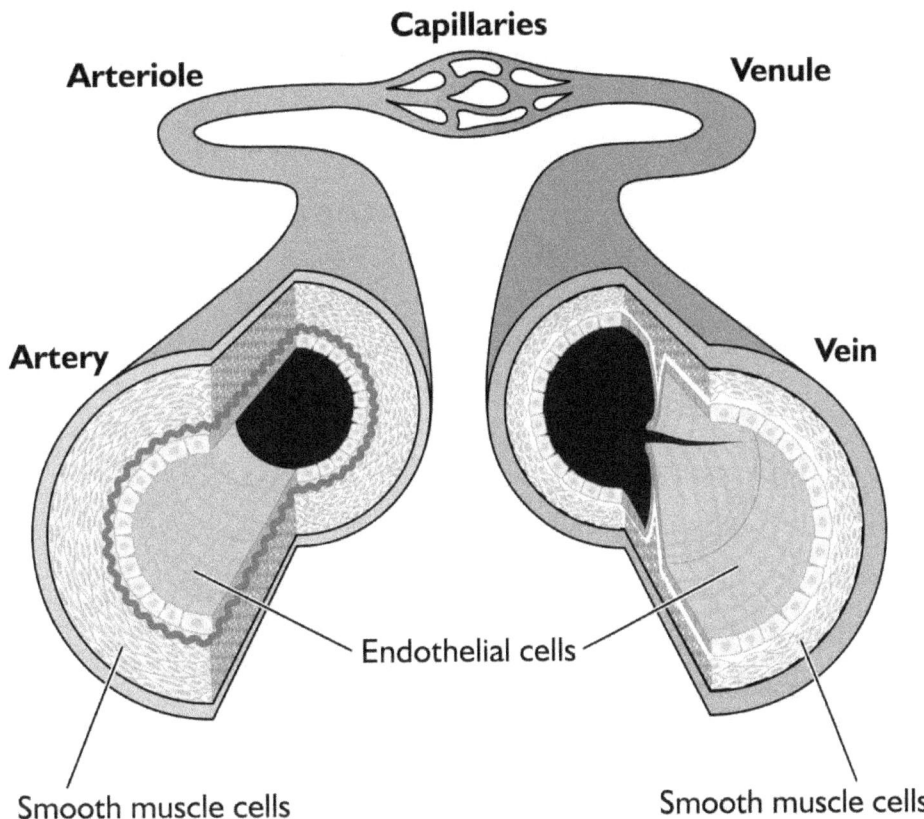

Heart

- Function - To circulate blood throughout the body
- Chambers - The two upper chambers are the right atrium and left atrium, and the two lower chambers are the right ventricle and the left ventricle

Valves

- Tricuspid - Lies between the right atrium and the right ventricle
- Pulmonary - Lies between the pulmonary artery and the right ventricle
- Aortic - Lies between the aorta and the left ventricle
- Bicuspid (Mitral) - Lies between the left atrium and the left ventricle

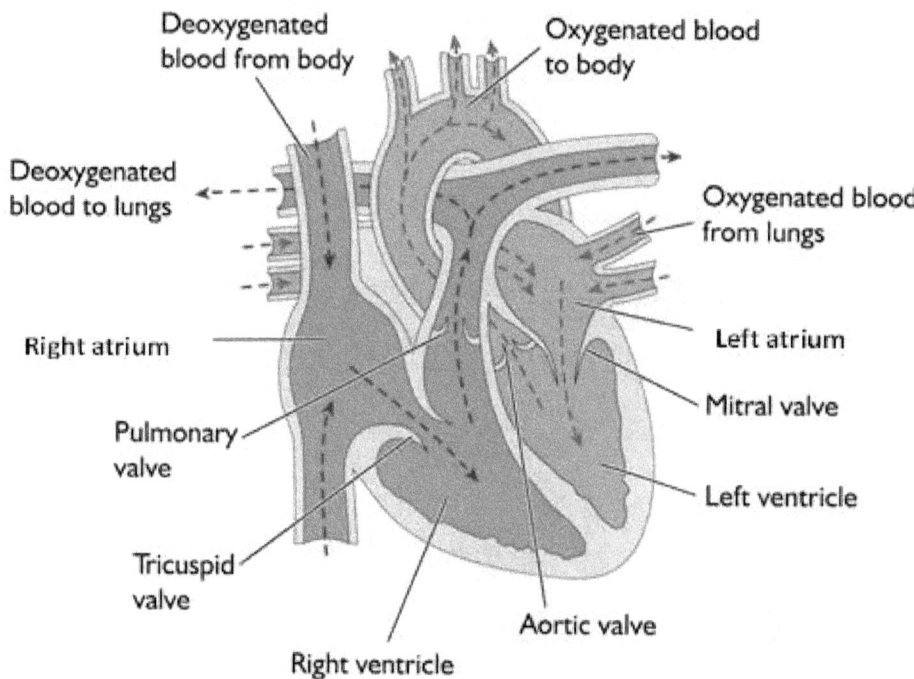

Terminology

- Aneurysm - Abnormal dilation of artery
- Angina - Chest pain described as spasmodic and choking
- Angiography - Diagnostic test on the blood vessels
- Angioplasty - Procedure used to dilate a vessel opening
- Atherectomy - Removal of plaque from an artery, which is done by a percutaneous method

- Bundle of His - Cardiac fibers that allow heart rhythm
- Circumflex - A coronary artery that encircles the heart
- Edema - Swelling due to fluid collection in the tissue
- Electrophysiology - The study of the heart's electrical system
- Embolectomy - Removal of an embolism or blockage from a vessel
- Epicardial - Over the heart
- Fistula - Opening from one area to the other or to the outside of the body
- Hemolysis - RBC breakdown
- Intracardiac - Inside the heart
- Thoracostomy - Incisions made into the chest wall to insert a chest tube
- Transvenous - Through a vein

Pathophysiology

- Coronary Artery Disease (CAD)
    - Also called: Ischemic Heart Disease
    - Cause - Hardening and thickening of the arterial intima (inner layer) with fibrous plaque and lipid accumulation (atherosclerosis)
    - Results - Produces peripheral vascular disease, stroke, aneurysms, coronary artery occlusion
    - Risk Factors - Advancing age, family history, hyperlipidemia, hypertension, cigarette smoking, diabetes, and obesity

- Myocardial Infarction (MI)
    - Also called - Heart Attack
    - Cause - Atherosclerosis of vessels lead to myocardial ischemia
    - Symptoms - Crushing chest pain and hypotension

- Hypertension
    - Also called - High Blood Pressure
    - Cause - Underlying disease that increases resistance in the heart and blood vessels
    - Symptoms - Often none, but can cause dizziness and headache

- Hypotension
    - Also Called - Low Blood Pressure
    - Cause - Drop in both systolic and diastolic arterial blood pressure and insufficient oxygen in blood
    - Symptoms - Dizziness, blurred vision, and syncope (fainting)

- Aneurysm
    - Cause - Dilation of an arterial vessel wall or heart chamber due to weakening or ballooning
    - Symptoms - Varies, depending on the site

- Thrombus
    - Also called - Blood Clot

- o Cause - Infection, inflammation, low blood pressure, obstruction, and atherosclerosis
- o Symptoms - Depends on the site

- Thrombophlebitis
    - o Description - Inflammation of the vessels
    - o Cause - Trauma, infection, and immobility
    - o Symptoms – Warmth, pain, and swelling

- Embolism
    - o Description - Mass that enters the bloodstream
    - o Types - Air, fat, bacteria, cancer cells, foreign substances, thrombus, and amniotic fluid

- Peripheral Arterial Disease
    - o Also called - Buerger's Disease
    - o Description - Inflammation of the peripheral arteries creating vasospasms
    - o Cause – Atherosclerosis
    - o Symptoms – Leg pain and tingling

- Varicose Veins
    - o Also called - Varicosities
    - o Description - Blood pools in the veins and distends them
    - o Symptoms - Swelling, pain, leg fatigue, and ulcerations

- Congestive Heart Failure (CHF)
    - o Description - The heart fails to generate adequate blood output
    - o Cause - Myocardial infarction, myocarditis, and cardiomyopathies
    - o Symptoms - Shortness of breath, fatigue, and exercise intolerance

- Arrhythmia
    - o Atrial Fibrillation (A. Fib) - Rapid, erratic contractions of the heart
    - o Atrial Flutter - Rapid regular heart contractions
    - o Ventricular fibrillation - Life-threatening rhythm of random electrical impulses through the ventricles

- Infective Endocarditis
    - o Description - Inflammation of the inner lining of the heart that causes permanent heart valve damage
    - o Cause - Bacteria, viruses, fungi, or parasites

- Pericarditis
    - Description - Inflammation of the heart pericardium
    - Types - Acute, pericardial effusion, and constrictive

- Rheumatic Heart Disease
    - Also called - Rheumatic Fever
    - Description - Inflammation of all layers of the heart, causing mitral or aortic valve disease (stenosis, regurgitation, insufficiency)
    - Risk Factors - History of carditis and family tendency

- Aortic Valve Stenosis
    - Description - Narrowing, thickening, stiffness, or blockage that creates resistance and increased pressure behind a valve
    - Cause - Degeneration, infection, and congenital malformation

- Mitral Valve Stenosis
    - Description - Impaired flow from the left atrium to the left ventricle
    - Cause - Bacterial infections or rheumatic fever

- Valvular Regurgitation
    - Description - Blood flow in the wrong direction
    - Types - Mitral, aortic, pulmonic, and tricuspid

- Cardiomyopathies
    - Description - Group of cardiac diseases that affect the myocardium
    - Cause - Idiopathic or an existing condition
    - Types - Dilated cardiomyopathy, hypertrophic cardiomyopathy, and restrictive cardiomyopathy

Notes
intentionally left blank

Notes
intentionally left blank

THE FEMALE REPRODUCTIVE SYSTEM

The female reproductive system protects the fertilized ovum (egg) for the nine-month gestation period. The external structures enhance sexual stimulation and protect the body from foreign materials. The internal structures produce and release the ovum.

Prefixes

- ante-   before
- dys-   painful
- ecto-   outside
- endo-   in
- extra-   outside
- in-   into
- intra-   within
- multi-   many
- neo -   new
- nulli-   none
- post-   after
- primi-   first
- pseudo-   false
- retr-   backwards

Suffixes

- -arche   beginning
- -cyesis   pregnancy
- -gravida   pregnancy
- -rrhexis   rupture
- -para   woman who has given birth
- -parous   to bear
- -rrhea   discharge
- -salpinx   uterine tube
- -tocia   labor

Combining Forms

- amni/o   amnion
- arche/o   first
- cervic/o   cervix
- chori/o   chorion
- colp/o   vagina
- crypt/o   hidden
- episi/o   vulva
- fet/o   fetus

- glact/o   milk
- gyn/o   female
- hyster/o   uterus
- lact/o   milk
- mamm/o   breast
- mast/o   breast
- men/o   menstruation
- metr/i   uterus
- nat/a   birth
- olig/o   few
- oo/o   egg
- ov/o   egg
- ovari/o   ovary
- peri/o   perineum
- phor/o   to bear
- top/o   place
- uter/o   uterus
- vagin/o   vagina

Anatomy

- Ovaries - Small structures that produce ova (eggs) and hormones
- Fallopian Tubes - Ducts that transport ova from the ovary to the uterus
- Uterus - Muscular organ with three layers: endometrium (inner mucosa), myometrium (middle layer), and perimetrium (outer layer)
- Vulva - External genitalia
- Vagina - Cavity that spans from the uterus to outside the body
- Breasts - Mammary glands and tissue that contain lactiferous ducts

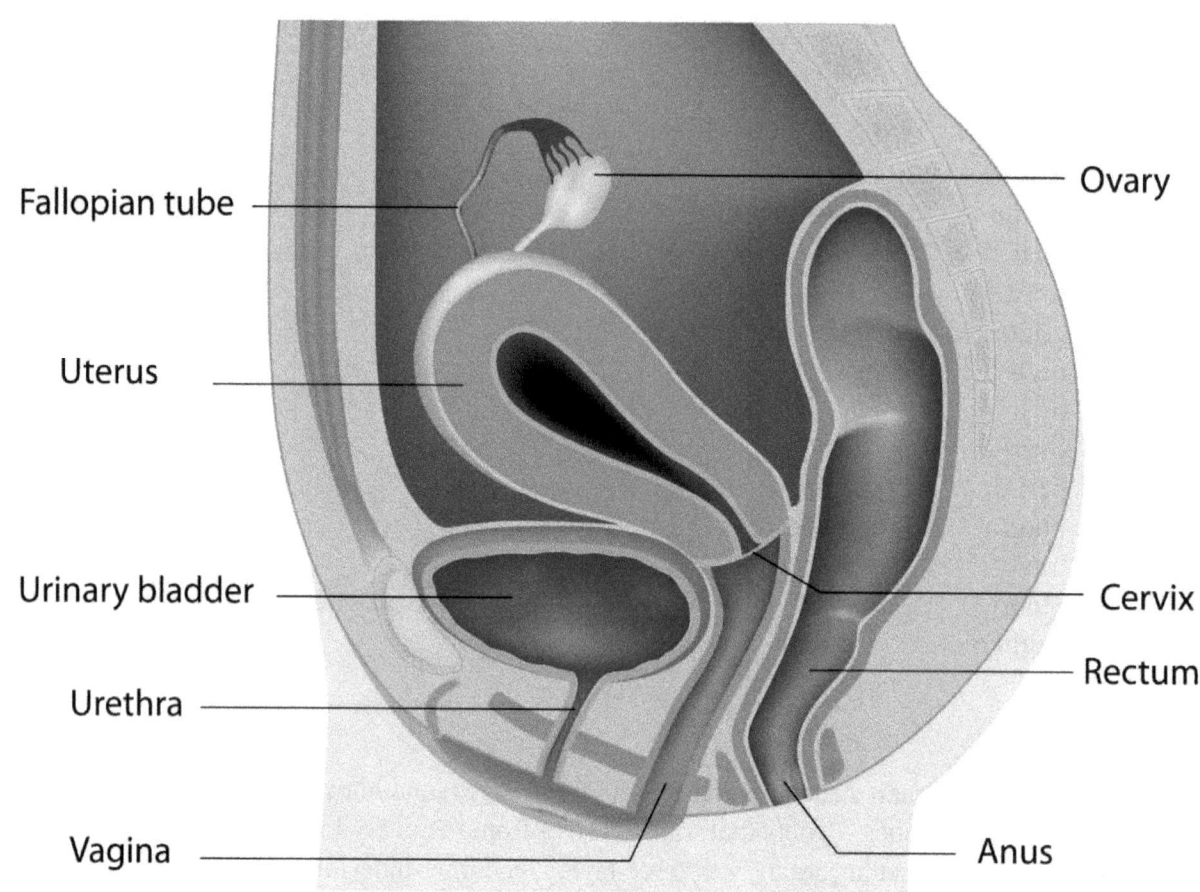

Menstruation

- Proliferation Phase   Days 1 - 5
- Endometrium Repair   Days 6 - 12
- Secretory Phase   Days 13 - 14
- Premenstruation   Days 15 - 28

Trimesters of Pregnancy

- First   (LMP - 12 weeks)
- Second   (13 - 27 weeks)
- Third   (28 weeks - EDD)
- Gestation Length   266 days

Terminology

- Abortion - Termination of a pregnancy

- Amniocentesis - Percutaneous aspiration of amniotic fluid
- Antepartum - Time before childbirth
- Cesarean - Surgical method of child delivery
- Chorionic villus sampling - Biopsy of the placenta
- Curettage - Scraping of the cavity using a special instrument
- Cystocele - Herniation of the bladder into the vagina
- Delivery - Birth of baby
- Dilation - Expansion
- Ectopic - Pregnancy that occurs outside the uterus
- Hysterectomy - Surgical removal of the uterus
- Introitus - Opening of the vagina
- Ligation - Binding of the fallopian tube
- Multipara - More than one pregnancy
- Perineum - Area between the vagina and anus
- Primigravida - First pregnancy

Pathophysiology

Menstrual Disorders

- Primary Dysmenorrhea
    - Description - Painful menstruation
    - Cause - Beginning menstruation
    - Symptoms - Pelvic cramping

- Secondary Dysmenorrhea
    - Description - Painful menstruation
    - Cause - Underlying condition, such as endometriosis, tumors, or polyps
    - Symptoms - Pelvic cramping

- Primary Amenorrhea
    - Description - Menstruation has never occurred
    - Cause - Genetic disorder
    - Symptoms – No menses

- Secondary Amenorrhea
    - Description - Menstruation ceases for 3 cycles or 6 months
    - Cause - Stress, tumors, eating disorders, strenuous exercise
    - Symptoms – Absence of menses

Abnormal Menstruation

- Metorrhagia - Bleeding in between cycles
- Menorrhagia - Increase in bleeding amount and duration of flow
- Oligomenorrhea - Bleeding in excess of 6 weeks between periods

- - Polymenorrhea - Less than 3 weeks between periods
  - Hypomenorrhea - Light or spotty flow
  - Menometrorrhagia - Irregular cycles of varying duration and amounts

- Endometriosis
  - Description - The development of endometrial tissue outside the uterus
  - Cause - Unknown
  - Symptoms - Inflammation, pain, and cramping

Sexually Transmitted Infections

- Pelvic Inflammatory Disease (PID)
  - Description - Infection and inflammation of the reproductive tract
  - Cause - Microorganisms
  - Symptoms - Pain with sex, pelvic pain, and vaginal discharge

- Candidiasis
  - Also called - Yeast infection
  - Description – Infection and inflammation of the vagina
  - Cause - Candida albicans
  - Symptoms - White curd-like discharge, pain with sex, and dysuria

- Chlamydia
  - Description – Infection of the reproductive tract
  - Cause - *Chlamydia trachomatis* bacteria
  - Symptoms - Mild vaginal or penis discharge and dysuria

- Gonorrhea
  - Description – Infection of the reproductive tract
  - Cause - *Neisseria gonorrhoeae* bacteria
  - Symptoms - Discharge and dysuria

- Condylomata Acuminata
  - Also called - Genital warts
  - Description – Warty growths of the reproductive structures
  - Cause - Human papillomavirus
  - Symptoms - Polyps, growths, and warty lesions

- Trichomoniasis
  - Description – Infection of the reproductive tract
  - Cause - *Trichomonas vaginalis* protozoan
  - Symptoms - Colored vaginal or penis discharge and dysuria

Benign Lesions

- Leiomyomas
    - Also called - Uterine fibroids
    - Occur - Beneath the endometrium (submucous), beneath the serosa (subserosa), or in the muscle wall (intramural)
    - Symptoms - Abnormal uterine bleeding, pelvic pain, and pelvic pressure

- Adenomyosis
    - Occur - Within the uterine myometrium
    - Symptoms - Enlarged uterus, abnormal menstrual bleeding, and pain

Malignant Lesions

- Carcinoma of the Breast
    - Also called - Breast cancer
    - Types - Invasive ductal carcinoma and invasive lobular carcinoma

- Carcinoma of Uterus
    - Also called - Endometrial Cancer
    - Symptoms - Abnormal uterine bleeding and postmenopausal bleeding

- Carcinoma of Cervix
    - Also called - Cervical cancer
    - Symptoms - Asymptomatic in early stages, but can cause bleeding and discharge in later stages

- Carcinoma of Ovary
    - Also called - Ovarian Cancer
    - Cause – Unknown
    - Symptoms - Usually asymptomatic in early stages, but can cause dysuria, vaginal bleeding, and pelvic pressure in later stages

Pregnancy Pathophysiology

- Placenta Previa - When the cervical opening is obstructed by placenta.
- Eclampsia - Condition of pregnancy characterized by edema, hypertension, and proteinuria.
- Ectopic Pregnancy - Implantation of a fertilized egg outside of the uterus.
- Spontaneous Abortion - Miscarriage that happens naturally.
- Dilation and Curettage (D & C) - Scraping of uterine lining to remove fetus.

Notes
intentionally left blank

Notes
intentionally left blank

THE MALE REPRODUCTIVE SYSTEM

The male reproductive system consists of testicles, the scrotum, epididymis, spermatic cords, seminal vesicles and ducts, the vas deferens, the bulbourethral gland, the prostate gland, and the penis. This system produces sperm cells for reproduction

Prefixes

- dys-   painful
- peri -   surrounding
- poly-   many
- retro-   behind

Suffixes

- -one   hormone
- -pexy   fixation
- -ectomy   removal
- -stomy   new opening

Combining Forms

- andr/o   male
- balan/o   glans of the penis
- cry/o   cold
- crypt/o   hidden
- gon/o   seed
- hydr/o   water or fluid
- orch/i   testicle
- prostat/o prostate gland
- semin/i   semen
- test/o   testicle
- varic/o   varicose vein
- vas/o   vas deferens

Anatomy

- Testes (Gonads) - Structures that produce sperm and testosterone
- Vas Deferens - Tubular structure at the end of the epididymis
- Prostate Gland - Structure that produces seminal fluid and activates sperm
- Bulbourethral Gland - Gland that secretes a tiny amount of seminal fluid
- Seminal Ducts - Structures that transport sperm from the testes to the exterior
- Seminal Vesicles - Structures that produce most seminal fluid
- Penis - External genital structure that encloses the urethra and passes urine and semen
- Scrotum - Sac that encloses the testes

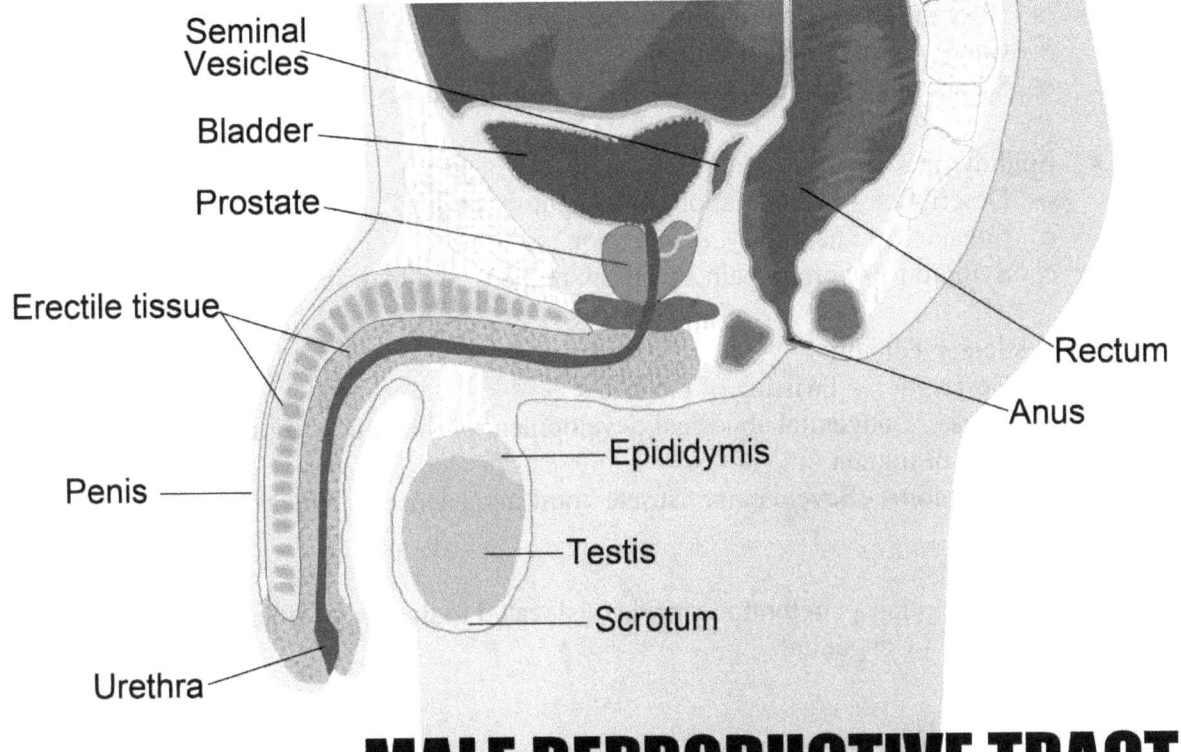

MALE REPRODUCTIVE TRACT

Terminology

- Cavernosa - The connection inside the penis
- Chordee - Condition where the penis is injured
- Corpora cavernosa - The two cavities of the penis
- Epididymis - Structure that holds sperm, located at the upper portion of the testes
- Orchiopexy - Surgical procedure to lower undescended testes
- Prostatotomy - Incision to the prostate
- Transurethral resection of the prostate (TURP) - Surgical procedure performed by way of cystoscopy to remove some or all of the prostate gland
- Varicocele - Swelling of a scrotal vein
- Vasectomy - Removal of a portion of the vas deferens
- Vesiculotomy - Incision into the seminal vesicle

Pathophysiology

- Cryptorchidism
  - Description - Undescended testes
  - Cause - Obstruction or other processes
  - Symptoms - Unilateral or bilateral

- Orchitis
  - Description - Inflammation of the testes
  - Cause - Virus, such as mumps
  - Symptoms - Atrophy, loss of sperm production, testicular pain, and swelling

- Epididymitis
  - Description - Inflammation of the epididymis
  - Cause - Trauma, injury, or infection
  - Symptoms - Scrotal pain, swelling, redness, and hydrocele

- Testicular Torsion
  - Description - Twisting of the testes
  - Cause - Congenital abnormal development of the tunica vaginalis and spermatic cord or trauma
  - Symptoms - Severe pain, nausea, vomiting, edema, and fever

- Epispadias
  - Description - Urethral meatus is mislocated to the dorsal side of penis
  - Cause - Congenital

- Hypospadias
  - Description - Urethral opening occurs on the ventral side of the penis
  - Cause - Congenital

- Urethritis
  - Description - Inflammation of the urethra
  - Cause - Infection from bacterial organisms
  - Symptoms - Penis discharge, dysuria, itching, and urgency

- Phimosis
  - Description - Foreskin is constricted and cannot be retracted
  - Cause - Chronic infection and poor hygiene
  - Symptoms - Erythema, edema, tenderness, and discharge

- Paraphimosis
  - Description: Condition where the foreskin is constricted and retracted over the penis
  - Cause - Congenital
  - Symptoms - Edema and pain

- Benign Prostatic Hypertrophy (BPG)
  - Description - Enlarged prostate gland
  - Cause - Increased levels of hormones and fibrous nodules
  - Symptoms - Nocturia, incontinence, hesitancy, and urinary urgency

- Prostatitis
    - Description - Inflammation of the prostate
    - Cause - E. coli and other bacteria
    - Symptoms - Fever, low back pain, perineal pain, dysuria, suprapubic tenderness, and urinary tract infection

Notes
intentionally left blank

Notes
intentionally left blank

THE URINARY SYSTEM

The urinary system includes the kidneys, ureters, urinary bladder, and urethra. These structures work together to remove metabolic waste materials from the body, such as uric acid, urea, nitrogenous waste, and creatinine. The urinary system also maintains electrolyte balance and assists the liver in body detoxification.

Prefixes

- dys-   painful
- peri - surrounding
- poly-   many
- retro- behind

Suffixes

- -eal   pertaining to
- -lithiasis condition of stones
- -lysis   separation
- -plasty   repair
- -tripsy   crush

Combining Forms

- azot/o   urea
- bacteri/o bacteria
- cali./o   calyx
- cyst/o   urinary
- dips/o   thirst
- glyc/o   sugar
- hydro/o   water
- ket/o   ketones
- lith/o   stone
- meat/o   meatus
- nephr/o   kidney
- loig/o   scant
- ren/o   kidney
- ur/o   urine
- vesic/o   bladder

<u>Anatomy</u>

- Kidneys - Two organs that control pH balance (acid/base), secrete renin, vitamin D, and erythropoietin, and stimulate red blood cell production
- Cortex - Outer layer of the kidney

- Medullar - Inner portion of the kidney
- Hilum - Middle section of the kidney
- Papilla - Inner part of the pyramids
- Nephrons - Operational units of the kidneys
- Ureters - Narrow tubules that transport urine from the kidneys to the bladder
- Urinary Bladder - Sac-like reservoir for the urine
- Urethra - Tube that transport urine from the bladder to outside the body.

ANATOMY OF THE KIDNEY

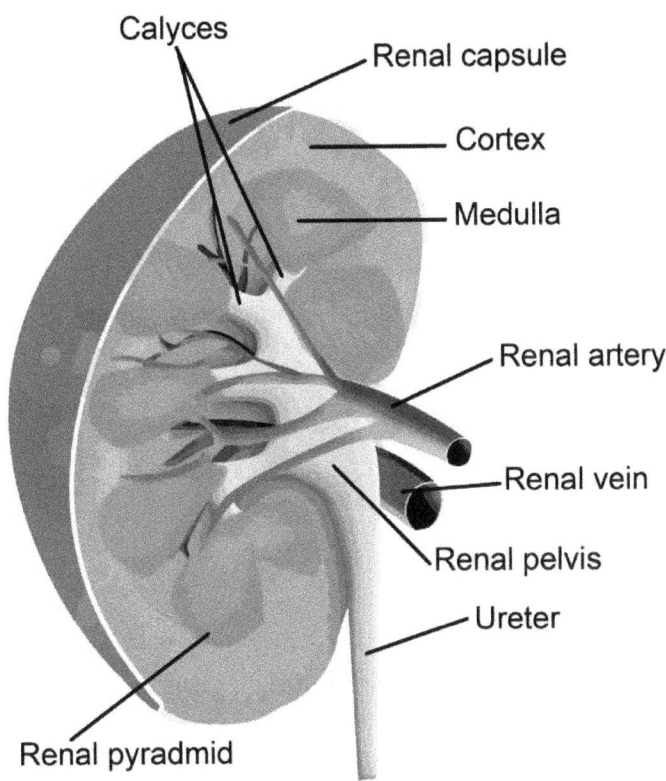

Terminology

- Bulbocavernosus - Muscle that constricts the female vagina and male urethra
- Bulbourethral - Gland that leads to the urethra
- Calculus - Kidney stone formed of minerals and salts
- Cystoplasty - Surgical reconstruction of bladder
- Cystoscopy - Use of a scope to view the bladder
- Cystotomy - Incision into the bladder
- Dysuria - Painful urination

- Extracorporeal - Occurs outside the body
- Hydrocele - Sac of fluid
- Nephrostomy - Surgical creation of a passage into the renal pelvis of the kidney
- Ureterectomy - Surgical removal of a ureter
- Ureterotomy - Incision into the ureter
- Urethroplasty - Surgical repair of the urethra
- Vesicostomy - Surgical creation of a bladder-to-skin connection

Pathophysiology

- Acute Renal Failure
  - Description - Sudden onset of kidney failure.
  - Cause - Trauma, infection, inflammation, toxicity, extreme hypotension, and obstructed vascular supply.
  - Types: Prerenal, intrarenal, and postrenal.

- Chronic Renal Failure
  - Description - Gradual, progressive loss of kidney function resulting in insufficiency
  - Cause - Nephrotoxins, diabetes, and hypertension
  - Symptoms - Polyuria, nausea, anorexia, dehydration, and confusion

- Cystitis
  - Description - Inflammation and infection of the urinary bladder
  - Cause - Bacteria
  - Symptoms - Low back pain, dysuria, frequency, and urgency

- Acute Pyelonephritis
  - Description - Infection of the kidney
  - Cause - Bacteria
  - Symptoms - Fever, groin pain, flank pain, dysuria, nausea, pyuria, and nocturia

- Chronic Pyelonephritis
  - Description - Recurrent kidney infection
  - Cause - Repeated infections and obstructive conditions.
  - Symptoms - Hypertension, dysuria, flank pain, and frequency

- Glomerulonephritis
  - Description - Inflammation of the glomerulus
  - Cause - Drugs, toxins, systemic disorders, vascular pathology, and immune disorders
  - Symptoms - Edema, protein loss, weight gain, pallor, and lipiduria

- Acute Post Streptococcal Glomerulonephritis (APSAGN)
  - Description - Inflammation of the glomerulus
  - Cause - Streptococcus
  - Symptoms - Back pain, flank pain, fatigue, headache, nausea, oliguria, elevated blood pressure, and malaise

- Nephrolithiasis
  - Also called - Renal Calculi and Kidney Stones
  - Description - Formations of minerals and salts
  - Cause - Buildup of minerals or salts
  - Symptoms - Nausea, vomiting, intense flank pain, and increased pulse rate

- Hydronephrosis
  - Description - Distention of the kidney with urine
  - Cause - Obstruction or kidney stone
  - Symptoms - Mild flank pain, asymptomatic, and infection

- Nephrosclerosis
  - Description - Hardening and thickening of the kidney vasculature
  - Cause - Genetic
  - Symptoms - Increased blood pressure and reduced blood supply

- Polycystic Kidney Disease (PKD)
  - Description - Numerous kidney cysts
  - Cause - Genetic
  - Symptoms - Usually asymptomatic

Notes
intentionally left blank

Notes
intentionally left blank

THE DIGESTIVE SYSTEM

The digestive system includes the gastrointestinal tract and various accessory organs. This system's functions include absorption, digestion, and elimination. The GI tract is regulated by a complex series of hormonal, neural, and local control systems.

Prefixes

dys-	painful
peri -	surrounding
poly-	many
retro-	behind

Suffixes

-ase	enzyme
-cele	hernia
-chezia	defecation
-lasis	abnormal condition
-phagia	eating
-prandial	meal

Combining Forms

abdomin/o	abdominal
an/o	anus
bil/i	bile
bucc/o	cheek
cheil/o	lip
chol/e	bile
col/o	colon
dent/i	tooth
enter/o	small intestine
faci/o	face
gastr/o	stomach
gloss/o	tongue
hepat/o	liver
ile/o	ileum
labi/o	lip
lith/o	stone
or/o	mouth
palat/o	palate
pharng/o	throat
proct/o	rectum
steat/o	fat

Anatomy

- Mouth – Includes the roof (hard palate, soft palate, and uvula) and the floor (tongue, muscles taste buds, and frenulum)
- Teeth – Adults have 32 permanent teeth
- Salivary Glands – The parotid, sublingual, and submandibular glands produce saliva
- Pharynx – The muscular tube that passes air, food, and water
- Esophagus – The muscular tube that carries food and water to the stomach
- Stomach – Digestive organ that contains the fundus (upper region), body (middle region), and antrum (lower region)
- Small Intestine – Slender, long, coiled tubular organ that contains the duodenum (2 inches), the jejunum (96 inches), and the ileum (132 inches)
- Large Intestine – 60 inch muscular organ that includes ascending colon, transverse colon, descending colon, and sigmoid colon
- Liver – Organ that produces bile and breaks down wastes
- Gallbladder - Small organ that stores bile
- Pancreas – Organ that produces enzymes for digestion
- Peritoneum – Serous membrane that lines the abdominal cavity

DIGESTIVE SYSTEM

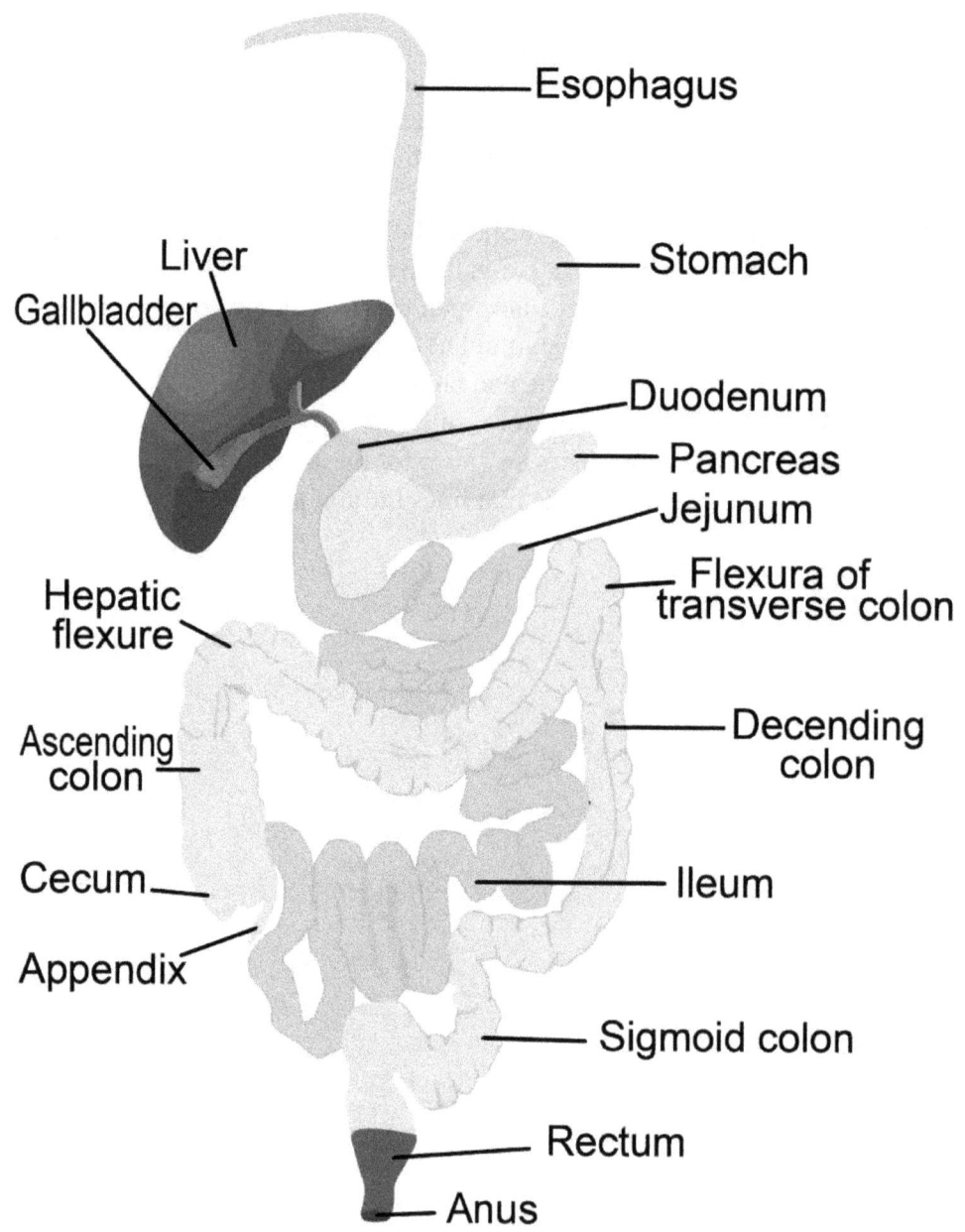

Terminology

- Anastomosis – Surgical connection of two body structures
- Cholecystectomy – Surgical removal of the gallbladder
- Colonoscopy – Fiberscopic examination of the colon
- Colostomy – Opening between the colon and the abdominal wall
- Diverticulum – Protrusion in the wall of the colon
- Dysphagia – Trouble swallowing
- Exstrophy – Condition where an organ is turned inside out
- Gastrostomy – Artificial opening between the stomach and the abdominal wall
- Hernia – Tissue or organ protruding through a cavity or the abdominal wall
- Laparoscopy – Exploratory procedure of the abdominal cavity using a small scope
- Lithotripsy – Procedure done to crush a kidney stone with sound waves
- Proctosigmoidoscopy – Procedure to examine the sigmoid colon and rectum with a small scope
- Varices – Varicose veins

Pathophysiology

- Ulceration
  - Also called – Canker sore, aphthous ulcer, or aphthous stomatitis
  - Description – Painful sore on the mouth or lips
  - Cause – Herpes simplex virus
  - Symptoms – Ulcers, tender sores, and redness

- Scleroderma
  - Also called – Progressive systemic sclerosis
  - Description – Atrophy of the lower esophagus smooth muscles.
  - Cause – Lower esophageal sphincter (LES) does not close properly
  - Symptoms – Esophageal reflux, dysphagia, and strictures

- Hiatal Hernia
  - Also called – Diaphragmatic hernia
  - Description – Condition where the diaphragm goes over the stomach
  - Cause – Part of the stomach protrudes through the diaphragm
  - Symptoms – Heartburn, belching, reflux, and chest discomfort

- Gastro Esophageal Reflux Disease (GERD)
  - Description – A disorder associated with hiatal hernia
  - Cause – Lower esophageal sphincter does not properly constrict
  - Symptoms – Heartburn, chest discomfort, and sour water reflux

- Gastritis
  - Description – Inflammation of the stomach mucosa
  - Cause – Infection, allergies, spicy foods, alcohol, or aspirin

- o Symptoms – Nausea, vomiting, bleeding, pain, and anorexia

- Peptic Ulcer
  - o Description - Erosive area on the gastric mucosa
  - o Cause – Smoking, alcohol, stress, aspirin, genetics, bacteria, and use of anti-inflammatory drugs
  - o Symptoms – Abdominal pain, dark tarry stools, and nausea

- Pyloric Stenosis
  - o Description – Infantile condition
  - o Cause – Pyloric sphincter narrowing
  - o Symptoms – Failure to thrive and projectile vomiting

- Appendicitis
  - o Description – Inflammation of the vermiform appendix that projects from the cecum
  - o Cause – Obstruction of the lumen results in infection
  - o Symptoms – Abdominal pain and fever

- Diverticulitis
  - o Description – Inflammation of the diverticula in the colon
  - o Cause – Aging condition caused by infection
  - o Symptoms – Diarrhea, gas, and abdominal pain

- Cirrhosis
  - o Description – Sever liver damage
  - o Cause – Alcohol use and liver damage from drugs or viruses
  - o Symptoms – Nausea, vomiting, fatigue, jaundice, and edema

- Pancreatitis
  - o Description – Inflammation of the pancreas
  - o Cause – Alcohol, biliary tract obstruction, drug use, gallstones, and viral infections
  - o Symptoms – Abdominal pain, fever, septicemia, and general sepsis

THE HEMIC AND LYMPHATIC SYSTEMS

The hemic and lymphatic systems includes the blood, lymph nodes, vessels, and small organs that remove excess tissue fluid from the body. Hemic refers to blood, and lymph is a colorless fluid that contains lymphocytes and monocytes.

Prefixes

hyper-	excess
inter-	between
retro-	behind

Suffixes

-ectomy	removal
-edema	swelling
-itis	inflammation
-megaly	enlargement
-old	resembling
-oma	tumor
-penia	deficient
-pexy	fixation
-poiesis	production

Combining Forms

aden/o	gland
axill/o	armpit/axilla
immun/o	immune
inguin/o	inguinal/groin region
splen/o	spleen
lymph/o	lymph
tox/o	poison

Anatomy

- Lymph – Sends leaked interstitial fluid into the venous system, assists in immune function, and helps with filtering blood
- Lymph nodes – Small structures of concentrated lymph tissue
- Spleen – Tiny organ located in the left upper abdomen area that filters blood
- Thymus – Tiny organ that secretes thymosins and matures the T cells
- Tonsils - Small tissue structures in the throat
- Bone marrow – Substance inside the bone that produces RBCs, WBCs, stem cells and platelets.

The Lymphatic System

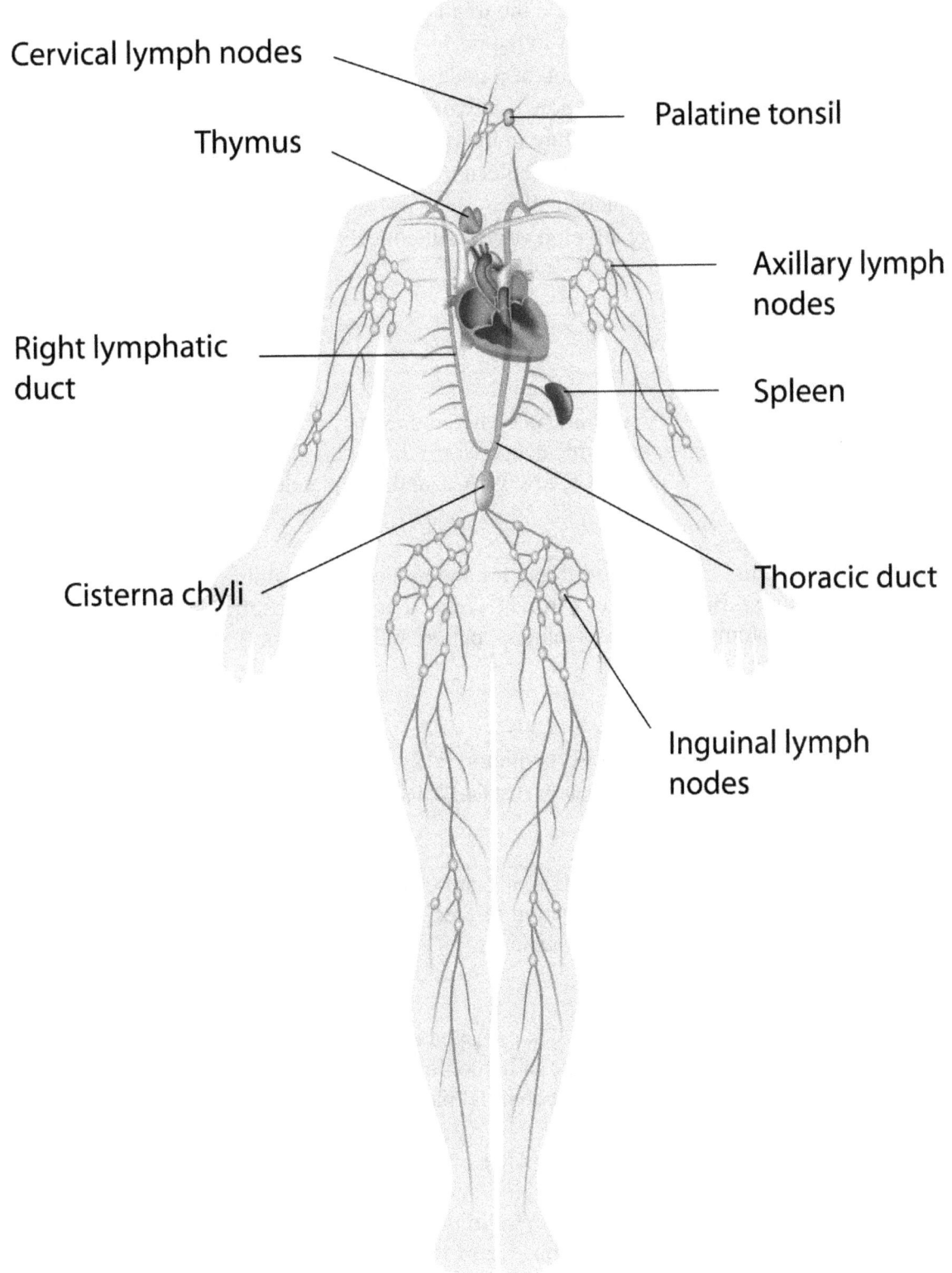

Terminology

- Axillary nodes – Lymph nodes in the armpits
- Inguinofemoral – Pertaining to the thigh or groin region
- Jugular nodes- Lymph nodes in the neck
- Lymphadenectomy – Excision of a node or nodes
- Lymphadenitis – Inflammation of a lymph node or nodes
- Parathyroid – A small structure in the brain that produces hormones
- Splenectomy – Removal of the spleen
- Stem cell – Immature blood cell
- Thoracic duct – Largest lymph vessel that collects lymph from areas below the diaphragm

Pathophysiology

- Aplastic Anemia
  - Description – Type of anemia where bone marrow failure occurs.
  - Cause – Genetics, chemical agents, irradiation, and immunologic factors.
  - Symptoms – Low RBCs, low WBCs, and low platelets.

- Iron Deficiency Anemia
  - Description – Small erythrocytes and reduced hemoglobin
  - Cause – Blood loss, low iron intake, and poor iron absorption
  - Symptoms – Fatigue, weakness, pallor, and headaches

- Pernicious Anemia
  - Description – Large stem cells
  - Cause – Inability to absorb vitamin B12
  - Symptoms – Pallor, weakness, and gastric discomfort

- Hemolytic Anemia
  - Description – Short survival of mature erythrocytes
  - Cause – Excessive destruction of RBCs
  - Symptoms – Pallor and weakness

- Sickle Cell Anemia
  - Description – Abnormal sickle-shaped erythrocytes
  - Cause – An abnormal type of hemoglobin
  - Symptoms – Arthralgia, abdominal pain, fatigue, and dyspnea

- Acute Myelogenous Leukemia (AML)
  - Description – Cancer of the blood that has a rapid onset and short survival time
  - Cause – Abnormal granulocytes in the bone marrow and blood
  - Symptoms – Fatigue, lymphadenopathy, and bone pain

- Acute Lymphocytic Leukemia (ALL)
  - Description – Cancer of the blood that occurs more often in children and adolescents
  - Cause – Immature lymphocytes
  - Symptoms – Fatigue, pallor, and abnormal blood values

- Chronic Myelogenous Leukemia (CML)
  - Description – Slow, progressive disease that occurs more often in those over 55
  Cause – Mature and immature granulocytes in the bone marrow and blood
  - Symptoms – Fatigue, weight loss, and fever

- Chronic Lymphocytic Leukemia (CLL)
  - Description – A slowly progressive cancer seen more often in older adults
  - Cause – Increased numbers of mature lymphocytes
  - Symptoms – Fatigue, fever, and weight loss

Notes
intentionally left blank

Notes
intentionally left blank

THE ENDOCRINE SYSTEM

The endocrine system is composed of various glands, including ductless endocrine glands that secrete hormones into the blood. This system manages the body by use of chemical messengers called hormones. Other components of this system are pineal gland, hypothalamus, pituitary gland, parathyroid gland, adrenals glands, the pancreas, ovaries, testes, and thymus.

Prefixes

eu-	good
oxy-	sharp
pan-	all
tropin-	act upon

Suffixes

-agon	assemble
-drome	run, to speed
-emia	blood condition
-in	a substance
-ine	a substance
-uria	urine

Combining Forms

andr/o	male
cortic/o	cortex
crin/o	secrete
dips/o	thirst
estr/o	female
gluc/o	sugar
gonad/o	testes or ovaries
home/o	same
kal/i	potassium
myx/o	mucus
natr/o	sodium
phys/o	growing
somat/o	body
thyr/o	thyroid gland
ur/o	urine

Anatomy

- Pituitary Gland
    - Also called: Master gland or hypophysis
    - Location: At the base of the brain near the sella turcica
    - Function: Releases numerous hormones

- Thyroid Gland
    - Location: Over the trachea
    - Function: Secretes thyroxine and triiodothyronine

- Parathyroid Glands
    - Location: On the posterior region of the thyroid gland
    - Function: Secretes parathyroid hormone

- Adrenal Glands
    - Location: On top of each kidney
    - Function: Secretes corticosteroids (cortisone, aldosterone, and androgens)

- Pancreas
    - Location: Behind the stomach
    - Function: Secretes insulin and glycogen

- Thymus
    - Location: Behind the sternum
    - Function: Produces thymosin

- Hypothalamus
    - Location: Above the pituitary gland
    - Function: Stimulates the pituitary gland to release hormones

- Pineal Gland
    - Location: Between the two brain cerebral hemispheres
    - Function: Secretes melatonin and various neurotransmitters

- Ovaries
    - Location: In the pelvic cavity
    - Function: Produce estrogen and progesterone, and release the egg for fertilization

- Testes
    - Location: Male genital region
    - Function: Secrete testosterone and sperm production

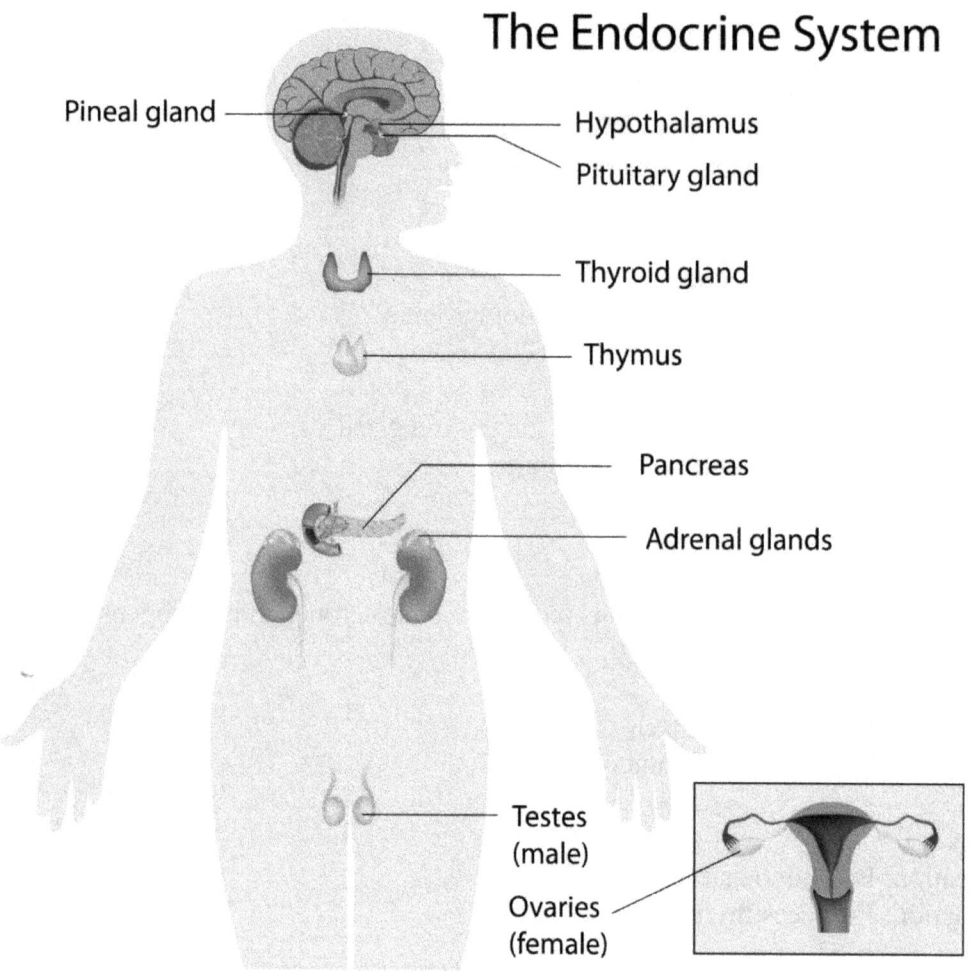

Terminology

- Contralateral – Opposite side
- Hormone – Chemical substance produced by various endocrine glands
- Isthmus – Connection of two structures or regions
- Isthmusectomy – Surgical removal of an isthmus
- Lobectomy – Surgical removal of a lobe
- Thymectomy – Surgical removal of the thymus
- Thyroglassal duct – An embryonic duct that is located between the thyroid gland and the posterior tongue
- Thyroidectomy – Surgical removal of the thyroid

Pathophysiology

- Diabetes Mellitus
    - Description: Chronic endocrine condition
    - Cause: A deficiency in insulin production or poor insulin usage
    - Types: Type 1 and Type 2
    - Symptoms: Polyuria, polydipsia, glycosuria, weight loss

- Disorders of the Pituitary Gland
    - Dwarfism – Hypopituitarism
    - Gigantism – Hyperpituitarism
    - Acromegaly – Hyperpituitarism
    - Diabetes Insipidus – Lac of antidiuretic hormone

- Hyperthyroidism
    - Also called: Thyrotoxicosis
    - Description: Excess production of thyroid hormone
    - Cause: Autoimmune process
    - Symptoms: Palpitations, goiter, dyspnea, nervousness, weight loss

- Hypothyroidism
    - Also called: Hashimoto's Disease
    - Description: Underactive thyroid gland
    - Cause: Inadequate amounts of thyroid stimulating hormone (TSH) or poor thyroid hormone production
    - Symptoms: Weight gain, mental sluggishness, fatigue, cold intolerance

- Cushing Syndrome
    - Also called: Hypercortisolism
    - Description: Excessive production of adrenocorticotropic hormone (ACTH)
    - Cause: Overactive adrenal cortex or long-term use of steroids
    - Symptoms: Weight gain, hypokalemia, hypernatremia, glucose intolerance

- Addison's Disease
    - Also called: Primary Adrenal Insufficiency
    - Description: Deficiency of adrenocortical hormones
    - Cause: Tumors, viruses, autoimmune disorders, infection, and tuberculosis
    - Symptoms: Fatigue, weight loss, loss of body hair, low blood pressure, infections

- Hyperaldosteronism
    - Description: Excess aldosterone from the adrenal cortex
    - Cause: Abnormality of the adrenal cortex or other adrenal stimuli
    - Symptoms: Hypokalemia, neuromuscular disorders, and hypertension

Notes
intentionally left blank

THE NERVOUS SYSTEM

The nervous system controls, regulates, and communicates with the body's various structures, organs, and body parts. It is made up of the central nervous system (CNS), which is the brain and spinal cord, and the peripheral nervous system (PNS), which involves the cranial and spinal nerves.

Prefixes

hemi-	half
per-	through
quadri-	four
tetra-	four

Suffixes

-algesia	pain
-algia	pain
-cele	hernia
-esthesia	feeling
-iatry	medical treatment

Combining Forms

crani/o	cranium
dur/o	dura mater
gangli/o	ganglion
gli/o	glial cells
lept/o	slender
ment/o	mind
mon/o	one
neur/o	nerve
phas/o	speech
phren/o	mind
poli/o	gray matter
rhiz/o	nerve root
vag/o	vagus nerve

<u>Anatomy</u>

- Neurons
    - Description: The primary cells of the nervous system
    - Types: Dendrites (receive nerve signals), Cell Body (nucleus), Axon (carries nerve signals), and Mylein Sheath (around the axon)

- Brain
  - Brainstem – Consists of the medulla oblongata, pons, and midbrain
  - Diencephalon – Consists of the hypothalamus and thalamus
  - Cerebellum – Structure that controls voluntary movement and balance
  - Cerebrum – Large portion of the brain
  - Lobes: Frontal, parietal, temporal, occipital, and insula

- Vertebral Column
  - Cervical – 7
  - Thoracic – 12
  - Lumbar – 5
  - Sacrum – 5
  - Coccyx – 4

- Nerves
  - Cranial – 12 pair
  - Spinal – 31 pair

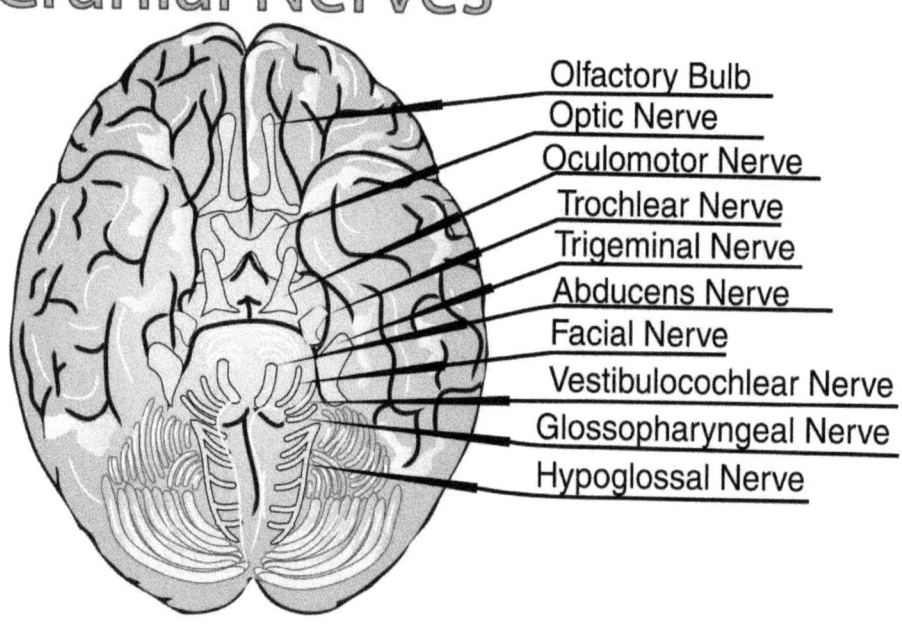

Terminology

- Burr – Drill used to enter the cranium
- Craniectomy – Partial, permanent removal of the skull
- Craniotomy – Opening into the skull
- Cranium – Skull

- Discectomy – Removal of a vertebral disc
- Electroencephalography – Diagnostic test that involves recording the electric currents of the brain
- Laminectomy – Surgical excision of the posterior region of the vertebra (spinal process)
- Shunt – An artificial passage
- Somatic nerve – Sensory nerve
- Stereotaxis – Method of identifying an area of the brain
- Trephination – Surgical removal of a disc
- Vertebrectomy – Removal of a vertebra

Pathophysiology

- Alzheimer's Disease
  - Description: The most common type of dementia
  - Cause: Thought to be genetic or autoimmune
  - Symptoms: Memory loss, personality changes, confusion, restlessness

- Amyotrophic Lateral Sclerosis (ALS)
  - Description: Lou Gehrig's disease involving deterioration of the motor neurons
  - Cause: Familial chromosome 21 aberration
  - Symptoms: Difficulty walking, talking, and breathing

- Multiple Sclerosis (MS)
  - Description – Demyelination of the central nervous system
  - Cause: Myelin damage and gliosis of white matter develops
    Symptoms: Vision problems, bladder disorders, paresthesia

- Myasthenia Gravis (MG)
  - Description: Grave muscle weakness
  - Cause: Autoimmune
  - Symptoms: Muscle weakness and muscle fatigue

- Spina Bifida
  - Description: Developmental birth defect where there is underdevelopment of the spinal cord and structures
  - Cause: Lack of nutrients during pregnancy, congenital, and genetics
  - Symptoms: Vertebrae over the spinal cord do not form or remain unfused or open

- Transient Ischemic Attack (TIA)
  - Description: Temporary reduction of blood flow to the brain causes stroke-like symptoms
  - Cause: Cerebrovascular disease
  - Symptoms: slurred speech, paresthesia of face, mental confusion

- Cerebrovascular Accident (CVA)
  - Description: Infarction of the brain due to lack of blood flow
  - Cause: Atherosclerotic disease, thrombus, embolus, or hemorrhage
  - Symptoms: Depends on the location of obstruction or damage

- Cerebral Aneurysm
  - Description: Dilatation of the artery
  - Cause: Atherosclerosis
  - Symptoms: Diplopia, headache, confusion, slurred speech

- Epilepsy
  - Description: A chronic seizure disorder
  - Cause: History of head trauma or brain disease, tumor, hemorrhage, infection, high fever, and brain edema
  - Symptoms: Aura, loss of awareness, incontinence, alternate contraction and relaxation

Notes
intentionally left blank

Notes
intentionally left blank

THE SENSES

The five senses are sight (eyes), smell (nose), hearing (ears), taste (tongue), and touch (skin). Various conditions and disorders of these structures result in loss of sense. Many procedures and services involve the sense organs and the five senses.

Prefixes

audi-	hearing
esco-	inward
exo-	outward

Suffixes

-opia	vision
-omia	smell
-tropia	to turn

Combining Forms

ambly/o	dim/dullness
aque/o	water
audi/o	hearing
blephar/o	eyelid
cor/o	pupil
cycl/o	ciliary body
dacry/o	tear
glauc/o	gray
ir/o	iris
mi/o	smaller
myring/o	eardrum
ocul/o	eye
opt/o	eye
ot/o	ear
papill/o	optic nerve
phac/o	eye lens
pot/o	light
presby/o	old age
scler/o	sclera
tympan/o	tympanic membrane
vitre/o	glassy
xer/o	dry

Anatomy

Eye/Sight

- Cornea – Outer layer of the eye that refracts light to focus on the posterior eye
- Sclera – The white of the eye that extends from the cornea to the optic nerve
- Choroid – The middle layer of the eye that contains pigment
- Retina – The inner layer of the eye that contains rods and cones
- Conjunctiva – The part of the eye that covers the sclera and lines the eyelid
- Lens – The section of the eye behind the pupil
- Aqueous humor – Fluid in front of the lens
- Vitreous humor – Fluid behind the lens
- Optic nerve – Transfers light rays from the brain to the rods and cones

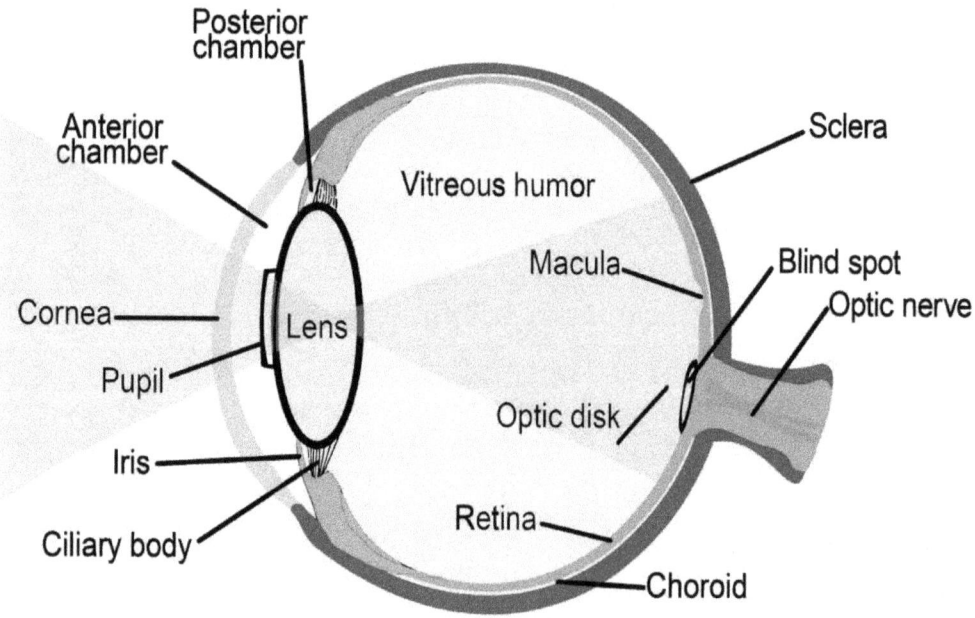

Ear/Hearing

- Auricle – Also called the pinna, this structure allows sound waves to enter the ear
- Auditory canal – The tunnel from the auricle to the middle ear
- Tympanic membrane – Inner ear eardrum
- Ossicles – Small inner ear bones: malleus, incus, and stapes
- Eustachian tube – Tube that goes from the inner ear to the pharynx
- Cochlea – Structure that conducts sound waves

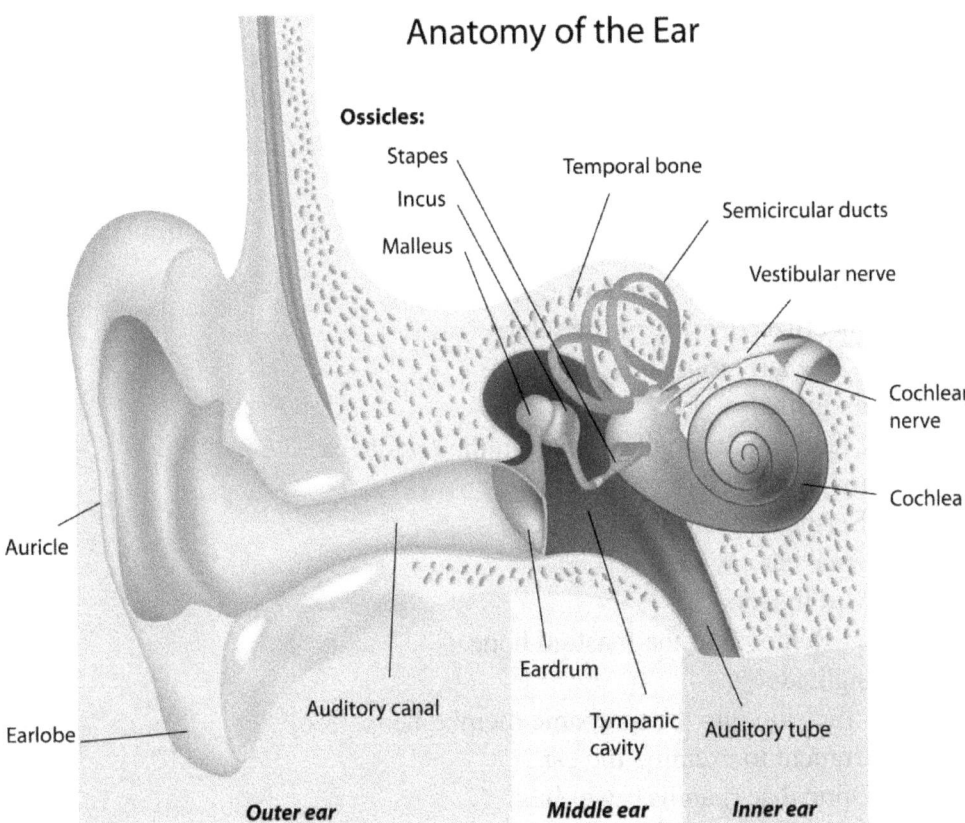

Nose/Smell

- Olfactory Sense Receptors – Located in the nasal cavity and associated with Cranial Nerve I (CNI).

Tongue/Taste

- Taste buds – Located on the anterior region of the tongue and associated with Cranial Nerves VII and IX (CNVII and CNIX).

Skin/Touch

- Mechanoreceptors – Involves the Meissner corpuscles (feel touch) and the Pacinian corpuscles (sense pressure)
- Proprioceptors – Control position and orientation
- Thermoreceptors – Lie under the skin and sense temperature changes
- Nociceptors – Pain sensors in the skin and organs

Terminology

- Apicectomy – Removal of a portion of the temporal bone
- Astigmatism – Condition where refractive surfaces of the eye are not equal
- Aural atresia – Congenital absence of the external auditory canal
- Blepharitis – Eyelid inflammation
- Dacryocystitis – Blocked nasolacrimal duct
- Dacryostenosis – Lacrimal duct narrowing.
- Ectropion – Eversion of the eyelid (sagging)
- Enucleation – Removal of an organ or organs
- Episclera – Connective covering of the sclera
- Exophthalmos – Eyeball protrusion
- Exostosis – Bony growth
- Fenestration – Creation of a small opening in the middle ear
- Hyperopia = Farsightedness
- Keratoplasty – Surgical repair of the cornea
- Labyrinth – Internal ear cavities
- Lacrimal – Related to tears
- Mastoidectomy – Removal of the mastoid bone
- Myopia – Nearsightedness
- Myringotomy – Incision into the tympanic membrane
- Otoscope – Instrument to examine the ear
- Papilledema – Optic disc (papilla) swelling
- Ptosis – Drooping of the upper eyelid
- Tarsorraphy – Suturing eyelids
- Tinnitus – Ringing in the ears
- Tympanolysis – Removal of adhesions from the tympanic membrane
- Tympanostomy – Insertion of tubes into the tympanum
- Vertigo – Dizziness

Pathophysiology

Visual Disturbances

- Astigmatism – Irregular curvature of the cornea or lens, which can occur from trauma, disease, congenital, or acquired
- Diplopia – Double vision
- Amblyopia – Dimness of vision
- Presbyopia – Age-related farsightedness
- Nystagmus – Rapid, involuntary eye movements
- Strabismus – Cross-eyed

Visual Conditions

- Conjunctivitis
    - Description: "Pink eye" where there is inflammation of the lining of the eyelid
    - Cause: Infection, allergy, or irritation
    - Symptoms: Pink sclera and drainage

- Hordeolum
    - Description: Stye on the eyelid
    - Cause: Bacterial infection of hair follicle
    - Symptoms: Red, tender mass on the eyelid

- Keratitis
    - Description: Corneal inflammation
    - Cause: HSV
    - Symptoms: Tearing and photophobia

- Macular Degeneration
    - Description: Destruction of the fovea centralis
    - Cause: Age-related
    - Symptoms: Loss of central vision

- Cataracts
    - Description: Clouding of the lens due to protein aggregate accumulation
    - Cause: Congenital, genetic, trauma, and age
    - Symptoms: Blurred vision and seeing halos around lights

- Glaucoma
    - Description: Accumulation of excess intraocular aqueous humor
    - Cause: Age-related
    - Symptoms: Often asymptomatic

Hearing Conditions

- Otitis Media
    - Description: Infection and inflammation of the middle ear
    - Cause: Viruses or bacteria
    - Symptoms: Hearing loss, ear pain, and vertigo

- Otitis Externa
    - Description: Swimmer's ear; infection and inflammation of the outer ear
    - Cause: Bacteria or fungus
    - Symptoms: Ear pain and discharge

- Conductive Hearing loss
    - Description: Loss of hearing due to defect of sound-conducting apparatus
    - Cause: Wax buildup or scarring of the tympanic membrane
    - Symptoms: Hearing loss

- Sensorineural Hearing Loss
    - Description: Loss of hearing due to lesion of the cochlea or neural path
    - Cause: Defect in receptors or vestibulocochlear nerve
    - Symptoms: Hearing loss

II. PSYCHOLOGY

GENERAL CONCEPTS

Universal mental health concepts include anxiety, stress, and self-esteem. Factors that influence reactions to stressors include cultural background, family dynamics, exposure to similar stressors in the past, and ongoing exposure to multiple or intense stress.

- Anxiety

    Anxiety is a common human phenomenon characterized by an intense fear or dread related to a known or unknown cause. All patients and most family members are vulnerable to feelings of anxiety. Typical anxiety is acute and can be useful for problem solving. Long-term, persistent anxiety is considered a mental health condition.

- Stress

    Stress is a relationship between a person and his or her environment that arises when he or she feels pressure or overwhelming feelings related to a situation, event, person, place, or thing. Resources to handle stress are considered coping and defense mechanisms. When confronting a physical danger, a person uses the fight-or-flight response to evade harm, such as with escaping a tornado or facing a wild animal in the forest.

- Self-Esteem

    Self-esteem is a person's judgment of his or her own worth and value. The patient's level of self-esteem can influence his or her adjustment to disease, illness, and injury. People with healthy self-esteem often face problems with a positive outlook, whereas those with low self-esteem have negative, pessimistic thoughts and feelings.

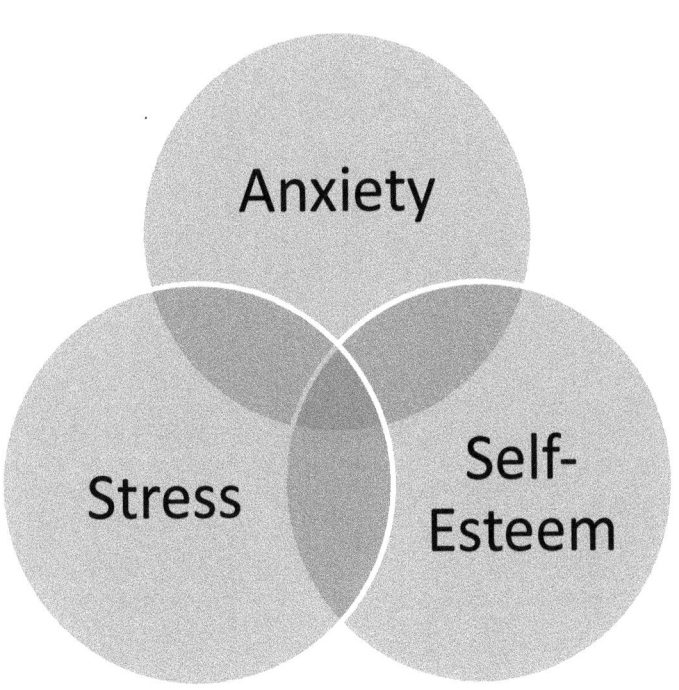

BEHAVIORAL THEORIES

Medical assistants often encounter patients who are suffering from various forms of behavior and emotional difficulties. Austrian physician Sigmund Freud was the first to label the hidden area of mind, naming it the unconscious. This area contained emotions, memories, and thoughts that people are not aware they have. Many other theories of behavior have been proposed over the last two centuries.

Erikson's Theory of Psychosocial Development

Erikson's theory of psychosocial development maintains that the human life cycle has eight ego development stages that span from birth to death. There is a psychosocial crisis that occurs for each stage, and the objective is to integrate the demands of physical growth, maturation, and society. Certain psychosocial tasks must be accomplished during the life cycle in order to maintain wellness with this theory.

Age	*Psychosocial Crisis*	*Task*	*Successful Resolution*	*Unsuccessful Resolution*
Birth to 18 Mo. Infancy	Trust Vs. Mistrust	Attachment to the mother	Trust in persons; faith in environment; hope for the future	Difficulties relating to others; suspicion/ fear of the future
18 Mo. to 3 Yr. Early Childhood	Autonomy Vs. Shame and Doubt	Gaining basic control over self and environment	Sense of self-control and adequacy	Independence-fear conflict; sense of self-doubt
3 to 6 Yr. Late Childhood	Initiative Vs. Guilt	Becoming purposeful and directive	Ability to initiate own activities; sense of purpose	Aggression-fear conflict; sense of inadequacy
6 to 12 Yr. School Aged	Industry Vs. Inferiority	Developing physical, social, and learning skills	Competence; ability to learn and work	Sense of inferiority; difficulty learning
12 to 20 Yr. Adolescence	Identity Vs. Role Confusion	Developing a sense of identity	Sense of personal identity	Confusion about self-identity; identity submerged in relationships or group attendance
20 to 35 Yr. Early Adulthood	Intimacy Vs. Isolation	Establishing intimate bonds and friendships	Ability to love and commit	Emotional isolation; egocentricity
35 to 65 Yr. Middle Adulthood	Generativity Vs. Stagnation	Fulfilling life goals related to career, family, and society	Ability to give and care for others	Self-absorption; inability to develop and grow

| 65 Yr. to Death Late Adulthood | Integrity Vs. Despair | Looking back over life and accepting meaning | Sense of integrity and fulfillment | Dissatisfaction with life (Varcarolis, 2006) |

Piaget's Theory of Developmental Learning

Piaget studied the basis for development of the mind, as well as learning and cognition. His theory holds that motor activity is stimulated by mental development and growth. Infants learn that motor activity can produce sound and that cognitive interaction is associated with the environment.

Developmental Period	*Age Group*	*Description*
Sensorimotor	Birth to 2 Years	Children learn through motor skills and senses.
Preoperational	2 to 6 Years	Children start to think symbolically and develop language skills, and thinking is self-centered.
Concrete Operational	7 to 11 Years	Children understand differences and begin to reason.
Formal Operations	12 to Adult	Children/adults grasp abstract concepts, set long-term goals, and related new material to the past (Martin, 2009).

Notes
intentionally left blank

Notes
intentionally left blank

DEATH AND DYING

Bereavement is the time period of mourning after a loved one has died. The amount of time varies from person to person, but it typically lasts 6 to 12 months or longer. Grief is a normal response to loss and mourning is the public expression of grief. The three types of grief are acute, chronic, and anticipatory. With chronic grief, the person is at risk for depression, which is characterized by feelings of sadness and changes in mood.

Loss is the absence of something wanted, available, and loved. With actual loss, others can identify situation or event, whereas with perceived loss, the patient experiences something others cannot comprehend or verify. Anticipatory loss is when the patient expects and experiences the loss before it occurs.

The medical assistant's role concerning grief and loss involves assisting the patient with various feelings and adjustments. Adequate communication with the patient and family is necessary, as is the provision of counseling and referrals to mental health professionals. The medical assistant must consider the survivor's religion, culture, family dynamics, coping skills, and support systems.

Stages of the Grief/Loss Response

- Stage 1: Shock and Disbelief – The survivor feels numb, has emotional outbursts, denies the situation or event, and isolates self.

- Stage 2: Experiencing the Loss – The survivor feels angry regarding the loss/death, bargains regarding this event, and suffers from depression.

- Stage 3: Reintegration – The survivor starts to reorganize his or her life, adapts to the situation/event, and accepts reality.

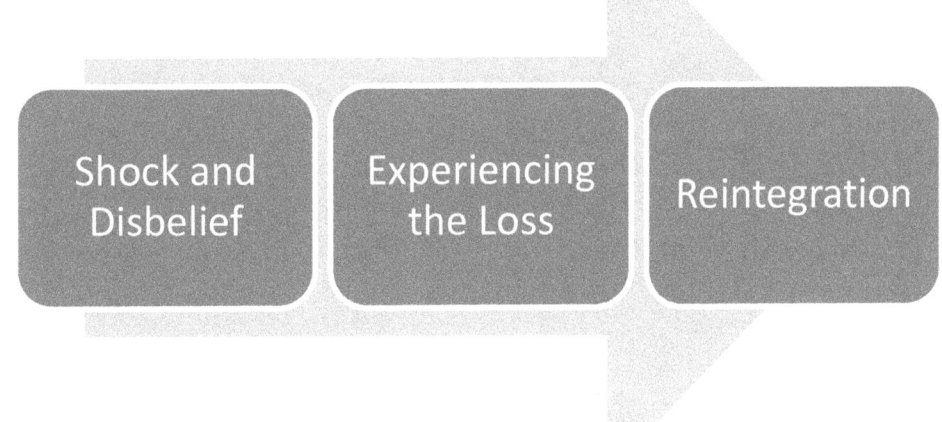

Situational Crises and Coping Mechanisms

For many patients, a serious illness and hospitalization constitutes a crisis. A crisis is the overwhelming events or series of events that create a situation that is perceived as threatening or unbearable. A situational crisis occurs when the unexpected event causes stress to a person or family, such as the development of an acute illness. The developmental stages of a crisis include:

- The person or family is in a state of homeostasis.
- The stressful event occurs
- Well-known coping skills fail to reduce the threat.
- A period of disequilibrium occurs.
- The problem is either resolved, or personal disintegration occurs.

A situational crisis is one in which the problem leads to disruption of normal psychological functioning. Examples of situational crisis include an unwanted pregnancy, a new baby, divorce, death of a loved one, onset or change in a disease process, loss of job or career, and being a victim of a violent act. Community situational crises are events that affect an entire community. These include terrorist attacks, floods, hurricanes, earthquakes, and tornadoes.

Phases of a Crisis

- Phase 1: External precipitating event – There is a situation that occurs or something happens.

- Phase 2: The threat – A perceived or actual threat causes increased anxiety where the patient copes or fails to cope.

- Phase 3: Failed coping – The patient fails to cope, which produces physical symptoms, relationship problems, and increases disorganization.

- Phase 4: Resolution – There is mobilization of internal and external resources, and the patient returns to the pre-crisis level of function.

Coping Mechanisms

Many patients respond to anxiety, stress, and crisis by using various coping skills they have learned over time. Coping mechanisms are learned external behaviors and internal thought processes that are used to decrease discomfort and pain. Coping behaviors can be emotion-focused or problem-focused. With emotion-focused behaviors, the patient alters a response to stress by thinking, saying or doing something that makes him or her feel happier or normal. These behaviors include crying, screaming, and talking with others. Problem-focused behaviors are done to alter the stressor in some way, such as investigating the facts of a problem or devising a plan to overcome the situation.

Self Defense Mechanisms

- Denial – Avoidance of a particular problem by refusing to recognize it or outright ignoring it.

- Displacement – Transfer of feelings for a threatening person, place, or thing to another neutral person, place, or thing.

- Intellectualization – Expressive thinking and logic adoption to avoid uncomfortable thoughts and feelings.

- Projection – Assignment of feelings or motivation to another person, place, or thing.

- Rationalization – Giving logical and acceptable explanations to hide a feeling, concern, or motive that is not socially acceptable.

- Regression – The demonstration of behavior characteristics from an earlier developmental stage.

III. PROFESSIONALISM

GENERAL CONCEPTS

A medical assistant must maintain a professional attitude and appearance at all times. The healthcare environment can be both stressful and humorous, but it is always best to maintain a sense of professionalism. This section covers professional attitude, job readiness, seeking employment, and working as a team member.

Displaying Professional Attitude

A professional attitude involves appropriate communication with patients, physicians, and other healthcare workers. Good communication skills include refraining from phrases that are considered slang or that are unfamiliar to patients and other healthcare workers. Speaking in a well-educated manner is crucial in order to portray a professional image of yourself and the facility where you work. It is important that a medical assistant is proficient in both written and spoken grammar.

Qualities of a Good Employee

After securing a position, the medical assistant must always look and do his or her best. An employer expects the employee to perform with increasing expertise as he or she gains experience. Certain qualities are important for holding a job. The desirable employee qualities that employers usually rank as most important are:

- Communication skills
- Dependability
- Cooperation
- Courteousness
- Enthusiasm
- Initiative
- Interest
- Punctuality
- Math skills
- Reading skills
- Time management skills
- Reliability
- Responsibility

Job Description

The job description is a document used in healthcare facilities to specify what is expected of employees. Each employee will have a detailed outline of job duties, giving particular information regarding the performance of these tasks and the position's responsibilities. The job description should contain:

- Title of the position
- Supervisor of the employee
- Summary of the position
- Primary duties of the job
- Expectations of the job
- Requirements of the position
- Qualifications for the job
- Additional criteria relevant to the facility

Employee Evaluation

Most employers require employees to have routine, regular evaluations regarding personal work performance. The time schedule varies from facility to facility, but typically, the reviews are held every three months for the first year, and then every 6 to 12 months after the first year. These employee evaluations should be regarded in a positive light. Some guidelines regarding this evaluation include:

- Let the supervisor know your intentions and goals.
- Ask questions regarding dress code, policies, and other important issues.
- Ask about your schedule and vacation during the meeting.
- Do not discuss personal problems or requests.
- Request a copy of the evaluation if it is not offered.
- Do not take suggests for improvements as insults

Working as a Team Member

In addition to physicians, the medical assistant will work with a variety of healthcare team members. Each person performs a specific set of duties for which he or she is trained. Many of these team members have direct contact with the medical assistant. It is necessary to be knowledgeable about various allied health professionals, such as:

- Admissions Clerk – An admissions clerk in a medical office has basic administrative office skills. He or she obtains basic medical history and information from patient when they come into the facility.

- Certified Nursing Assistant (CNA) – A CAN provides basic nursing skills and patient care to people in adult day care centers, nursing homes, office settings, and hospitals. This person is registered and/or licensed.

- Emergency Medical Technician (EMT) – An EMT is a person trained in the administration of emergency care and transportation of patients to the medical facility.

- Laboratory Technician – Often called a medical technologist, a laboratory technician is someone who works under the supervision of a pathologist or physician. These healthcare workers perform chemical, microscopic, and/or bacteriologic testing on blood and body tissues.

- Licensed Practical Nurse (LPN) – An LPN is a one-year nurse who is trained in patient care and licensed by the state.

- Registered Nurse (RN) – An RN is a two- or four-year nurse who is trained in patient care and licensed by the state.

- Nurse Practitioner (NP) – An NP is a RN who has advanced training to diagnose and treat patients in the healthcare environment.

- Phlebotomist – Also called an accessioning technician, a phlebotomist is a person who is trained in drawing blood.

- Physician Assistant (PA) – A PA is a person trained to practice medicine under the supervision of a physician.

Radiologic Technologist (RT) – Also called an x-ray technician, an RT is a person who is trained to operate radiologic equipment under the supervision of a physician.

Notes
intentionally left blank

Notes
intentionally left blank

JOB READINESS AND SEEKING EMPLOYMENT

Once the medical assistant completes his or her education and obtains certification, it is time to start looking for a job. When seeking employment, it is necessary to understand the components of a resume and cover letter, as well as the interview process.

Resume Overview

The personal resume is an outline or summary of your experience, knowledge, and abilities. One of the first steps to obtaining employment is developing and presenting a resume. The resume should include professional affiliations, previous work experience, community service, and employment objectives. It should not include your age, marital status, race, religion, or any other personal facts.

Resume Styles

- Traditional - The traditional approach to a resume is a chronological ordered listing of your information.
- Career objective - With this style, you show the reader your career choice and list your qualifications.
- Functional - With this type of resume, you show attention to your achievements and strengths.
- Targeted - The targeted approach is used for a precise field of employment, showing expertise in a particular area.

Cover Letter

A cover letter should state why the medical assistant desires employment and why he or she should be hired for a particular position. Personalizing the letter is one approach that gives the letter more attention. Finding the name of the office manager can be accomplished by making a phone call to the office or facility. Be sure to make the letter simple and direct, request an interview, and specify when and how you can be reached. The cover letter should be error-free, so be sure to check it well for grammatical errors and spelling mistakes.

The Interview

An interview is a face-to-face meeting with the person who hires personnel. Some general guidelines for the interview include:

- Dress professionally
- Do not chew gum
- Avoid excessive makeup and jewelry
- Do not take anyone along
- Introduce yourself and shake hands
- Answer questions honestly and directly
- Avoid rambling

Common Interview Questions

So that you are prepared for the interview, here are some commonly asked interview questions:

- What were your favorite subjects in school?
- What are your qualifications for employment?
- Do you plan to continue your education? If so, what are your plans?
- Why are you seeking employment with our organization?
- Do you work well under pressure?
- What are your strengths and your weaknesses?
- How would you describe yourself?
- What motivates you to do your best?
- What make you decide to enter the healthcare field?
- What are your long-term goals?
- What two things are the most important to you in a job?

Questions for the Applicant

Here are some questions you can ask during the interview:

- Can I see a job description?
- What are the office hours and holiday schedule?
- Do you offer health and dental insurance?
- What is the rate of pay?
- Are there any chances for promotion or advancement?
- Do you offer tuition reimbursement or a retirement plan?
- How frequent are the job performance evaluations?

IV. COMMUNICATIONS, LAWS AND PRIVACY

GENERAL COMMUNICATIONS CONCEPTS

The care of patients involves many different individuals and all types of healthcare providers. Therefore, it is necessary for there to be effective and meaningful communication in order to ensure healthcare delivery. Communication systems are formal and informal structures used to support the communication needs within an organization. Elements of these systems are the communication channel, type of message, policies, agent, services, device, interaction mode, and security protocol. Also, effective communication relies on useful style and principles of sharing information, negotiation concepts and strategies, and communication processes that support safe patient care.

Communication Systems

Communication systems are structures used by the healthcare facility to support exchange of information. The can be either formal or informal, involve people or groups, and use technology or other modes of transfer. The elements of a communications system includes:

- Communication channel – The "pipeline" along which a message must travel that runs from the initiator to the recipient. These include telephone, email, reports, staff meetings, board meetings, presentation, one-on-one conversation, consumer feedback, and patient/family council.

- Types of message – Messages can be structured (formal) or unstructured (informal). When messages are sent via a computerized email or telephone recording, they will usually be in a standard format.

- Policies – Communication policies are used to shape the communication system performance, which is independent to the technologies used.

- Agents – The agent is the person who is responsible for transmission of information from person to person or from one to a group.

- Services – There are numerous computer software applications for providing communication services. These include faxing, voice mail, and text messages.

- Device – Examples of communication devices include fax machine, telephone, and personal digital assistant (PDA).

- Interaction mode – The way the interaction is designed relies on the information system. Some modes of interaction require that the message recipient pays attention, such as the ring tone of a phone.

- Security protocol – In the healthcare environment, patient privacy concerns make it important that unintended recipients do not gain access to clinical records or patient information. The facility uses a security protocol to reflect the degree of risk associated with the message content.

Communication Styles

Five well-known communication styles include:

- Persuasive – This style encourages others to view ideas as beneficial to their needs, displays authority to build trust, and reassures staff by creating an emotive and empathetic connection.

- Assertive – This style involves standing up for personal rights and expressing feelings, beliefs, and thoughts in an honest, direct, and appropriate way which does not violate another individual's rights.

- Passive – This style involves violation of your own rights by failing to express feelings, beliefs, and thoughts and allowing others to violate your rights. This is often done in a timid, apologetic manner.

- Aggressive – This style involves violation of the rights of others by directly standing up for your personal rights in an inappropriate manner.

- Passive-aggressive – This style involves expressing your feelings, beliefs, and thoughts in a confusing and unclear way.

Types of Communication

Communication is verbal, nonverbal, and written. The purposes of communication are to inquire, inform, and persuade. A medical assistant can inquire through verbal or written communication and by phone or in person. Informational communication is a key component of many medical-related transactions, and insurance companies must be updated and informed regarding patients' health conditions, progress, and treatment plans. Other than the patient and family, the medical assistant communicates with insurance companies, physicians, and other healthcare team members.

Verbal communication refers to spoken words. If the information is obtained, provided, and shared with ease, this enhances the communication process. Words should be kept simple and in the appropriate vernacular. The medical assistant should avoid using abbreviated names, technical jargon, or medical terminology that is unfamiliar to the patient or family. A successful medical assistant can synthesize and articulate information without the need for constant clarifications and explanations. Common difficulties of verbal communication include:

- Hearing impairment
- Language barriers
- Developmental, cognitive, and/or psychological impairment.

Communicating with Others in the Healthcare Environment

When communicating with other healthcare workers, a medical assistant should react and respond only to facts – not feelings – to avoid confrontation and biased decision-making. Professional communication skills that facilitate team communication include active listening, asking questions to clarify rather than challenge someone's ideas, respecting others' opinions, and not interpreting others' statements or interrupt others to give unsolicited advice.

When communicating with a patient, both non-verbal and verbal responses give the medical assistant useful information and can be of equal importance. When someone is not telling the truth or does not want to answer a question, he or she may look away, become tense, and remain silent. Therefore, information obtained during an interview should not include only the patient's factual responses but concerns, attitudes, and non-verbal responses, as well. The medical assistant should attempt to ask open-ended questions whenever possible. Also, rephrasing a patient's statement and providing a list of options are two strategies that encourage the patient to give more detailed information.

Interview Techniques

One of the essential skills for a medical assistant is interviewing. Many interviews are conducted face-to-face, by telephone, by electronic mail, or in writing. Some interviews involve only the CMA and the patient, but the family is often included. Preparation for the interview will ensure that the goals and objectives of the interview are met and that the flow of the process is organized and purposeful.

Strategies for Interview Preparation

- Know the purpose of the interview, what you intend to accomplish, and what the expected outcomes are.
- Outline the information that should be obtained and provided, and collect all necessary forms before the interview process.
- Obtain education regarding the main facts and topics of the interview.
- Make an appointment for the interview to show respect and ensure that the patient and family will have time to prepare.
- Arrange the interview room for the comfort of the patient and attempt to minimize noise and distractions.

The Interview Process

- Greet the participant(s) and introduce yourself and others present.
- Explain the relationship and/or role of all concerned parties.
- If you plan to take notes or write during the process, inform all participants of this.
- Use a conversational style, vary your questions, and attempt to ask open-ended questions when possible.

- Only ask one question at a time and save personal questions for the end of the interview.
- Keep the objectives of the interview in mind and avoid turning the process into a question-answer session.
- Show empathy and understanding and practice active listening.
- Give participants a chance to ask questions.
- Close the interview with a review of the discussed information and facts collected.
- Thank all participants for their time and assistance.

Telephone Techniques

The telephone is the most used technology for patient interaction with the medical office. For telephone communication to be effective, office workers use specific skills and guidelines.

Telephone Voice Qualities

- Enunciation – Speak clearly.
- Pronunciation - Speak words correctly.
- Speed - Speak at a normal rate.
- Volume - Use a normal voice.
- Infection - Use correct pitch and tone.
- Courtesy - Speak politely.
- Attention - Focus on the caller

Office Calls

- Answer before the fourth ring.
- Greet the caller with "Good morning" or "good afternoon."
- Provide the name of the facility, as well as your name.
- Use a standard closing, such as "thank you for calling."
- Allow the caller to hang up first.

Directing Multiple Incoming Calls

- Ask the first caller if he or she minds being placed on hold. Be sure to explain that you have another call.
- Ask the second caller to wait and allow time for a response before placing him or her on hold.
- Attempt to respond within 30 seconds, but provide options if the hold will be longer.
- Thank callers for waiting.

Screening Calls

- Manage physicians' time by referring necessary calls only and taking messages for other calls.

- Know who and where to refer patients for assistance.

Routing Calls

- Tell the caller who you are forwarding the call to.
- Provide the forwarding number in case of disconnection.
- Inform the caller if the party does not respond, the person may leave a voice mail.

Dealing with Emergencies

- Notify the physician of the emergency immediately.
- Activate the emergency medical system (EMS).
- Instruct the caller to hang up and call 911.
- Provide EMS with necessary information, including advance directives.

Managing Difficult Callers

- Keep voice at a normal tone and remain calm when speaking with angry callers.
- Notify the appropriate staff member after determining the problem.
- Follow up with the patient to be sure the problem was addressed.
- Notify the office manager, administrator, or physician of irate callers of callers with unresolved issues.
- Obtain the identity of threatening callers and notify appropriate supervisor.

Telephone Confidentiality

According to HIPAA standards, certain guidelines apply to the telephone. These include:

- Verify that the caller is indeed the patient.
- Give information only to the patient.
- Be sure the conversation is not heard by other patients.
- Avoid discussing telephone conversations around patients.
- Do not leave information on a patient's voice mail.

LEGAL GUIDELINES AND REQUIREMENTS

This section covers law, ethics, healthcare duties, obligations, and reportable incidences.

Law and Ethics

Laws are rules that govern actions, regulate conduct, punish offenders, and remedy wrongs. They are enforced by an agency. The two types of law are criminal law and civil law.

- Criminal Laws - These rules and regulations apply to crimes committed against an individual, society, or an organization. The state or government brings charges against a person or persons and issues a punishment.

- Civil Laws - These rules and regulations apply to crimes committed against an individual or property. The individual or his representative brings charges against a person or persons and seeks some form of compensation. The three types of civil law are tort law, contract law, and administrative law.

Tort Laws

Tort laws involve accidental or intentional harm to a person or property, which results from the wrongdoing of a person or persons. A tort is a wrongful civil act. Negligence is a type of tort, defined as failure to offer an acceptable standard of care that is comparable and reasonable to what a competent medical assistant, nurse, or other healthcare worker would provide in a similar situation. The four types of negligence include:

- Nonfeasance - The failure to act that results in or causes harm.

- Misfeasance - Improper action that results in or causes harm.

- Malfeasance - The performance of an improper act that results in or causes harm.

- Malpractice - The failure to act or improper action that results in serious damage or death to an individual. For malpractice to occur, four things must occur: the patient-physician relationship was established (duty), the professional neglected to act or acted improperly (dereliction), a negative outcome occurred from an action or lack of an action (direct cause), and the patient sustained harm (damages.)

Contract Laws

Contract laws involve the rights and obligations of contracts, which are promises of obligation. A contract is an obligatory agreement between two or more parties. For a contract to be legal and binding, five things must occur: (1) an offer was made, (2) the offer was accepted, (3) an exchange of something of value (consideration), (4) all parties were legally capable to accept the terms (capacity), and (5) the intent was legal.

Consent for Medical Services and Care

Consent for various medical services and health care involves the patient giving verbal or written permission. Consents are contracts, which can be implied or expressed, except in life-threatening circumstances and medical emergencies. Consent must be informed, which requires a trained healthcare worker explaining the necessary information to the patient so he or she can make an educated decision. Components of the consent involve an explanation of the test or procedure, the reason for the test or procedure, the possible side effects, risks, and complications, alternative therapies and their side effects, risks, and complications, the prognosis with or without the test or procedure, and any additional information that assists in the decision making process.

Only certain people can give consent for medical services and care. They include:

- Patient
- Legal competent adult in charge of patient's care
- Emancipated minor
- Minors in the armed forces
- Minors seeking services for sexually transmitted infections (STIs)

- Minor parent with custody of his/her minor child

Patient Self-Determination Act

The federal Patient Self-Determination Act of 1989 requires that patients under Medicare and Medicaid be provided with information concerning their rights to determine and make healthcare decisions. This legislation is intended to improve the use of advance directives and increase the appropriateness of care while ensuring the patient has the right to make various decisions. This Act encourages patients to decide about the extent of medical care they want early in the care process.

With the PSDA, the patient can choose which treatments and care activities he or she wishes to accept or refuse. Also, this Act requires that all healthcare organizations recognize the advance directive(s). Under the PSDA, the facility must explain to the patient his or her rights under state law. The information given to the patient includes issues about the state's laws concerning patients' rights to make medical care decisions, such as refusing or accepting treatment options. Additionally the patient is entitled to receive information regarding his or her right to create an advance directive.

Advance Directives

Advance directives are documents that state the patient's wishes for medical decisions used in the event he or she becomes incapable of making decisions. These documents must be signed by the patient, witnessed by state policy, and notarized by a legal notary. Examples of advance directives include:

- Living Will - A document that specified means to sustain the patient in case of terminal conditions.

- Durable Power of Attorney - Document that states who the patient designates necessary medical decisions regarding withholding medical treatment.

- Organ Donation - A document that specifies the patient choses to donate organ(s) to a specified organization (Houser & Sesser, 2008).

Administrative Laws

Administrative laws are rules and regulations established, maintained, and enforced by government agencies, such as the Food and Drug Administration (FDA) and the Drug Enforcement Agency (DEA), as well as various licensing boards and certification organizations. Some laws and regulations that affect medical practice include:

- Clinical Laboratory Improvement Amendments (CLIA) - Rules and standards for healthcare facilities that perform certain laboratory tests.

- Occupational Safety and Health Administration (OSHA) - Organization that regulates workplace safety and health.

- Americans with Disabilities Act (ADA) - Rules and regulations that protect people with disabilities from discrimination, such as the provision of handicap-accessible bathrooms and entrances.

- Equal Employment Opportunity Act (EEOA) - Rules and regulation that protect employees from discrimination because of race, age, religion, sex, or national origin.

Healthcare Credentialing

- Licensure – This is the credential required to practice a profession, which is issued by an official state agency or department. The physician's license to practice medicine is issued by the state's medical board and is regulated by the medical practice acts. Medical licensure is obtained through examination (written test), endorsement (acceptance by the state board), and reciprocity (acceptance of a valid license from another state).

- Certification – Various healthcare occupations are subject to certification or registration. Sometimes this process is mandatory, and other times, it is voluntary. Examples are nurses, paramedics, laboratory technicians, and medical assistants.

- Accreditation – This is a type of credentialing, which typically involves a healthcare facility, agency, or organization. This voluntary process involves standards that are specific to the person or facility. One example is The Joint Commission on Accreditation of Healthcare Organizations (JCAHO.)

The Uniform Anatomical Gift Act

In 1968, the U.S. government passed the Uniform Anatomical Gift Act, which specified that any person of sound mind and legal age could donate any part(s) of the body after death, whether to research or for transplantation purposes. Most states allow residents to sign the back of their driver's license to notify medical personnel of their donor status. No money can be exchanged for organ(s), and organs cannot be sold for profit.

Healthcare Duties, Obligations, and Reportable Incidences

Medical assistants are often the main agents in the chain of custody of evidence and specimens in the event such as rape or battery to a patient. The medical assistant should not allow anyone to touch the evidence or tamper with specimens. This also applies to routine drug testing. Additionally, all drug and alcohol information is under federal jurisdiction of the Public Service Act, and this information cannot be disclosed without the patient's permission.

Medical assistants are mandated by the state to report neglect and/or abuse of children, adults, or elderly persons. Child abuse involves neglect, abandonment, sexual assault, physical assault, and psychological abuse. Abuse to elderly persons can be of various natures, including emotional, financial, physical, sexual, and neglect.

In the medical office setting, the medical assistant is often the designated person who reports communicable diseases and vital statistics to the public or local health department. Reportable diseases include mumps, measles, polio, chlamydia, gonorrhea, syphilis, tuberculosis, and HIV, all of which are tracked for epidemics and trends by the state health department and Centers for Disease Control and Prevention (CDC). The medical assistant should be aware of the rules and regulations of communicable disease reporting in his or her state.

Public Duty and Mandatory Reporting

States require physicians and other health care personnel to report certain things for the safety, welfare, and health of the public.

- Birth certificates - Must be completed and submitted to the designated local or state agency by the birth attendant.
- Death certificates - Completed by the attending physician.
- Deaths reported to the medical examiner - Death from an undetermined cause, death resulting from criminal or violent activity, death without prior medical care, and death within 24 hours of admission to a healthcare facility.
- Communicable diseases - Any occurrence of specified communicable diseases such as tuberculosis, sexually transmitted diseases, and vaccine-preventable diseases.
- Vaccine administration - Must be reported to a designated local or state agency, including date, vaccine lot number, manufacturer, administering person's name, any adverse reaction.
- Phenylketonuria (PKU) - Must be reported to state agency.

MEDICAL RECORDS AND PRIVACY

The employee should review confidentiality policies every year, and all employees are responsible for keeping patient records secure and confidential. The decision to disclose patient information is the patient's choice. The physician cannot refuse to release records if the patient request disclosure to another party. However, each party to whom a physician discloses information requires a new authorization. Also, the patient has the right to rescind an authorization of record release, which is best done with a written and dated request. A physician needs permission to disclose records unless:

- He or she is issued a court subpoena.
- He or she is being sued by a patient.
- He or she believes disclosure of the information will protect the welfare of the patient or a third party.

Health Insurance Portability and Accountability Act (HIPAA)

In 1996, the federal government of the U.S. enacted the Health Insurance Portability and Accountability Act (HIPAA). A section of this act is concerned with the security and protection of the electronic medical record (EMR). Also, HIPAA specifies what is considered to be confidential information, including:

- Patient and family names
- Geographic areas
- Dates of birth, death, admission, and discharge
- Telephone and fax numbers
- Home and email addresses
- Social security numbers
- Health plan beneficiary members
- Vehicle, device, and equipment numbers
- Medical records and account numbers
- Photographs
- Biometric identifiers
- Any unique identifying number, code, or characteristic

Medical Records Management

The medical assistant is sometimes responsible for the medical records of patients. The medical record is all patient information that is relevant to health care, which is usually in the form of paper, medical imaging films, disks, photographs, and electronic printouts. Most medical record systems are color-coded, using letters and/or numbers. Regarding hard copy medical records retention, the typical guidelines for state and federal statute of limitations is 7 to 10 years for adults, and retention for minors is the age of majority plus 7 to 10 years.

Functions of Medical Assistant

- Assembling – Constructing the file in correct order.
- Filing – Putting the medical record in a secure storage area.
- Maintaining – Filing all medical record documentation.
- Retrieving – Recovering the medical record from storage when needed.
- Transferring – Sending the medical record (copy) to another physician's office.
- Protecting – Keeping the medical record secure at all times.
- Retaining – Keeping the medical record for a specified length of time.
- Purging – Removing medical records that are beyond the time of the statute of limitations.
- Destroying – Shredding the medical record

Types of Patient Files

- Active – Patient has been seen within 3 - 5 years (depending on the practice's policy).
- Inactive – Patient has not been seen within the past 3 - 5 years (depending on the practice's policy).
- Closed – The patient is deceased, has moved, or has reached legal age limit (pediatrics.)

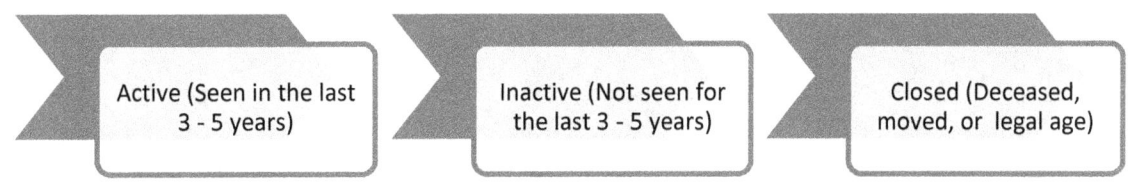

The HITECH Act

The Health Information Technology for Economic and Clinical Health (HITECH) Act was enacted under a section of the American Recovery and Reinvestment act of 2009. The HITECH Act promotes the adoption of health information technology and electronic medical records (EMR). The federal government created an incentive program to encourage medical practices to use EMR technology. Areas affected include medical billing, patient records, and employee communication. The goal is to make better use of technology for patient care and affordability (HealthIT.gov, 2013).

The Patient Protection and Affordable Care Act (PPACA)

The Patient Protection and Affordable Care Act (PPACA) of 2010 mandates the protection of privacy using the EMR system. With this legislation, insurance agencies are no longer able to drop patients due to pre-existing health conditions.

Chief Complaint

When entering a chief complaint (CC), think of the six Cs :

- Client's own words
- Clear
- Concise
- Complete
- Chronologic order
- Confidential

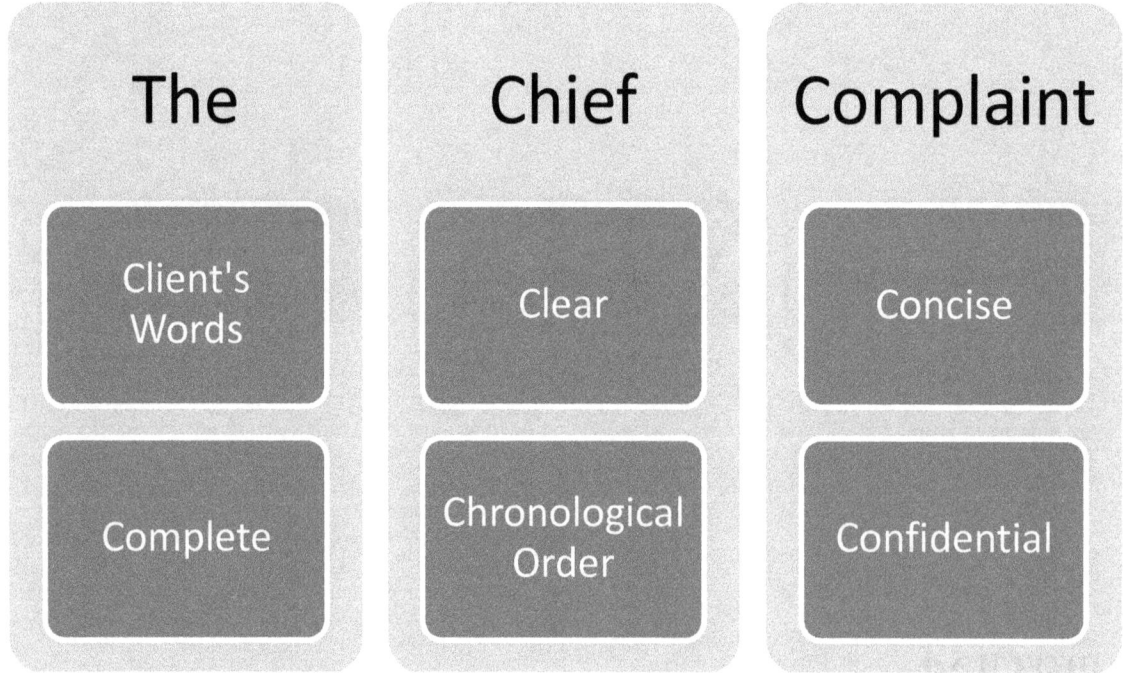

RESPONSIBILITIES, RIGHTS AND ETHICS

The medical assistant has the responsibility of providing appropriate and acceptable medical care under the direct supervision of a physician. The medical assistant has the right to be free from sexual discrimination or harassment. This could involve being refused employment, being paid less for the same work, or being treated inferior. Also, unwelcomed sexual advances or physical conduct is not to be tolerated in the work place under the Civil Rights Act of 1964. If this occurs, the medical assistant should consult with a supervisor or manager.

Patient Responsibilities and Rights

The American Hospital Association (AHA) formulated the Patient's Bill of Rights in 1973. This document outlines the various rights, which include the right to:

- Receive respectful, considerate, and appropriate care.
- Expect privacy and confidentiality.
- Consult the physician of his or her choice.
- Make decisions regarding healthcare.
- Receive all information regarding diagnosis(es), treatment, and prognosis.
- Refuse treatment.
- Make informed decisions related to healthcare.
- Obtain copies of his or her medical record.
- Participate or refuse to participate in research.
- Receive continuity of care

Physician Responsibility and Rights

The physician has the right to refuse to accept a patient into the practice, or to terminate the patient-physician relationship. Also, the physician may refuse to offer emergency services if he or she does not have the appropriate office setting for this. Physicians can establish their own working hours, determine fee charges, and change the office location. If the physician choses to dismiss a patient from the practice, he or she must send a letter of dismissal by certified mail, and a copy should be retained for the medical record.

Ethics

Ethics are moral principles, values, and duties. Whereas laws are enforceable regulations set forth by the government, ethics are moral guidelines set forth and formally or informally enforced by peers, the community, and professional organizations. A "norm" is short for "normal," which is a behavior or conduct that is valued and usually expected. Duties are commitments or obligations to act in an ethical and moral manner. The code of ethics is a statement of the expected behaviors of its members. This code also sets standards and disciplinary actions for violations, including suspension, censure, fines, or expulsion. The American Medical Association (AMA) code of ethics was written in 1847, has been revised many times, and specifies the physician's ethical duty to the patient.

AAMA Code of Ethics

The American Association of Medical Assistants (AAMA) sets forth principles of moral and ethical conduct for the practice of medical assisting. Medical assistants pledge to:

- Uphold the honor and principles of the profession.
- Accept the profession's disciplines.
- Render service with full respect for human dignity.
- Respect confidential information.
- Participate in additional service activities for the improvement of community health

Notes
intentionally left blank

Notes
intentionally left blank

V. ADMINISTRATIVE CONCEPTS

COMPUTERS, DATA ENTRY AND OFFICE EQUIPMENT

Administrative concepts include the use of computers, data entry, operation of office equipment, records management, screening and processing mail, scheduling and monitoring appointments, resource information and community services, maintaining the office environment, office policies, procedures, and protocols, and practice finances.

Data is information that includes facts, numbers, letters, or symbols that the computer processes. A medical assistant usually enters this data. It includes patient demographic information, insurance information, diagnosis codes, procedure codes, and various transactions.

Software Applications

Software applications are programs on the computer that perform important functions for the medical office. Applications areas include:

- Word Processing - Software used to write physician notes, reports, memos, transcripts, and letters.
- Graphics - Software that produces information using pictures.
- Database - Software that provides templates for office activities, such as progress notes, laboratory information medication lists, and health histories.
- Spreadsheet - Software that produces a spreadsheet of numeric calculations from data entered, such as financial reports, invoices, and budgets.
- Utility - Software that maintains the function of the computer system.
- Communication - Software used to communicate with other healthcare workers or facilities.

Equipment

- Computers - The computer is used to maintain data, schedule appointments, bill patient encounters, and maintain office finances.
- Telephones - Telephone systems in the office setting are used to communicate with coworkers, as well as patients, other physicians, laboratories, hospitals, and businesses outside of the office. The reception area typically has more than one telephone, and most offices have phones in the physician's office(s), the laboratory, and in patient hallways.
- Fax Machines - The fax machine is used to send necessary patient information to insurance companies, other physicians, and referrals. A cover sheet must be used to specify that the material is of a confidential nature to alert the recipient of the fax and the sensitivity of the information. This is done using a disclaimer.

- Calculators - Calculators can be on the computer or free-standing. They are used to calculate bank deposits, dose calculations, and other mathematical purposes.
- Photocopiers and Scanners - A patient may request a copy of his or her medical record, or a hard copy may be needed for referral purposes. A photocopier or scanner is used to make necessary copies of documents or blank forms that are routinely used in the office setting.
- Shredder - A paper shredder is essential for destruction of confidential medical records, as well as financial documents and purged information.

Computer Concepts

- Hardware - The central processing unit, hard drive, disk drive, motherboard, keyboard, and monitor.
- Central processing unit (CPU) - Circuit on a microchip that processes data.
- Random access memory (RAM) – This is the main memory bank of the computer located on the motherboard.
- Hard drive - The box that contains the computer's data files and programs.
- Keyboard - The keys of the computer.
- Monitor - The visual display terminal.
- Disk drive - The device that allows the information to be accessed from a compact disc (CD).
- Modem - A device connecting the computer to the telephone line.
- Software - Computer programs that tell the computer what to do.
- Digital video disc (DVD) - A high-density optical disc with contents which are displayed on a computer or TV screen.
- Universal serial bus (USB) - A small, lightweight data storage device, which is also called a flash drive, thumb drive, memory stick, and USB key.
- File format - A mechanism used by the computer to store and retrieve certain computer data, such as text or pictures, such as document files (DOC), joint photographic experts group (JPEG), rich text files (RTF), and graphics interchange format (GIF).
- Local area network (LAN) - A computer network used to connect computers, which is usually associated with a single organization.
- Wide area network (WAN) - A computer network that uses telephone systems and coaxial cables, and connects the computers of a geographic area. The Internet is an example of a WAN.
- Hyper-text makeup language (HTML) - The language used to transfer documents on the Internet.
- Hyper-text transfer protocol (HTTP) - The process of transferring and formatting messages over the Internet.
- Search engine - An extensive program that allows searches for websites and information, such as Google and Yahoo.
- Uniform resource locator (URL) - System that identifies the address and domain to access website pages.

Notes
intentionally left blank

RECORDS MANAGEMENT

Medical record management involves the assembling, filing, maintenance, retrieval, transferring, protecting, retention, purging, and destruction of files. This section covers filing systems, filing guidelines, and medical records.

Filing Systems

The term medical record also refers to the patient's chart or patient's files. The medical record contains all information and documentation relative to the patient's medical care. There are three types of files: active, inactive, and closed. Shelving units are used to house the medical records, whereas electronic medical records are located on a network. Types of systems include:

- Alphabetic filing system – With this system, medical records are filed by the units of the patient's name. Unit 1 is the last name, letter by letter, unit 2 is the first name, letter by letter, unit 3 is the middle initial or name, letter by letter, and unit 4 is the prefixes and suffixes, such as Sr., Jr., Dr., and Mrs.

- Numeric filing system – With this system, each patient is assigned a medical record number through a computerized or manual means, and the numbers are cross-referenced with an alphabetic file (the master file).

- Color coding system – With this system, medical records are filed in coordination with numbers and/or letters. Each letter, group of letters, number, or group of numbers is designated with a specific color, used for easy location of the file (Houser & Sesser, 2008).

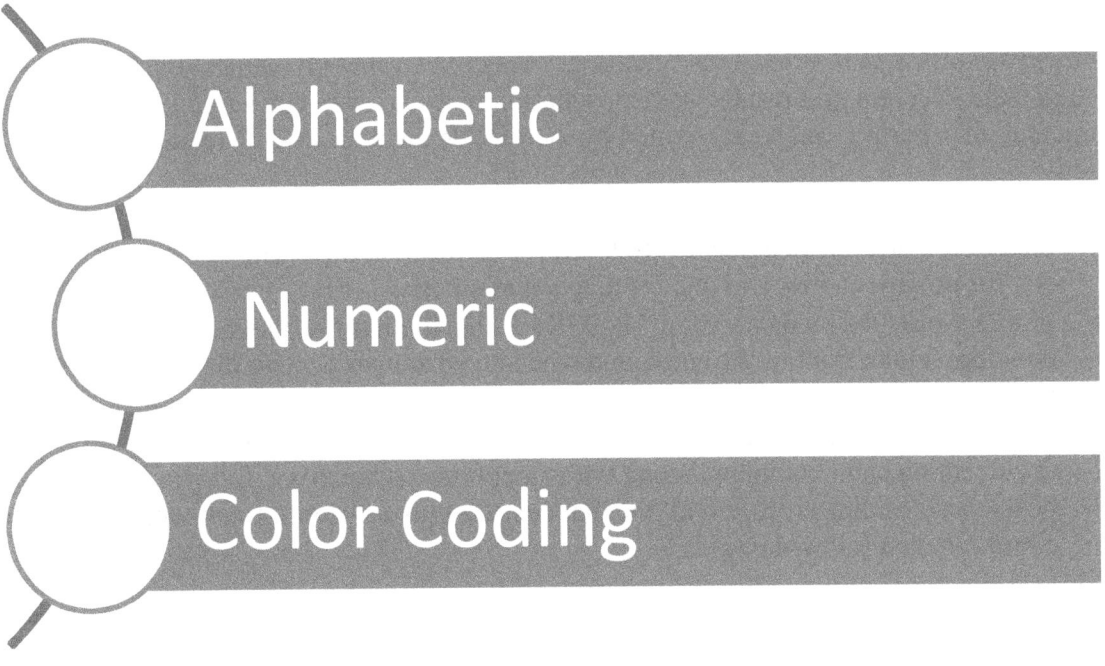

Medical Records

The individual medical record includes all information related to a patient who receives or has received care at the physician's office. This information functions as a quality of care monitor, provides a resource for education, provide legal protection for the healthcare providers and patient, and facilitates good medical care through continuity.

Medical Record Sequencing

The determination of record organization and sequence is associated with:

A. Type of practice
B. Frequency of access
C. Physician preference

Potential Legal and Ethical Dilemmas

- Breach of confidentiality
- Withdrawal from care
- Broken appointments
- Improper information release
- Patient noncompliance
- Missing information
- Illegible entries
- Lost notes or files

Documentation and Reporting

Documentation is often referred to as "charting." This is information medical workers enter into the record. Reports, test results, and consultation notes are also considered documentation. Charting can be performed by the SOMR method, POMR method, or SOAP method:

- Source-oriented medical record (SOMR) – The file is divided into two sections, with one for progress notes, and one for diagnostic reports.
- Problem-oriented medical record (POMR) – This file has the patient's problems listed on a form at the front of the chart, and when an encounter occurs, that number and problem is noted.
- Subjective/Objective/Assessment/Plan (SOAP) – This format involves first documenting chief complaint along with symptoms (subjective), followed by the physician's findings (objective), the diagnosis(es) (assessment), treatment, tests, education, and follow-up (plan.)

Notes
intentionally left blank

Notes
intentionally left blank

MAIL ADMINISTRATION AND SCHEDULING APPOINTMENTS

This section covers basic mail concepts, postal delivery services, and opening and sorting mail.

Basic Mail Concepts

- Envelopes - For mail correspondence, always use a business-size envelope.
- Labels - Address labels can be computerized or printed on a label machine. These should be used for business mail and referrals.
- Invoices and Statements - Medical assistants are often responsible for mailing out monthly invoices and statements. The amount due will be printed somewhere on the document, and most are due within 30 days. Superbills are other types of forms that the medical assistant has to handle on a daily basis. These documents often need to be mailed to billing personnel or companies.
- Folding 8 x 11 paper - When preparing mail for the envelope, fold the document down one-third of the way and up one third of the way. Make sure that address appears in the window if necessary.

Postal Delivery Services

- First-class mail - This mail must weigh 13 ounces or less, and most mail will be sent in this manner.
- Second-class mail - This class is used for mailing periodicals or newspapers.
- Third--class - This class is used for bulk mail, such as catalogs, books, and other printed material that weighs less than 16 ounces.
- Fourth-class - This is for third-class mail that weighs more than a pound.
- Express - This mail is delivered faster than other classes, and it is available as next-day or second-day delivery.
- Certified mail - This service guarantees that the item is received by the person on the address. A certified mail signature card is a legal document, which can be used in court if necessary.
- Overnight delivery - Various carriers offer overnight, quick delivery, including UPS, Federal Express, and DHL.

Opening and Sorting Mail

The medical assistant is often required to open and/or sort mail. The office will have general guidelines to follow, such as:

- Check the address to be sure the item is supposed to be delivered to the office.
- Sort the mile by priority, with top priority being certified mail, overnight mail, or special delivery.
- Second-priority mail is confidential and personal, and should be set aside and given to the addressee.
- Once sorted, deliver the mail to the appropriate recipients.
- Stamp all bills and statements with a dated stamp.

Scheduling Appointments

Appointments are scheduled either manually, using and appointment book, or by computer with scheduling software. Appointments are usually scheduled at 10, 15, 20, or 30 minute intervals. An initial appointment will take longer than that for a returning patient. When scheduling appointments, provide the patient's full name, use correct spelling, list the patient's date of birth, and obtain both home and work telephone numbers. Also, depending on office policy, obtain the purpose of the visit.

Scheduling of two or more patients for the same appointment slot is called double-booking. This is done to help accommodate patients with medical conditions and specific needs that cannot wait for another day. Cluster scheduling is the grouping of similar appointments together during the day or week, and advanced scheduling involves scheduling patients weeks or months in advance. Underbooking occurs when there are too many gaps between appointments, an can be costly to the practice. Attempt to avoid this by maintaining a regular schedule.

Notes
intentionally left blank

Notes
intentionally left blank

RESOURCE INFORMATION AND COMMUNITY SERVICES

This section covers various resource information and community services, as well as the medical assistant's role as a patient advocate and the referral process.

Patient Advocate

Advocates are those who represent or plead the cause of those who cannot speak for themselves. Medical assistants are often considered "patient advocates" because they serve in this role for patients. However, medical assistants cannot always act as a patient advocate when their values are at odds with the patient's choice.

Services Available

Supportive therapy allows patients to express various feelings, explore solutions and alternatives, and make decisions and resolutions in a safe, caring environment. Many patients turn to family and friends as a means of support, while others value the help of psychologists, social workers, nurses, and physicians. Group therapy involves a therapist leading a small number of people who have individual problems and goals. The stages of group development include an initial stage (members are unclear of goals and purpose), working stage (members accomplish goals), and the termination stage (members learn to deal with problems and accept group end.)

Support groups are based on the premise that people who have experienced similar problems are able to help other individuals with that same problem. A prototype support group is Alcoholics Anonymous (AA), where alcoholics support each other's' recovery, and assist members of the group during meetings and socially. Other support groups are Adult Children of Alcoholics, Gamblers Anonymous, Narcotics Anonymous, Overeaters Anonymous, Bereavement groups, mental illness support groups, and recovery groups.

Referrals

When the physician refers a patient to a specialty practice, the medical assistant usually executes this. The physician may request a particular practice, or the patient may specify where he or she wants to be referred. Patients who have HMO or PPO insurance plans must be referred to physicians that are associated with that plan. A referral form must be completed and sent to the insurance agency per protocol, as well as a copy to the specialist and for the patient's record.

Notes
intentionally left blank

OFFICE POLICIES, PROCEDURES AND PROTOCOLS

Maintaining the Office Environment

This section covers the physical office environment and maintaining equipment and inventory.

Physical Environment

The medical office is a place where workers and patients should feel safe and secure. An environmentally friendly workplace is efficiently designed, friendly, and follows the principles of ergonomics. Safety in the reception room requires carefully placed furniture, which as stable legs and seats. Electrical cords and lamps should be examined regularly to assure adequate lighting and safety.

In the reception area, file drawers should not remain open, and wall cupboards must be secure. All office equipment should operate correctly with no evidence of damage or electrical shorts. All laboratory equipment should contain labels regarding biohazardous waste. Also, chemicals that are volatile should not be kept beyond their expiration date and should be stored appropriately.

Equipment and Supply Inventory

The medical assistant may be responsible to maintain an inventory of administrative and clinical supplies. The best method of organizing supplies is to prepare a separate inventory card for each frequently used item. Keep the name, phone number and address of the supplier, as well as the cost of each item.

Certain office equipment and devices require regular maintenance and cleaning in order to work effectively. Typewriters and computers must be covered when not in use, sphygmomanometers must be calibrated and checked periodically, and autoclaves require regular scheduled service and cleaning. Various lighted scopes and instruments should be checked regularly for working bulbs, and the bulbs must be replaced as needed.

Policy and Procedure Manual

The policy and procedure manual contains all rules and protocols relevant to the medical office. The office manager is responsible for the development and maintenance of the policy and procedure manual for the office. Usually, there are regular staff meetings regarding this manual, and employees have the opportunity to give input and exchange ideas. The medical assistant should keep written records or minutes related to this meeting if he or she is the responsible party.

Personnel Manuals and Records

All employees follow certain job descriptions and personnel policies in the medical office setting. Most full-time employees receive benefits in addition to a salary. These could include health and dental insurance, profit sharing, paid holidays, and paid vacation time.

The office manager is responsible for maintaining these personnel records, as well as the personnel manual.

Notes
intentionally left blank

Notes
intentionally left blank

FINANCIAL MANAGEMENT

Because financial management is an essential aspect of the medical office, medical assistants must be familiar with business activities, such as third-party reimbursement, claim preparation and processing, and basic accounting principles. Most payers are from government-funded programs or employer-sponsored coverage. However, some patients do not have health insurance that covers their particular ailment, and they will pay by check, cash, debit card, credit card, or in payments.

Principles of Bookkeeping

Physician Fee Schedules

The office will have a list of fees changed for various services and products used in the practice. This list is reviewed each year or when state or federal systems change. The list is based on overhead costs, such as rent, equipment, utilities, and supplies. The practice must set and maintain fees above actual cost of service to remain open and profitable. The physician rates are usually verified against state- and national-specific charges that are usual and customary. The U.S. government publishes Relative Value Units (RVUs) that identify a range of charges for various office activities and procedures.

Accounting

Daily financial management in the primary care setting involves bookkeeping and accounting procedures. Encounter forms identify any and all services and products for which the patient or third-party payer will be charged. Accurate record keeping is a crucial component of financial management as it ensures that the physician is paid for services and that patients are credited for payments. The medical assistant may have to handle accounts receivable balances to ensure that cash flow covers necessary expenses and generates a profit. Accounts payable involve all money that is due for various goods and services provided to the office, such as payroll costs, rent, consumable supplies, housekeeping, and utilities.

Patient Accounts

Most offices track patient accounts with computerized systems. This method offers versatility, reduces the need for record entries, and allows for easier accounting measures. The encounter form is called a superbill or charge slip. It is usually a three-part form that offers the patient a record of account activity for the day and serves for billing procedures. The information on the encounter form includes the amount of the transaction, procedure codes, and diagnosis codes, all which is necessary to file an insurance claim. The form also has the patient's demographic information and the practice or physician's name, telephone number, and address.

A software management program allows for the creation of a charge slip, and calculates the charges for a monthly billing statement. In addition, this program keeps a daily log, transfers data to produce insurance forms, and allows for the creation of statements, billing cycle lists, and billing statements.

Coding and Billing

Forms

The CMS-1500 form is used for billing physician services provided in an outpatient setting. Medicare Part B services are reported using this form. Diagnosis codes are reported in file location 21 on this form. These codes are linked to service/procedure codes, which are derived using the Current Procedural Terminology (CPT) and Healthcare Common Procedure Coding System (HCPCS). Procedure/service codes are reported in lines 1 through 6 of field location 24D.

The CMS-1450 form is used for submitting healthcare facility claims. Medicare Part A services are reported using this form. The ICD-10-CM diagnosis code for the admitting diagnosis is placed in the field location 69, and the main diagnosis code is placed in field location 67, with 67A through 67Q used for additional diagnoses. The ICD-10-PCS procedure code for the main procedure is reported in field location 74, and additional procedure codes are reported on filed locations 74A through 74E.

Inpatient Prospective Payment System

Each prospective payment system has its own way of using codes for reimbursement purposes. The CMS website is an excellent website for coders. Also, Medicare Conditions of Participation (CoPs) and Conditions for Coverage (CfCs) both provide standards that healthcare providers must meet in order to receive reimbursement for Medicare.

The inpatient prospective payment system (IPPS) is used for acute care hospital admissions. The payment rate is fixed based on the Medicare Severity-Diagnosis Related Groups (MS-DRGs), which identify the set payment amount based on the average cost of specified groupings of procedures and diagnoses. Each MS-DRG is associated with a standardized payment amount, which is based on the average resources used in the treatment of Medicare patients for those particular diagnoses and procedures.

The IPPS payment has two parts: the labor-related share and the non-labor share. The labor-related share is adjusted to the wage index of the facility's location to account for variation in labor costs. The calculated base payment rate is multiplied by the MS-DRG's relative weight, accounting for the variance in the case mix of patients.

Uniform Hospital Discharge Data Set (UHDDS)

The Uniform Hospital Discharge Data Set (UHDDS) is a standard data set adopted by the federal government for collection of data for Medicare and Medicaid. Coders sometimes need to report some of the elements of UHDDS when they code. These elements enable coders to describe the patient, as well as the circumstances.

Outpatient Prospective Payment System (OPPS)

With the outpatient prospective payment system (OPPS), CPT and HCPCS codes are used to justify medical necessity. All hospital outpatient services are classified as ambulatory payment classifications (APCs), and each code for procedures or services is assigned an associated APC. A payment rate is assigned to each APC, and diagnoses are reported using the ICD-10-CM codes.

Other Prospective Payment Systems

- *Physician Office* - The Resource-Based Relative Value Scale (RBRVS) physician fee schedule was implemented by Medicare in 1992. This payment system uses a relative value for physician services and is based on commonly used resources for each level of service. Associated with CPT codes are the values of work expense, practice expense, and professional liability insurance expense, which are calculated to determine payment.

- *Home Health* - The Home Health Prospective Payment System (HH PPS) was implemented by Medicare in 2000. It consists of various base payments, which are adjusted for care needs and patient health condition. HHPPS payments are given for each 60-day period of care. Also, the Outcome and Assessment Information Set (OASIS) instrument is used to document an assessment of the patient. The data from this assessment are used to determine the case-mix adjustment relative to standard payment. For patient classification related to clinical presentation, service utilization, and functional factors, there are 80 case-mix groups, which are referred to as Home Health Resource Groups (HHRGs.)

- *Long-Term Care Hospital* - Long-term care hospital prospective payment system (LTCH PPS) went into effect in 2002. This system is a diagnosis-related group patient classification system, which reflects variations in patient resources and costs. Long-term care diagnostic-related groups (LTC-DRGs) are the same DRGs used for IPPS with adjustments related to resources necessary to treat patients who are in long-term facilities. Payment adjustments are made based on area wage modifications, DRG weights, geographic classification, outliers, updates, and share adjustment.

- *Skilled Nursing Facilities* - In 1998, the PPS for Medicare skilled nursing facility (SNF) services became effective. SNF PPS uses standard rates with adjustments for geographic location and case-mix. Resource utilization groups (RUGs) are associated with skilled nursing and therapy services. The SNF PPS data reflects the residents' functional capabilities.

- *Inpatient Rehabilitation Facilities* - Inpatient rehabilitation facilities (IRFs) are reimbursed under the inpatient rehabilitation facility prospective payment system (IRF PPS). This system incorporates information from a patient assessment instrument and classifies patients based on their anticipated resource needs and clinical characteristics. Each IRF PPS group has a separate payment, adjusted for facility and case level.

Third-Party Billing

Traditional Indemnity Health Insurance/ Commercial Insurance Carriers

There are many different types of private health insurance. Traditional indemnity policies provide coverage on a fee-for-service coverage. The insurer pays the provider a fee based on the cost of service, and the insurance company creates a chart of customary charges for each type of services. The patient or the employer pays a monthly premium for the insurance. Many employer-sponsored health plans provide group coverage, which allow family members to be covered. Most of these plans have a deductible that must be met, and after it is met, the patient or covered family member must pay a co-pay.

Medical insurance is usually either basic insurance or major medical insurance. The basic form covers a specific amount for hospital care, physician feeds, surgery, and/or anesthesia. Major medical insurance covers the costs of catastrophic expenses from injury, trauma, or serious illness. Some policies only cover visits where there is an actual disease, illness, or condition, and not routine examinations. Other insurance plans cover routine preventive care and physical examinations.

Prepaid Health Insurance Options

Managed care is a popular method used to reimburse for healthcare services. Managed care systems require the policy holder to seek medical care only from select preferred providers, which are under contract with the insurance company. Patients pay lower copays and premiums when they use a preferred provider. Managed care organizations (MCOs) include health maintenance organizations (HMOs) and preferred provider organizations (PPOs). MCOs offer cost-effective services by using primary care providers who channel patients to the most affordable, quality care options. Also, they use specific treatment guidelines and utilize selective contracting with institutions and providers to achieve a discounted rate.

Integrated delivery systems are groups of provider sites that offer full and/or specialty services to members. The affiliated providers often include clinics, physician practices, hospitals, surgical centers, and ancillary allied health facilities. These systems negotiate group rates for all providers with various insurance companies.

Medicare

The federal government funds health insurance coverage for adults over age 65 years and disabled persons under the Medicare program. Medicare was developed in 1965 and is administered by the Centers for Medicare and Medicaid Services (CMS). Part A covers hospital care, home health care, and skilled nursing home care, and Part B covers outpatient care and physician services. Medicare pays 80 percent and the patient pays the remaining 20 percent. The patient must meet a $100 deductible before Medicare begins to pay for services.

The basic structure of the Medicare program is:

- Part A – Hospital and institutional Care Coverage: Hospitals submit electronic claims on a UB-04 form. Covered expenses are semiprivate rooms, meals and special diets, and all medical necessary services, such as skilled nursing, home health, hospice, and rehabilitation.

- Part B – Supplemental and Nonhospital Care Coverage: Pays for services and supplies that are not covered under Part A. These include outpatient services, ambulatory surgical services, home health care, and medically necessary equipment and supplies.

- Part C – Medicare Advantage Organization (MAO) Plans: This includes Medicare Health Maintenance Organizations (HMOs), Medicare Preferred Provider Organizations (PPOs), Medicare Private Fee-for-Service Plans (PPFSs), and Medicare Medical Savings Account Plans (MSAs).

- Part D – Prescription Drug Plan (PDP) – This includes Medicare Advantage Plans (MA-PDs), Private Prescription Drug Plans (PDPs), and premiums paid by the beneficiary (Martin, 2009).

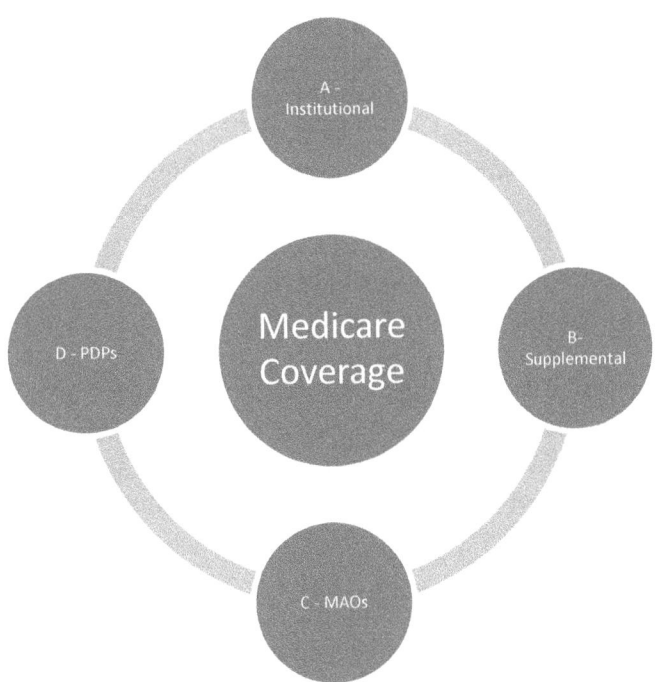

Medicaid

The Medicaid program is a government insurance plan for people who are unable to work due to life circumstances, disabilities, or serious illness. It is also available for children and is income-based. Each state has a unique list of covered benefits related to Medicaid coverage. Eligibility depends on state-specific requirements.

TRICARE and CHAMPVA

Active-duty military personnel who are stationed on a military base are covered by healthcare workers employed by the military. Their spouses and children are covered under TRICARE, which covers active-duty personnel families, as well as retired members, dependents of retired members, dependents of personnel who died during active duty, personnel serving in the Reserve, and active-duty military members stationed away from a major military base. CHAMPVA covers spouses and unmarried dependent children of veterans with permanent total disabilities from injuries related to service or duty. Both of these military insurance plans are billed after all other coverage, except when the patient has Medicaid.

Workers' Compensation

Workers' compensation insurance pays for medical care costs and a portion of lost wages when a worker is injured or becomes ill on the job. Employers are required to pay premiums to an insurance carrier for the entire worker's compensation insurance policy. The premium is based on the degree of occupational risks for the employees, as well as the number of workers employed. A patient covered under workers' compensation pays no co-insurance, co-pay, deductible, or bill, as this insurance covers 100 percent of services.

Billing and Claims Processing

The consumer (patient) usually wants to know in advance what charges to expect from the office visit. Billing and collections is best when it is customized to the practice and the patient is respected. Accurate billing techniques make cash flow and collections smoother, and the best time for collection is at the time of service. This is done to eliminate further bookkeeping work, assure prompt collection and provide adequate cash flow for the office.

Primary care and ambulatory office settings may charge interest for installment arrangements, so the patient must be informed of these practices. The Truth-in Lending Act (also known as the Consumer Credit Protection Act) specifies that providers of installment credit state the fees clearly in writing and designate the annual rate of interest.

Billing System Formats

- Monthly - All accounts are billed at the same time each month. This is more common in smaller medical offices.
- Cyclic - All accounts are divided alphabetically into groups, with each group billed at a different time. This allows for easier processing for office personnel.

Preparing Medical Claims

It is the responsibility of the medical coder to ensure accurate coding based on provided services and documentation. Payment involves knowledge of both the reimbursement policies and coding guidelines.

Notes
intentionally left blank

CODING

ICD-9-CM Codes

International Classification of Diseases (ICD) ninth revision (9) Clinical Modifications (CM) codes are used for reporting various diagnoses. Volume 1 is called "Diseases, Tabular," Volume 2 is called "Diseases, Index," and Volume 3 is the hospital version. The use of ICD-9-CM allow for tracking of patients and healthcare costs. A diagnosis establishes medical necessity and is reported on the CMS-1500 form in block 21 and 24E (Buck, 2013).

Volume 1: Diseases, Tabular List

There are two major divisions of the Tabular List: classification of diseases and injuries (codes 001.0 – 999.9) and supplementary classification (V and E codes). The main portion of the ICD-9-CM consists of diagnosis codes and most chapters are subdivided by body systems (Buck, 2013).

Volume 2: Diseases, Alphabetic Index

The Alphabetic Index of the ICD-9-CM manual lists main terms in body type, as well as sub terms indented below the main terms. Nonessential modifiers are enclosed in parentheses to clarify diagnosis. Coders are not to code from the index, as mandatory fifth digits only appear as notes (Buck, 2013).

ICD-9-CM Conventions

Conventions are symbols, punctuation, abbreviations, and notations, as well as cross reference notes.

- Common abbreviations – Two abbreviations commonly used are Not Elsewhere Classifiable (NEC) and Not Otherwise Specified (NOS).

- [ ] Brackets – These are used to enclose synonyms, explanatory phrases, or alternative wording.

- ( ) Parentheses – These are used to contain nonessential modifiers, and they do not affect code assignment.

- : Colons – These are used to complete statements with one or more modifiers.

- } Brace – This precedes a modifying statement.

- **Bold Type** – Indicates codes and code titles.

- *Italicized Type* – Indicates codes NOT used as a principal diagnosis.

- Cross References – Includes "see," "see also," and "see category."

- Notes – Give further coding instructions, such as when to use mandatory fifth digits (Buck, 2013).

ICD-9-CM Manual Sections

There are three sections of the ICD-9-CM manual:

- Section 1: Index to Diseases and Injuries – This is the largest part of the manual, which includes the main terms and sub terms.

- Section 2: Table of Drugs and Chemicals – This is located after the Index to Diseases and Injuries section. It contains classification of various medications and substances used to identify adverse effects and poisoning.

- Section 3: Index to External Causes of Injuries and Poisoning (E Codes) – These codes are used to provide additional information regarding the exact nature of injury or poisoning (Buck, 2013).

Includes and Excludes Notes and Inclusion Terms

- Includes Note: This appears immediately under a 3-digit code title, and its purpose is to further define or give examples of the content.

- Excludes Note: This indicates that the terms excluded from the code should be used somewhere else. In some cases, however, the codes for the excluded terms should not be used along with the code from which it is excluded.

    - Example: A congenital condition excluded from an acquired form of the same condition, where the congenital and acquired codes should not be used together. In other cases, the excluded terms may be used together with an excluded code.

    - Example: Fracture of two different bones may be used together if both types of fractures are present.

- Inclusion Terms: This is a list of terms included under certain 4 and 5-digit codes. These terms specify the conditions for which that code number is to be used. The terms are either synonyms of the code title, or "other specified" code terms indicating various conditions assigned to that code.

Steps to Diagnosis Coding

The basic steps for diagnosis coding are:

1. Identify the main term.
2. Locate the main term in the Alphabetic Index.
3. Review sub terms for any that apply.
4. Follow all cross-reference instructions.
5. Verify the code(s) in the Tabular Index.
6. List the code on form (Buck, 2013).

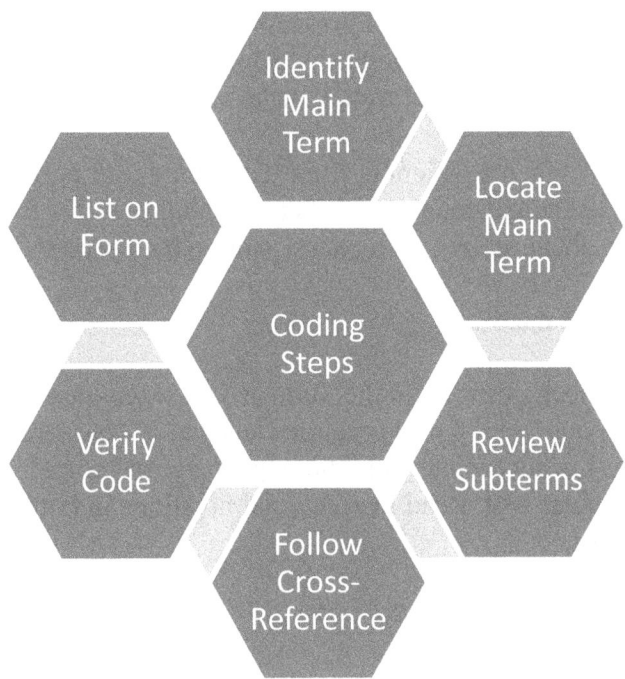

Official ICD-9-CM Guidelines

The Uniform Hospital Discharge Data Set (UHDDS) definition of principal diagnosis applies only to inpatients in acute, short-term, long-term care and psychiatric hospitals. Coding guidelines for inconclusive diagnoses (suspected, probable, rule out, etc.) were developed do not apply to outpatients.

The general guidelines are called the "ICD-9-CM Official Guidelines for Coding and Reporting." A coder must understand and follow the guidelines when assigning diagnoses codes. The ICD-9-CM official guidelines were developed by four cooperating parties:

- American Health Information Management Association (AHIMA)
- American Hospital Association (AHA)
- Centers for Medicare and Medicaid Services (CMS)
- National Center for Health Statistics (NCHS) (Buck, 2013)

1. Selection of First-Listed Diagnosis

In the outpatient setting, the term "first-listed diagnosis" is used in lieu of the term "principal diagnosis," and the term "first-listed code" is used instead of the term "principal code." In ICD-9-CM, the general and disease-specific guidelines take precedence over the outpatient guidelines when determining the first-listed diagnosis. Diagnoses in the office or other outpatient setting often are not established at the time of the initial visit. It may take two or more visits before the diagnosis is made.

- Outpatient Surgery – When a patient presents for outpatient surgery, code the reason for the surgery as the first-listed diagnosis, which is the reason for the encounter. Do this even if the surgery is not performed due to a complication or contraindication.

- Observation Stay – When a patient is admitted to the hospital for observation, assign first a code for the medical condition. When a patient presents for outpatient surgery and develops complications requiring admission to the hospital.

2. Use of ICD-9-CM Manual

Use both the Alphabetic Index and the Tabular List when locating and assigning a code. Reliance on only one of these sections leads to coding errors and less specificity in code selection. Locate each term in the Alphabetic Index and verify the code selected in the Tabular List. Read instructional notations in both the Alphabetic Index and the Tabular List.

3. Selection of Codes 001.0 - V91.99

Codes 001.0 through V91.99 are used to identify diagnoses, symptoms, conditions, problems, complaints, or other reason(s) for the encounter.

4. Documentation of Diagnosis

The documentation should describe the patient's condition, list a diagnosis, and include symptoms, problems, and reasons for the visit. Each diagnostic statement should be as informative as possible for classifying the condition to the most specific category. If no definite diagnosis has been made at the end of an encounter, code with the information that permits the greatest degree of specificity related to the condition.

5. Selection of Codes 001.0 – 999.9

Codes in this section are often used to report the reason for the visit. List first the ICD-9-CM code that shows the reason for encounter/visit as shown in the medical record to be chiefly responsible for the services provided. List any additional secondary codes that describe any coexisting conditions. In some cases the first-listed diagnosis may be a symptom when a diagnosis has not been established by the physician.

6. Symptoms and Signs

Codes that describe the signs and symptoms rather than a diagnosis are only used when no diagnosis is established or confirmed by a physician. For someone who may not currently be sick or who receives limited services, the details or circumstances should be recorded as the main condition.

7. Encounters for Reasons other than a Disease or Injury

The Supplementary Classification of Factors Influencing Health Status and Contact with Health Services (V01.0- V91.99) is used when circumstances other than a disease or injury are recorded as problems. These codes are used in circumstances other than the disease, condition, or injury.

8. Level of Detail in Coding

ICD-9-CM is composed of codes with either 3, 4, or 5 digits. Codes with 3 digits are included as the heading of a category, and they may be further subdivided by the use of 4th or 5th digits, which provide greater specificity. A 3-digit code is to be used only if it is not further subdivided. If 4th-digit subcategories and/or 5th-digit sub-classifications are provided, they must be used. A code is invalid if it has not been coded to the full number of digits required.

9. Uncertain Diagnosis

Do NOT code any diagnosis that is listed as "suspected," "probable," "possible," "rule out," or "questionable." Instead, code the condition(s) to the highest degree of certainty for that encounter, such as signs, symptoms, abnormal test results, or other reason for the visit.

10. Chronic Diseases

Chronic condition codes can be used over again and continuously, as long as the patient is receiving care for that diagnosis.

11. Conditions that Coexist

The coder must code for all documented conditions that exist at the time of the encounter, and that require or affect patient treatment. Avoid use of codes for reporting conditions no longer being treated. "History of" codes (V10-V19) are used as secondary codes, as long as they impact current treatment or care.

12. Diagnostic Services Only

   For a patient receiving therapeutic or diagnostic services, the coder should assign first for the diagnosis, problem, or condition and list secondary codes for chronic or coexisting conditions.

13. Routine Diagnostic Services

   For routine laboratory/radiology testing in the absence of signs, symptoms, or associated diagnosis, assign V72.5 and/or a code from subcategory V72.6. If routine testing is performed during the same encounter to evaluate a sign, symptom, or diagnosis, assign the V code first, followed by a secondary code describing the reason for the non-routine test.

14. Confirmed Diagnosis on Diagnostic Tests

   For diagnostic tests that have been interpreted by a physician, and the final report was used, code first any confirmed or definitive diagnoses documented in the interpretation. Do NOT code signs and symptoms as secondary diagnoses.

15. Chemotherapy, Radiation, and Rehabilitation Services

   For a patient who is receiving chemotherapy, radiation therapy, or rehabilitation, use an appropriate V code first, followed by a secondary code for the diagnosis or problem that requires treatment.

16. Preoperative Evaluations Only

   For a patient who is receiving preoperative evaluation, the coder should code first from category V72.8, Other specified examinations, followed by a secondary code for the reason for surgery.

17. Ambulatory Surgery

   For a patient who is receiving ambulatory surgery or an outpatient procedure, the coder should use the diagnosis that required the ambulatory surgery, unless the postoperative diagnosis differs from the initial diagnosis.

18. Routine Outpatient Prenatal Visits

   For a patient who is being seen for a routine prenatal visit with no complications, the coder should use codes V22.0, Supervision of normal first pregnancy, or V22.1, Supervision of other normal pregnancy.

19. Multiple Conditions

> When an episode of healthcare involves a number of related conditions, the one that is clearly more severe and demands the most resources should be recorded as the first-listed diagnosis. Where no one condition predominates, use a code that incorporate multiple conditions as the "main" code (Buck, 2013).

National Correct Coding Initiative (NCCI)

The National Correct Coding Initiative (NCCI) was developed by CMS to promote national coding methods and control improper coding and reimbursement. This includes "unbundling," which is billing multiple procedure codes for services covered by a single comprehensive code. The Federal Registrar is a government publication that lists updates, revisions, and deletions in laws: http://www.gpo.gov/fdsys/.

Quality Improvement Organizations (QIOs)

Quality Improvement Organizations (QIOs) were established by CMS to ensure quality of patient care, see that Medicare only pays for necessary and reasonable services, and protect the beneficiaries. The reviews include oversight of admission, discharge, quality of care, Medicare Severity Diagnosis-Related Groups (MS-DRGs), coverage, and procedures.

Resource-Based Relative Value Scale (RBRVS)

The Resource-Based Relative Value Scale (RBRVS) is a form of physician payment reform implemented in 1992. This established the National Fee Schedule (NFS), which is a RBRVS payment method that allows payment of 80 percent. It is used by both suppliers and physicians. Relative Value Units (RVUs) are national unit values assigned to each CPT code. These involve malpractice costs, overhead costs, and the work and skilled required for the procedure.

ACCOUNTING AND BANKING PROCEDURES

Accounting

Accounts are financial transaction records and the resulting balances during a fiscal period, which is usually January 1st through December 31st. Most medical offices have two types of accounts: accounts receivable and accounts payable.

Accounting Functions

- Entries - Recording each transaction.
- Postings - Transferring information from the journal (day sheet) to the accounts receivable ledger or to the individual patients' ledgers
- Adjustments - Changes made to the amount of money owed for reasons other than additional payments or services.
- Billing - Records of charges sent to the patient in the form of statements to show balance due and to request payment.
- Balancing - Ensuring accuracy in totals by comparing them to set criteria.

Components of Accounts Receivable

- Day Sheet - A daily record of the services rendered and payments received.
- Journal - A chronologic collection of the day sheets, which has a running total for a specified period.
- Patient Ledger - A patient statement or itemized statement that is an individual for of each patient's accounts
- Charge Slip - A form given to the patient to indicate the charges for services. (This is often a copy of the superbill).
- Receipt - A numbered form that indicates the payments a patient has made.
- Pegboard System - A system of layered forms that allows all transactions to be completed at one time.

Collections

Collections are the efforts made by office staff to obtain money that is owed to the medical practice. Office efforts can include payment by check, cash, debit card, or credit card at the time of service. A collection agency is an outside company that is independent of the medical office. This agency is contracted to obtain payment for delinquent bills after internal efforts were not sufficient. After a bill has been sent to a collection agency, the office does not make further collection efforts. Most of these agencies receive 50 percent of the amount collected.

Components of Accounts Payable

- Purchase Order - A document sent to a vendor via fax, mail, email, or the Internet to purchase equipment and supplies for the medical office.
- Invoice - A bill sent from the vendor stating what was purchased and the charges.
- Materials - All items received should be compared and verified to the invoice and purchase order.
- Bill - Statements sent to the medical office requesting payment for services or materials.
- Payment - Money sent from the medical office for services or materials.
- Petty Cash - A small amount of money (around $100 to $200) used for incidental expenses.

Banking Terms and Concepts

- Payee - The person or organization to whom a check is written, and who receives the money.
- Payer - The person or organization giving the money to the payee.
- Acceptable checks - personal checks with the proper identification, money order, cashier's check, certified check, and traveler's check.
- Unacceptable checks - Third-party checks, payroll checks, and personal checks without identification.
- Voided check - A check written but not used because of an error or other reason. With these situations, write VOID across the front of the check.
- Endorsement - Signing the back of the check as the payee for the amount represented on the front.
- Nonsufficient funds (NSF) - A term that indicates that the checking account does not hold enough money to honor the amount of the check.
- Deposits - Checks and cash paid to the medical office and placed into a checking account at the bank.
- Check register - Also called the checkbook, this is a computer program or book that has a chronologic listing of all checks written, deposits made, and balance.
- Bank statements - Reports sent from the bank that list all account activities, including deposits, checks written and cashed, bank charges, and balances.
- Reconciliation - Also called balancing, this process is a means of verifying the information on the bank statement and tallying it with the information in the check register.

Payroll

W-4 forms are called the Employee's Withholding Allowance Certificate. They are completed by all employees, and the office manager has the responsibility to prepare payroll checks for each employee and record all deductions. To comply with government regulations, an up-to-date record on each employee must be available. The employee file has a copy of an I-9 form, a copy of the social security card, the employee's salary information, and the number of exemptions claimed on the W-4.

Paycheck Data

- Date of the pay periods
- Date of the check
- Number of hour worked
- Gross salary
- Itemized deductions for income tax, social security tax, state tax, and local tax
- Itemized deductions for disability and health insurance
- Other deductions (loan payments, child support, etc.)

Common Tax Concepts

- Federal Income Tax - A specified percentage of income withheld and based on total amount earned.
- W-2 Form - A federal tax form prepared for each office employee containing all income and deductions from the previous year.
- W-4 Form - A federal tax form for each employee that shows the number of tax exemptions claimed.
- Federal Insurance and Contribution Act (FICA) - A percentage of income withhold from Social Security and Medicare.
- Federal Unemployment Tax Act (FUTA) - A percentage of each employee's income paid by employer for an unemployment fund.

VI. CLINICAL CONCEPTS

Clinical concepts include the principles of infection control and environmental safety, the treatment area, patient preparation and assisting the physician, patient history interview, minor surgical procedures, laboratory specimens and diagnostic testing, preparing and administering medications, emergencies, and nutrition and oral hydration.

INFECTION CONTROL

The safety and infection control section involves protecting patients and healthcare personnel from health and environmental hazards. This section covers the process of infection, infection control, and environmental safety.

The Process of Infection

When an organism establishes an opportunistic relationship with a host, the process is called infection. The process of infection starts with the transmission of organisms and ends with the development of infectious disease. Infections can be mild or severe, and the acuteness of an infection relies on the disease-causing potential (pathogenicity) (Murray & Ellis, 2010).

Chain of Infection

The relationship between human and organism can be intricate and valuable, or illness-producing when the parasite sustains life at the expense of the host. The chain of infection includes a causative organism, a reservoir, a mode of exit from the reservoir, a mode of transmission from reservoir to host, a susceptible host, and a mode of entry into the host.

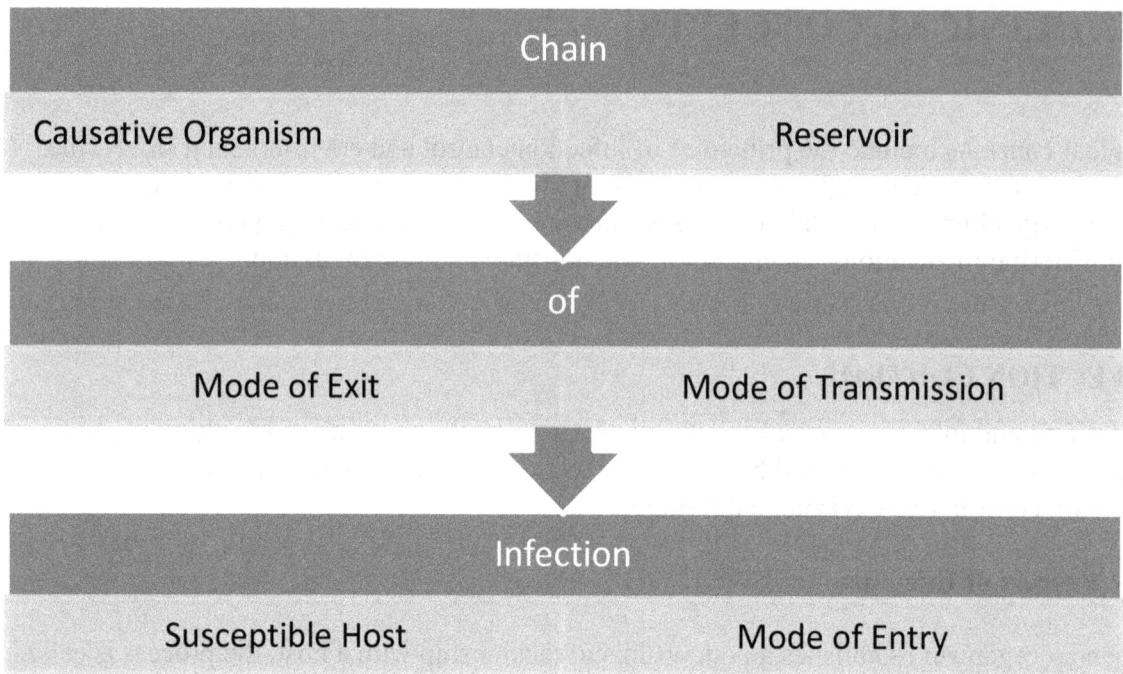

The Infectious Process

Only a few body structures are sterile. Beneficial bacteria, called normal flora, reside in and on the body. Infectious disease occurs when pathogenic bacteria enter the body from an outside source or the normal flora on the skin or in the gastrointestinal tract. The inflammatory response is a method in which the body attacks and destroys microorganisms and renovates tissue after injury, damage, or death. There are two phases of this process: the vascular phase and the cellular phase.

Normal Flora

- Mouth – Includes anaerobic spirochetes, Prevotella, and fusobacteria.
- Skin – Includes anaerobic streptococci and clostridia.
- Vagina – Includes bacteroides, anaerobic streptococci, and fusobacteria

Mouth	Skin	Vagina
Anaerobic spirochetes	Anaerobic streptococci	Bacterioides
Prevotella	Clostridia	Aneorobic streptococci
Fusobacteria		Fusobacteria

Four Stages of the Infectious Process

The four stages of the infections process include: incubation period, prodromal stage, acute illness, and convalescent stage:

- Incubation Period – The organisms establish presence inside the susceptible host.
- Prodromal Stage – The symptoms of infection begin to appear.
- Acute Illness – The organisms are growing and spreading quickly inside the host.
- Convalescent Stage – The damaged tissue begins healing, and symptoms resolve.

The Five Indications of Local Inflammation

1. Redness
2. Warmth
3. Swelling
4. Pain
5. Loss of function

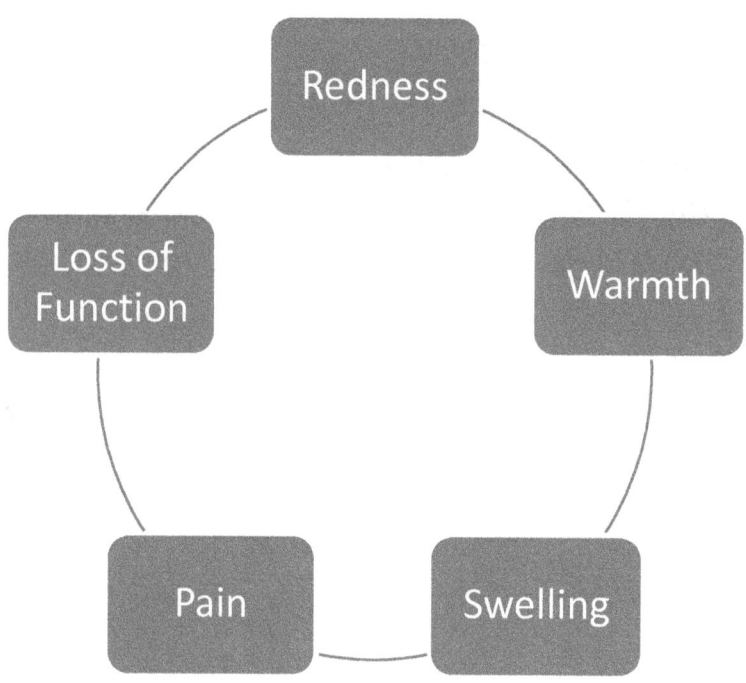

The Two Indications of Systemic Inflammation

1. Fever
2. Leukocytosis

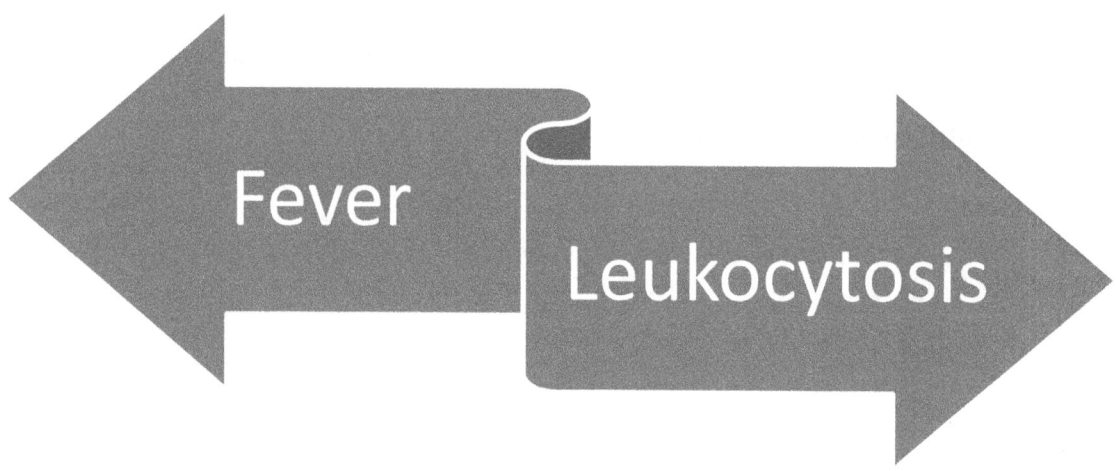

Infection Control

The incidence of antibiotic-resistant pathogens remains a problem in healthcare. Community-acquired methicillin-resistant *Staphylococcus aureus* (MRSA) infections are commonplace worldwide, so medical assistants must understand the principles of proper anti-infective treatment, infection control measures, and preventive disease precautions. An infectious disease is any disease that occurs because of growth of pathogenic microbes in the body. True pathogens lead to infectious disease regardless of the body's immune function and normal defenses. Therefore, healthcare workers have to be able to recognize infectious causes and treatment for serious, contagious, and common infections. The goal of infection control is to interact at the point where infection is most likely to protect others using necessary resources.

Hand Hygiene

To properly control and prevent infection, nurses must practice adequate hand hygiene. Successful hand washing requires 15 seconds or more of vigorous scrubbing, where particular attention is given to the areas around nail beds and between fingers. In addition, healthcare workers should use alcohol-based antiseptic agents (hand sanitizers) in between patients when hands are not visibly soiled and should not have artificial fingernails or nail polish when providing care.

When to Wash
- After contact with patient if hands are not visibly soiled.
- When moving from a contaminated to a clean body site.

Always Wash Hands
- After contact with inanimate objects in the room.
- Before caring for immune suppressed patients.

Use Sanitizer
- Before donning sterile gloves.
- After removing gloves

Standard Precautions

Also called universal precautions, standard precautions hold that all patients are infected or colonized with microorganisms, whether or not there are symptoms and written diagnoses, and that a uniform level of caution should be used when caring for any given patient.

Standard precautions decrease the risk of transmission of microorganisms from blood and body fluids containing blood, since many patients with HIV, hepatitis B, and hepatitis often have no visible symptoms. This set of principles is used by all healthcare workers who have direct or indirect contact with patients.

Transmission-Based Precautions

There are three types of transmission-based precautions: contact precautions, droplet precautions, and airborne precautions. These precautions are devised for the care of patients with known infections or illness or those who are colonized with infective microorganisms.

- Contact precautions – These decrease the risk of pathogenic spread by direct or indirect contact by wearing gloves, gowns, and shoe covers, as well as designating equipment for use with a single patient. These kinds of precautions are used for patients with infectious diarrhea or a major abscess.

- Droplet precautions - These protect against the spread of disease through droplet in the air and involve wearing masks, face shields, and goggles to prevent droplets from making contact with the conjunctivae or the mucous membranes of the eyes, nose, or mouth. These measures are used in the care and treatment of the patient with diphtheria or meningitis.

- Airborne precautions - These protect against pathogenic agents that are spread through particles that remain suspended in the air and can be inhaled or otherwise deposited to a host. Personal respiratory masks called respirators are engineered to combat these types of diseases. These measures are needed for the treatment of the patient with TB, smallpox, measles, or varicella.

Personal Protective Equipment (PPE)

Personal protective equipment (PPE) is any item necessary for the prevention of microorganism transmission. PPE includes gloves, gowns, goggles, eye shields, and masks. Gloves and gowns help prevent the spread of pathogens from patients or equipment in the environment to other patients or equipment. The CDC recommends healthcare workers remove fluid-resistant gowns before leaving a patient's room and before performing hand hygiene. Masks, goggles, and face shields should be used by healthcare workers when there is a likelihood of blood or body fluid splashes. All of these PPE devices protect the mucous membranes of the mouth, nose, and eyes from infected particles.

Surgical Asepsis

Asepsis is the absence of infectious organisms. In the operating room, aseptic techniques include measures and practices that minimize or prevent contamination due to infectious pathogens. Asepsis principles involve sterilization processes to completely eliminate all microorganisms, as well as appropriate delivery of items. Surgical aseptic practice is based on the premise that most infections occur due to exogenous organisms or pathogens that are external from the body. Medical assistants can monitor the surgical field to decrease patient risk.

ENVIRONMENTAL SAFETY

Fire Safety Measures

Although rare, fires in physician offices do occur. The medical assistant should be aware of certain fire safety measures, including:

- Keep open spaces free of clutter.
- Mark fire exits.
- Know the locations of fire exits, alarms, and extinguishers.
- Know the fire drill and evacuation plan of the healthcare facility.
- Don't use the elevator when a fire occurs.
- Turn off oxygen in the vicinity of the fire.

Electrical Safety Measures

Before use, electrical equipment should be inspected for defects and safety. This involves the use of three-pronged outlets and reading warning labels. Any electrical cords that are exposed, damaged, or frayed should be discarded, and circuits should not be overloaded. Safety measures include:

- Never run electrical wiring under carpets.
- Don't pull a plug by using the cord.
- Never use electrical appliances near bathtubs, sinks, or other water sources.
- Disconnect a plug from the outlet before cleaning appliances or equipment.
- Never operate unfamiliar equipment.

Radiation Safety Measures

Radiation safety involves the use of various protocols and guidelines of the healthcare facility. Radiation exposure is monitored with a film badge. Safety measures include:

- Label potentially radioactive material.
- Limit time spent near the source.
- Use a shielding device to protect vital organs.
- Place the patient with radiation implants in private room.

Poison Safety Measures

A poison is any substance that destroys or impairs health or life when inhaled, ingested, or otherwise absorbed by the body. The reversibility of the poison effect is determined by the capacity of the body tissue to recover from the poison. Poisonous substances can alter various body systems, including the respiratory, central nervous, circulatory, hepatic, renal, and gastrointestinal systems. Safety measures include:

- Keep the Poison Control Center phone number visible.
- Remove obvious substances/materials from patient's mouth, eyes, or body area.
- If the patient vomits, save the vomitus for examination.
- Never induce vomiting unless specified in poison control policies.
- Never induce vomiting in an unconscious patient.

Notes
intentionally left blank

Notes
intentionally left blank

THE TREATMENT AREA

This section covers basic instruments and equipment, autoclave and sterilization, casting, electrocardiography, mobility/immobility assistive devices, and durable medical equipment.

Basic Instruments and Equipment

- Otoscope - A device used to examine the inside of the ears. It has disposable covers that should be changed after each patient. It can be handheld or mounted to the wall. Portable units should be fully charged and ready for use each morning.

- Ophthalmoscope - A device used to examine the eyes. It is usually mounted to the wall along with the otoscope. It can be portable, as well.

- Nasal speculum - A device that dilates the nares for examination. It must be cleaned between patients.

- Tongue depressor - A flat wooden stick used to depress the tongue so the throat can be evaluated.

- Reflex hammer - A small rubber head hammer used to test reflexes.

- Tuning fork - A metal device used to test for auditory acuity and bone vibration.

- Stethoscope - A long, tube-like device used to assess blood pressure and heart rate, as well as listen to lung, heart, and abdominal sounds.

- Gloves - Disposable latex or vinyl items of various sizes used for examinations.

- Lubricant - Water-soluble gel substance used for rectal and vaginal examinations.

- Tape measure - A disposable paper that measures various body parts, wounds, ulcers, and skin rashes.

Autoclave and Sterilization

Sterilization is the process of destroying living organisms. Two types of heat are used:

- Dry heat - Used for sterilizing instruments that corrode easily, and requires one hour of heat at 320 degrees F. Chemical sterilization is also known as cold sterilization, and is used for heat-sensitive equipment, such as endoscopes. The equipment is soaked in closed containers with strong chemical agents.

- Steam heat - Also known as autoclaving, this type of sterilization is the most common method used in the medical office. The steam achieves high temperatures under pressure, usually between 250 to 254 degrees F. Time required will vary from 20 to 40 minutes, depending on how tightly items are wrapped.

Autoclave Wrapping Process

If an item is wrapped loosely, it requires less time than one that is tightly wrapped.

- Place cleaned and dried instruments in the center of a wrap.
- Position opened wrap on flat surface in a diamond shape with a point toward you.
- Fold the corner closest to you over the instrument.
- Fold the first side corner toward the center, covering the instrument.
- Fold the extra material to form a tab and repeat with the second side corner.
- Fold the last corner toward center and completely cover the instrument.
- Fasten the packet with sterilization tape.

Cast Equipment and Materials

The application of a cast to an extremity is often done in the physician office. Most of the medical assistant's responsibility in the casting process is assisting the physician with supplies and application of the cast. Also, the patient should be educated regarding cast care and the signs and symptoms of infection. The types of casts include:

- Plaster – Plaster is comprised of rolls of casting material that are moistened with warm water before being applied in a rolling manner. The extremity will be covered first with a stockinet and cast padding. Once the casting material is applied, it can be molded to the extremity and allowed to harden.

- Fiberglass – A fiberglass cast is applied just like the plaster type, but it is fairly waterproof and lighter.

- Air – An air cast is a plastic envelope cast, which is inflated, easily applied, and removable.

Electrocardiography

Electrocardiography involves heart activity. The electrical activity of the heart follows a conductive pathway resulting in the cardiac cycle (heart pumping blood). There are three types of cardiac polarity: polarization, depolarization, and repolarization. Polarity is the electrical status of cardiac muscle cells in an attempt to maintain electronegativity inside the cells for distribution of ions, such as potassium, sodium, and chloride. Polarization is resting of the cardiac muscles cells, depolarization is charging and contracting of these cells, and repolarization is recovery of the cells.

The cardiac cycle involves pumping to the heart in a rhythmic cycle of contraction and reaction. Normally, the adult heart beats between 60 to 100 beats each minute, which are considered cycles. The phases of contractions are called systole and the phases of relaxation are called diastole.

ECG Complex

A full cardiac electrical cycle is one heartbeat, represented by P, Q, R, S, and T waves on the electrocardiogram.

- P wave - An upward curve that represents atrial contraction and used to measure the atrial rate
- Q wave - A downward deflection of the P wave
- R wave - A large upward spike that occurs after the Q wave
- S wave - A downward deflection that follows the R wave
- T wave - An upward curve that occurs after the S wave, and shows repolarization and ventricle resting
- U wave - A small upward curve that occurs after the T wave and shows slow repolarization
- QRS complex - The Q, R, and S waves together, which represents contraction of the two ventricles
- PR interval - The P and R waves, which represents the time the electrical impulse travels from the sinoatrial (SA) node to the atrioventricular (AV) node
- QT interval - The QRST waves that represent a full cardiac cycle
- ST segment - An upward line that connects the QRS complex to the T wave, and shows the time between ventricular contraction and relaxation

Placement of Electrodes

Electrodes are sensors attached to the shin. A lead is the view of the heart produced by combination of all electrodes. The 12-lead ECG uses 10 electrodes, which should never be placed over clothing or bony prominences. Electrodes and leads include:

- Chest Electrodes (6)
    - V1 - Fourth intercostal space, just right of the sternum
    - V2 - Fourth intercostal space, just left of the sternum
    - V3 - Midway between V2 and V4
    - V4 - Fifth intercostal space, at the left midclavicular line
    - V5 - Midway between V4 and V6
    - V6 - Fifth intercostal space, at the left midaxillary line

- Limb Electrodes (4)
    - RA - Right arm
    - LA - Left arm
    - RL - Right leg
    - LL - Left leg

- Bipolar Limb Leads - Record cardiac electrical activity between two electrodes.

    - Lead I - Heart view between LA and RA electrodes
    - Lead II - Heart view between LL and RA electrodes
    - Lead III - Heart view between LL and LA electrodes

- Unipolar Limb Leads - Called augmented voltage.

    - aVR - RA electrode
    - aVL - LA electrode
    - aVF - LL electrode

- Chest Leads - Also called precordial leads, these six leads are equate to the six chest electrodes (V1, V2, V3, V4, V5, and V6.)

ECG Paper

The ECG paper is standardized and has a combination of large and small blocks. These blocks are used to measure the cardiac electrical activity as shown on the graph. The horizontal line means time, and the vertical line signifies voltage or amplitude. The small bloc is 1 mm X 1 mm and it represents 0.1 millivolt (mV) on the vertical axis and 0.04 second on the horizontal axis. The large block is 5 mm X 5 mm, and it represents 0.5 mV on the vertical axis, with five large horizontal blocks being one second.

The ECG paper speed is 22 mm per second, and the calibration is 10 mm vertical mark or two large blocks. The stylus is the pen-line device that receives impulses via electrodes, moves across the ECG paper, and records the heart electrical activity.

Cardiac Arrhythmias

Cardiac arrhythmias are irregular heart activities, which include:

- Bradycardia - Slow heartbeat (less than 60 beats per minute)
- Tachycardia - Fast heartbeat (more than 100 beats per minute)
- Asystole - Absence of a heart rate (flat line)
- Ectopic beat - A beat that originates outside of the heart's pacemaker (SA node)
- Premature ventricular contraction (PVC) - A contraction of ventricles that occurs early
- Ventricular fibrillation - Uncoordinated ventricular contractions (quivering of the heart)
- Ventricular flutter - A ventricular rate of 150 to 300 beats per minute (considered life-threatening)
- Premature atrial contraction (PAC) - Atrial contraction that occurs early
- Paroxysmal atrial tachycardia (PAT) - Atrial tachycardia that occurs and subsides suddenly
- Atrial fibrillation - Atrial rate of 350 to 500 beats per minute

- Atrial flutter - Atrial rate of 250 to 350 beats per minute that produces a "saw tooth" pattern

Artifacts

Artifacts are interruptions or disturbances in the ECG strip that results from activity outside the heart, such as somatic tremors, wandering baseline, and alternating current interference. Somatic tremors are involuntary or voluntary muscle or other movement by the patient. A wandering baseline is movement of the stylus from the center of the paper in a "wandering" fashion, which results from electrodes that are too loose or too tight, dirty electrodes, or from oil on the patient's skin. Alternating current interference occurs from other sources of electricity in the room, such as improper grounding or equipment.

Mobility/Immobility Assistive Devices

Patients who have been injured or those with chronic conditions are often placed on bed rest or have their activities restricted. Immobility causes many common problems, such as weakened muscles, joint contractures, and joint deformity. Each joint has a certain range of motion, and when that motion is limited, the joint and muscles cannot function appropriately and deformity occurs. Deformed joints are immobile, painful, and stiff. If a person cannot exercise or move the joint as they should, contractures occur. A joint contracture is a shortening of the tendon and muscle which limits joint mobility.

Patients who cannot bear weight on one extremity are often prescribed crutches. Muscle groups used for crutch walking include the shoulder depressors, shoulder abductors, arm flexors, extensors, and abductors, forearm extensors, wrist extensors, and finger and thumb extensors. The medical assistant can assist the patient to use these assistive devices. To sit down with crutches, the patient needs to grasp the crutches on the hand pieces, bend forward and assume the sitting position, and place the affected leg forward to prevent flexion and weight-bearing. To stand up, the patient must move to the edge of the chair, place both crutches in the hand on the side of the affected leg, and push down on the hand piece while assuming the standing position.

A walker is used for stability and support during ambulation. A pick-up walker is picked up and moved as the patient steps forward. This walker is useful for patients with poor balance and those who cannot use crutches. The rolling walker permits a natural walking pattern and is used by patients who cannot lift or carry the pick-up walker. To ambulate with a walker, the patient must hold the hand grips for stability, be able to come to a standing position, and support the body weight on the hands while balancing.

Durable Medical Equipment (DME)

Durable medical equipment is the term used to describe any assistive device or piece of equipment or technology that is used in the patient's home or community setting, as well as an institution that meets the requirements of the insurance company. DME can be furnished on a rental basis or purchased. For Medicare to cover DME, it must be approved by the insurance company and ordered by one of the patient's physicians. Medicare will only cover DME if the physician or supplier is enrolled in the Medicare program. When the supplier is not enrolled with federal Medicare services, Medicare cannot limit how much the supplier charges for the DME.

DME Categories

DME is sometimes called home medical equipment (HME) and is categorized into four groups:

- Basic mobility aids – Includes canes, crutches, and walkers
- Assistive devices for independence with ADLs – Includes shower chairs, hand rails, kitchen equipment, wound care supplies, and ostomy care supplies
- Mobility aids – Includes electric beds and wheelchairs
- High-technology equipment – Includes ventilators, IV pumps, infusion pumps, apnea/sleep monitors, and special electric beds

Notes
intentionally left blank

Notes
intentionally left blank

PATIENT PREPARATION AND ASSISTING THE PHYSICIAN

This section covers vital signs, examinations, the physical exam, and patient education.

<u>Vital Signs</u>

Vital signs change with age, illness, injury, and health status. Vital signs are often monitored in the healthcare environment, including body temperature, heart and pulse rate, respiratory rate, and blood pressure.

Body Temperature

Normal body temperature is 98.6 degrees Fahrenheit but the range is between 97.8 to 99.1 degrees. Body temperature can be measured with a thermometer by various routes, such as oral, axillary, forehead, or rectal. Normal body temperature is harder to control as a person gets older due to a decreased amount of subcutaneous fat below the skin. Also, aging decreases a person's ability to sweat, making them at risk for hyperthermia or heat stroke.

Elevated temperature (fever) is often a symptom of infection or inflammation, but some elderly people do not exhibit a high body temperature with illness. Conditions that often raise body temperature include infection, stress, dehydration, exercise, the environment, and thyroid disorders. When someone gets cold from weather, exposure to the elements, or experiences shock or a thyroid disorder, a drop in body temperature occurs. Any temperature of 95 degrees Fahrenheit or lower is defined as hypothermia.

Condition	*Causes*
Fever	Infection Stress Dehydration Exercise Environment Thyroid disorders
Hypothermia	Shock Environment Exposure to elements Thyroid disorders

Heart and Pulse Rate

The heart beats a certain number of times each minute. This is considered the heart or pulse rate. The normal adult pulse rate at rest is from 60 to 100 beats per minute. A rapid heart rate occurs from infection, dehydration, shock, anemia, stress, anxiety, thyroid conditions, and heart conditions. A slow pulse rate can occur from certain medications (beta blockers and digoxin), a vasovagal response, and various cardiac conditions.

Condition	Cause
Rapid Pulse	Infection Dehydration Shock Anemia Stress Thyroid and heart conditions
Slow Pulse	Medications Vasovagal response Cardiac conditions

Respiratory Rate

A person's respiratory rate is the number of breaths taken per minute. The normal respiratory rate is 12 to 20 breaths per minute. Conditions that can elevate the respiratory rate include acute respiratory distress, asthma, COPD, pneumonia, heart failure, bronchitis, and tuberculosis. Use of narcotics, drug overdose, or a diabetic coma can lower the respiratory rate.

Condition	Cause
High Respiratory Rate	Acute respiratory distress COPD Asthma Pneumonia Heart failure Bronchitis Tuberculosis
Low Respiratory Rate	Narcotic use Drug overdose Diabetic coma

Blood Pressure

Blood pressure (BP) is the measurement of the force of blood as it flows against the walls of the arteries. Written as two numbers, a healthy blood pressure is a systolic value of 100 to 139 and a diastolic value of 60 to 79. High blood pressure is called hypertension. Factors that can elevate blood pressure include smoking, stress, exercise, eating, caffeine, certain medications, salt intake, and a full bladder. Prolonged hypertension can result in atherosclerosis, stroke, and heart failure. Hypotension (low BP) can be caused by hypothermia, shock, and syncope. Also, older people often experience orthostatic hypotension, which occurs when standing up too quickly. Other factors that cause hypotension include arrhythmias like atrial fibrillation and bradycardia, diuretics, and digitalis.

Condition	Cause
Elevated BP	Smoking
	Stress
	Eating
	Caffeine
	Medications
	Salt
	Full bladder
Low BP	Hypothermia
	Shock
	Syncope
	Standing too quickly
	Medications
	Arrhythmias

Examinations

Height

The patient's height is assessed by using a fixed bar on the weight scale or wall. Measurements are recorded in feet (ft.) and inches (in.), or by converting inches to centimeters (2.5 cm equals 1 inch.)

Weight

The patient's weight is measured using a balanced scale and recorded in pounds (lb.) or kilograms (kg.) Conversion is 2.2 lb. per kg.

Examination Positions

- Supine - Patient lies on his or her back with arms to the sides.
- Dorsal Recumbent - Patient lies on his or her back with knees bent and feet flat on the table.
- Lithotomy - Patient lies on his or her back with buttocks on the edge of the lower end of the table, legs elevated, and feet in stirrups.
- Sims' - Patient lies on his or her left side with the left leg flexed, left arm resting behind the body, right leg flexed, and right arm at the chest.
- Prone - Patient lies on his or her stomach.
- Fowler's - Patient lies face up with his or her upper body elevated at 45 to 90 degrees.
- Semi-Fowler's - Same as the Fowler's position, except the upper body is only elevated between 30 to 45 degrees.

Examination Techniques

- Observation - Visual review of the patient's body, assessing for abnormalities, skin color and condition, and symmetry.
- Palpation - Use of hands and fingertips to assess/feel for positions and sizes of organs, masses, lumps, or other abnormalities, skin moisture and temperature, and joint flexibility.
- Percussion - The process of assessing density of body structures by sound produced by external tapping.
- Auscultation - Listening to body regions with a stethoscope, assessing for abnormalities.
- Manipulation - Passive movement of the patient's joints to assess extent of movement.
- Mensuration - Measurement of height and weight.

The Physical Exam

The purpose of the physical examination is to assess the patient's state of health and wellness and to determine the cause of the chief complaint. The medical assistant must greet the patient, obtain necessary vital signs and measurements, document the chief complaint, interview the patient, and provide the patient with a sense of support and security. Your role as the medical assistant is to assist the physician by:

- Preparing the exam room and necessary equipment.
- Making sure the exam room is clean and free of clutter.
- Preparing the patient for the exam by giving instructions.
- Helping with draping/gowning.
- Assisting the physician with the exam

Patient Education

Some educational plans require little preparation and planning, such as simple medication instructions. Other plans require a multidisciplinary approach, such as physician office workers, physical therapists, and home health workers. Depending on the patient's needs, the steps of education planning are:

- Identify the topic and purpose.
- Assess the patient's abilities and needs.
- Develop the plan and decide who will do what and how it will be done.
- Implement the plan.
- Evaluate the patient's understanding.
- Document the education in the medical record.
- Reevaluate the plan on follow-up.

Factors that Affect Learning

  A. Motivation
  B. Adaption to disease or illness
  C. Age
  D. Hearing or sight impairment
  E. Pain
  F. Language
  G. Socioeconomic barriers
  H. Cultural barriers
  I. Ability of the educator

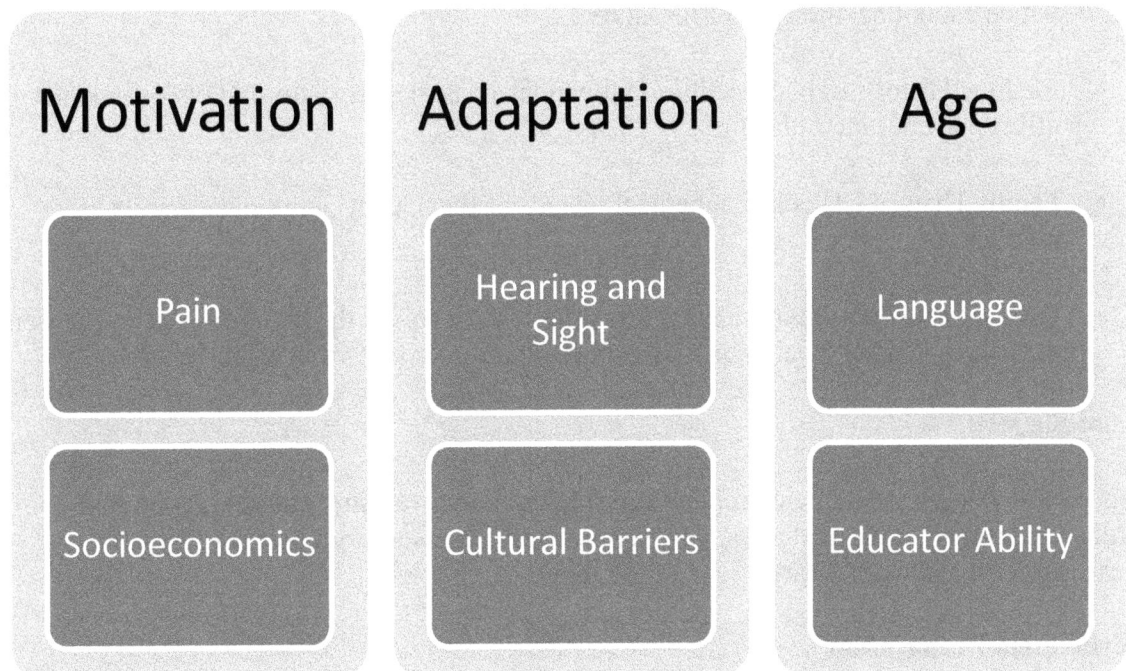

Teaching Aids

- Pamphlets
- Videos
- Audiotapes
- Oral discussion
- Anatomical models
- Support groups
- Patient journals
- Posters and illustrations

The Patient History Interview

The medical assistant is often the first member of the healthcare team to communicate with the patient. From the moment of contact, the medical assistant observes the patient and documents obtained information.

- Chief Complaint - This is a summary of the patient's own words, explaining why he or she seeks care and services. A good way to do this is to ask "What brings you in today?"

- Symptoms - These are subjective descriptions and altered health indicators, some of which cannot be observed or measured.

- Medical History - This describes that patient's past health status and exposures that affect current state of health.

- Family History - This is the medical history of the patient's biological family members.

- Psychosocial and Environmental History - This involves the patient's past and present exposures and personal habits, as well as emotional issues that affect health.

<u>Minor Surgery</u>

This section covers sterile field preparation, surgical hand washing, patient preparation, surgical instruments, surgical trays, endoscopic exam, cryosurgery, laser surgery, electrosurgery, and wound care.

Sterile Field Preparation

The sterile field is a pathogen-free area that contains the sterile instruments, solutions, and other items that will be used in the procedure. This also includes the hands and anterior neck to waist region of the physician and assistants.

- Check for sterile indicators and dates on all items before opening them and putting them on the sterile field.
- Examine each item for breaks in packaging or for moisture.
- Open the packages per instructions.
- Maintain a border of one inch between non-sterile and sterile areas.
- Do not reach over the sterile field.
- Do not cough, talk, or sneeze over the sterile field.

Surgical Hand Washing

- Remove all jewelry.

- Wash hands, wrists, and forearms at foot- or knee-controlled faucet.
- Cleanse for 10 minutes.
- Hold hands in an upward position while rinsing.
- Dry with a sterile towel.
- Apply sterile gloves

Patient Preparation

- Hair Removal - Shave or cut the hair from the surgical site with a disposable blade.
- Skin Cleaning - Use an antiseptic skin cleansing solution, such as Betadine, on the surgical site, using a circular motion from the point of the incision outward.
- Draping - Drape the patient with a fenestrated sterile towel or sheet.

Common Surgical Instruments

- Curette - A sharp, spoon-shaped tool used to scrape tissue or substances on the body.
- Dilator - A solid long instrument used to widen or stretch an opening.
- Forceps - A two-handled tool used to grasp, crimp, and move tissue.
- Hemostat - A straight or curved tool used to compress vessels or tissue.
- Needle Holder - A two-handed tool used to clasp a suture needle.
- Scalpels - Knives of varying blades and sizes used to cut, dissect, and incise skin.
- Scissors - A two-bladed tool used to cut tissue, skin, and materials.

Surgical Trays

- General Minor Surgery Tray - Used for lesion/mass removal procedures. Contains: 4 towel clips, scalpel, curved and straight hemostats, scissors, forceps, needle holder, sponges, sutures, and drapes.

- Suture Tray - Used for suturing various wounds. Contains: towel clips, curved hemostat, forceps with teeth, thumb forceps, sutures, scissors, needle holder, gauze, and drape.

- Suture Removal Tray - Used to remove sutures. Contains: scissors, thumb forceps, and gauze.

- Staple Removal Tray - Used to remove staples. Contains: staple remover and gauze.

Endoscopic Examination

An endoscope is a special instrument used to examine the inside of the body, such as the respiratory or gastrointestinal tract. This scope contains fiberoptic technology, allowing for lighting and videoing, as well as biopsies and procedures.

Electrosurgery

The electrosurgery method involves cutting and cauterization of the skin and tissues using an electric current directed to a specific anatomic region, The power source is controlled by a small box-shaped unit that transmit electrical current to a hand piece that comes in contact with the surgical site.

Cryosurgery

The cryosurgery method involves destroying tissue by cryogenics (freezing), which employs liquid nitrogen applied to the surgical site for the purpose of lesion removal or tissue destruction.

Laser Surgery

The laser method of surgery uses electromagnetic radiation in narrow beams for diagnostic and treatment applications. Common types of lasers include KTP, YAG, Q-Switched, Pulsed Wave, Continous Wave, and Argon.

Types of Wounds

Wounds are injuries and traumas to the skin and body tissues. The type of wound determines the treatment. Dirty wounds are those that occur under contaminated conditions.

- Abrasion - Outer layers of the skin are removed from scraping, which causes a small amount of clear or thin, blood-tinged drainage.

- Contusion - The top layers of skin are bruised, and bleeding occurs below unbroken skin from blunt trauma.

- Incision - A smooth cut from surgery or a razor.

- Laceration - A traumatic, jagged cut that results in irregular wound edges.

- Puncture - A small, round hole in the skin and tissues from a sharp, pointed object.

Laboratory Specimens and Diagnostic Testing

The medical assistant must be familiar with the laboratory specimen collection procedure, as well as any special instructions for handling and storage of the specimen. To avoid errors, the patient should be properly identified and the specimen must be labeled as soon as it is obtained. The label should be placed on the container, not the specimen bag.

Venous Blood Collection

- Ask the patient if he or she has latex or tape allergies.
- Assess the antecubital region of both arms.
- Place the tourniquet three to four inches above the site of puncture.
- Do NOT leave the tourniquet on for longer than one minute.
- Cleanse the site with an antiseptic solution.
- Insert the safety needle and obtain the specimen.
- Release the tourniquet.
- Apply a clean gauze dressing to the site.
- Gently invert the collection tube(s) 10 times.

Order of Blood Draw

According to the National Committee for Clinical Laboratory Standards, the recommended order of blood draw is:

- Yellow top - Contains sodium polyanethole sulfonate and is used for blood cultures.
- Red top - This tube contains non additive and is used for blood chemistry, serologic tests, viral studies, blood grouping, and blood typing.
- Red/gray (tiger) top - Contains a silicone serum separator and is used for tests requiring blood serum.
- Blue top - Contains anticoagulant sodium citrate and is for coagulation studies.
- Lavender top - Contains ethylenediaminetraacetic acid (EDTA) and is used for hematology studies.
- Green top - Contains the anticoagulant sodium heparin and is for arterial blood gases and electrolyte studies.
- Pink top - Contains EDTA and is used for hematology studies.
- Gray top - Contains the anticoagulant potassium oxalate or sodium fluoride and is used for blood glucose evaluation.

Capillary Blood Specimen

A capillary blood specimen is collected using a small sample tube, usually for testing hematocrit, hemoglobin, and glucose. The skin of the finger or heel is punctured and the blood is drained into the container. When collecting a capillary specimen, do not milk the site if possible. Capillary puncture for adults and children is best when obtained from the third or fourth finger, and for infants, use the heel or big toe.

The skin puncture is performed using a semiautomatic disposable lancet, which is spring-loaded and plastic. The blade is usually 3.0 mm for adults and 2.4 mm for children and infants. Before obtaining the specimen, make sure the patient is seated comfortably. Gently massage the area or used warm water to increase blood flow by dilation of vessels. Cleanse the site with alcohol and allow it to dry before puncture.

Quality Control

The Clinical Laboratory Improvement Amendments (CLIA) is legislation passed by Congress in 1988. It was developed to improve the quality of laboratory testing, and under this, all laboratories must follow certain quality assurance standards. Quality control and assurance requirements include employee training, written policies, documented maintenance of instruments, equipment, and procedures, and proficiency testing. Quality assurance does not apply to CLIA waived tests, however, but it does apply to moderate complexity, high-complexity, and performed microscopy tests.

Quality control measures allow for testing accuracy through careful monitoring of various procedures. The laboratory must follow these procedures, which include control samples, calibration, reagent control, maintenance, and documentation. Calibration involves testing procedures where the equipment generates a result set by a known value. Control samples are specimens with known values, used to check for testing accuracy. Reagents are chemicals that react in specific ways when exposed to known substances. A reagent control log documents quality of reagents. Documentation of all quality control measures depends on facility policy, as well as CLIA standards and requirements.

CLIA Waived Tests

- Urinalysis, dipstick
- Urinalysis, tablet reagent
- Fecal occult blood (guaiac)
- Urine pregnancy test
- Blood glucose
- Erythrocyte sedimentation rate (ESR)
- Hemoglobin (Hgb)
- Hematocrit (Hct)
- Strep A test
- Ovulation testing

Moderate-Complexity Tests

- Blood chemistry performed with automated analyzer
- Hematology performed with automated analyzer
- Pinworm preparation
- Gram staining
- Microscopic analysis of urine sediment

High-Complexity Tests

- Cytology testing
- Blood cross matching
- Blood typing

- Pap smears (Houser & Sesser, 2008)

OSHA Standards

The Occupational Safety and Health Administration (OSHA) Blood borne Pathogens Standards of 1991 was created to reduce the risk to healthcare employees from infectious disease exposure. OSHA standards include:

- Hand Washing - Done before and after donning clean gloves.
- Biohazard Container - Closable, leak-proof container, used for infectious waste, as well as used to transport specimens.
- Clean Disposable Gloves - Used by all healthcare workers when in contact with blood, non-intact skin, mucous membranes, and contaminated surfaces.
- Protective Clothing - Worn to protect the face and body (gowns, goggles, lab coats, etc.)

Performing Selected Laboratory Tests

Urine Specimen Collection

Urine is assessed for various reasons in the medical office. It is composed of 95 percent water and 5 percent organic and inorganic waste products. Analysis of urine occurs by physical, chemical, and microscopic means. The urine is assessed for color, clarity, pH, specific gravity, glucose, ketones, nitrites, white blood cells, and red blood cells. The medical assistant should collect 30 to 50 ml of urine for specimens.

The random specimen is collected in a dry, clean container. The first-voided morning specimen is often brought in by the patient after being collected at home. A clean catch midstream specimen is obtained in a sterile container after the patient cleanses himself of herself with an antiseptic towelette. The urine must be neither the first voided nor the last voided. A two-hour postprandial urine is collected two hours after a meal, and it is used for diabetic screening. A 24-hour specimen measures various components, such as creatinine, protein, urea, and calcium, and it is collected at home in a 3000 ml container that is kept on ice or refrigerated.

Hematology

- Erythrocyte sedimentation rate (ESR) – This test assesses the rate at which erythrocytes settle out of anticoagulated blood in one hour. Normal value is 0 to 30 mm/hr.

- Hemoglobin – This test determines the level of hemoglobin in the blood. Normal values include 14 to 16.5 g/dL (adult male) and 12 to 15 g/dL (adult female).

- Hematocrit – This test shows red blood cell mass. Normal values include 42% to 52% (adult male) and 35% to 47% (adult female).

- Serum iron – This test assess the level of iron in the blood. Normal values include 65 to 175 mcg/dL (adult male) and 50 to 170 mcg/dL (adult female).

- Red blood cells – RBCs function in hemoglobin transport, which assists with oxygen delivery to organs and body tissues. Normal values include 4.5 to 6.2 million (adult male) and 4.0 to 5.5 million (adult female).

- White blood cell count – WBCs function as an immune defense system. A "left shift" indicates an increased number of immature neutrophils. A low total WBC count indicates a recovery from bone marrow or an infection. With a "right shift," cells have more nuclear segments than usual.

Coagulation Studies

- Activated partial thromboplastin time (aPTT) – This test evaluates the coagulation sequence function by measuring he amount of time it takes in seconds for plasma to clot after partial thromboplastin is added to it. Normal value is 20 to 36 seconds.

- Prothrombin time (PT) with international normalized ration (INR) – This test measures the amount of time it takes in seconds for a clot to form. A PT value within 2 seconds of the control is a normal value. Normal values for PT: 9.6 to 11.8 seconds (adult male) and 9.5 to 11.3 seconds (adult female). Normal values for INR: 2.0 to 3.0 standard warfarin therapy and 3.0 to 4.5 for high-dose warfarin therapy.

- Platelet count – This test measures platelets, which assist with the coagulation process. Normal value is 150,000 to 400,000 cells/mm^3.

Blood Chemistry

- Serum sodium – This electrolyte maintains osmotic pressure and acid-base balance, assists in the transmission of nerve impulses, is absorbed from the small intestine, and is excreted in the urine. Normal adult sodium values are between 135 and 145 mEq/L.

- Serum potassium – This electrolyte regulates the cellular water balance, acid-base balance, and electrical conduction in muscle cells. Potassium levels are used to assess for renal, cardiac, and gastrointestinal function. Normal adult potassium values are between 3.5 and 5.1 mEq/L.

- Serum chloride – This electrolyte functions to balance cations (positively charged ions), acts as a buffer during oxygen-carbon dioxide exchange, and aids in maintenance of osmatic pressure. Normal adult chloride values are between 98 and 107 mEq/L.

- Serum bicarbonate – This electrolyte is responsible for regulating the pH of body fluids. Normal adult sodium bicarbonate values are between 22 and 29 mEq/L.

Immunology

- Mono Test – This test assesses for the mononucleosis virus.
- Strep Test – This test evaluates for Streptococcus.
- C-Reactive Protein (CRP) – This blood test assesses the level of CRP.
- Pregnancy Test - The urine is assessed for the presence of human chorionic gonadotropin (hCG)

Microbiology

On occasion, the physician will examine a specimen under the microscope to identify microorganisms. Preparation for specimens includes:

- Smear - Use a swab applicator to collect a small amount of the specimen and apply it to the glass slide.

- Wet Mount - After a slide is smeared, apply a drop of normal saline to the smear and cover with a glass slide.

- Potassium Hydroxide (KOH) Mount - After a slide is smeared, apply a drop of KOH to the smear and cover with a glass slide.

- Stains - After smearing a slide, heat the slide and apply a staining material.
    - Purple stain - Used for gram-positive bacteria.
    - Red stain - Used for gram-negative bacteria.
    - Acid-fast - Used for certain bacteria that do not respond to color stain.

- Sensitivity - Special testing used to determine if a pathogen's is susceptible to antibiotics.

- Culture - Collecting a specimen with an applicator swab for the purpose of growing pathogens form the inoculated substance. The transport media is in a tube structure.

Tuberculosis Testing

The Mantoux tuberculin test (also called purified protein derivative or PPD) is a type of intradermal skin test. To perform this test, the healthcare worker injects a small amount of tubercle bacillus into the patient's skin and reads the result in 48 to 72 hours. A "positive" result involves induration, which is a raised, hardening of the skin around the injection site. Further testing involves X-ray of the chest and sputum analysis and culture.

Guaiac Testing

Fecal occult blood (FOB) testing (commonly referred to as guaiac testing) is used to detect blood in the stool (feces). The patient collects a stool sample on a reagent card with paper, and returns the card to the laboratory in a leak-proof envelope or biohazard bag. The medical assistant instills a few drops of developer on the specimen. A bluish discoloration is an indication of the presence of blood.

Performing Diagnostic Tests

Electrocardiogram

An electrocardiogram (EKG or ECG) is a noninvasive test that records the electrical activity of the heart and detects cardiac dysrhythmias. Medical assistant interventions for electrocardiography include reassuring the patient regarding no electrical shock and instructing on normal breathing.

Stress Test

A stress test is also called an exercise test, and this noninvasive exam studies the heart during activity to detect coronary artery disease. Medical assistant interventions include instructing the patient to notify staff of any dizziness, chest pain, and/or shortness of breath and discussing pre- and post-procedure instructions.

Colonoscopy

A colonoscopy is an invasive procedure done to visually examine and take biopsies from the gastrointestinal tract. Medical assistant interventions include instructing on NPO after midnight status, monitoring for signs of bowel perforation, and administering medications as prescribed.

Bronchoscopy

For direct visual examination of the larynx, bronchi, and trachea, the bronchoscopy involves the use of a special scope. Medical assistant interventions involve maintaining NPO status until the gag reflex returns, monitoring sputum and respiratory status, and patient education.

Vision Testing

Visual acuity is the measurement of eyesight and vision. The Snellen chart is used for adults, and the E chart is used for children. The patient closes or covers one eye, while the other is measured. Normal vision is 20/20, with the top number (numerator) indicating the distance the patient is from the chart, and the bottom number (denominator) indicating the distance at which people with normal visual acuity can read the last line.

Hearing Testing

- Audiometry - This is a hearing test that measures the patient's response to various tones, which are recorded in decibels (db.) and frequencies.

- Impedance Audiometry - This is a hearing test using an ear probe to measure the ossicle and tympanic membrane mobility.

- Whisper Test - Gross measurement of hearing done when the healthcare worker whispers behind the patient and asks what was said.

- Startle Test - This gross hearing measurement for infants is done by eliciting a loud clap or bang and assessing the infant for a cry or jerk reaction.

Pulmonary Testing

Pulse Oximetry

A pulse oximeter (pulse ox) is a small device used to assess blood oxygen concentration. Pulse oximetry is the measurement of the percentage of oxygen in the blood. This is a simple, noninvasive test.

Pulmonary Function Test

A pulmonary function test (PFT) is a means of respiratory testing where volume and the flow of air are measured by using a spirometer. The spirometer is a small device attached to a computer that assesses lung capacity and ability.

Medical Imaging

Radiographic tests are used to visualize internal structures for the purpose of diagnosis. A radiograph (X-ray) is a permanent record produced on radiographic film. Contrast medium is used to make internal organs and structures visible on the radiograph. X-rays are directed from the front to the back of the body, which is referred to as anteroposterior viewing. A lateral view is where the X-ray beam passes form one side of the patient's body to the other side. An oblique view is obtained when the body is situated at an angle or semilateral position.

Types of Radiographic Tests

- X-ray - Basic radiograph performed in many physician's offices.
- Angiography - Insertion of a catheter into the patient's artery or vein so that dye and X-ray viewing can be used for diagnostic purposes.
- Computed Tomography (CT) - Detailed radiograph that permits cross-sectional views of a body region, acquired as a camera rotates around the patient.
- Magnetic Resonance Imaging (MRI) - A combination of nonionizing radiation and a magnetic field that permits examination of the internal body structures.
- Ultrasound (US) - Use of high-frequency inaudible sound waves to produce images based on echoes.

PREPARING AND ADMINISTERING MEDICATIONS

For the 50 most commonly used medications, see the "Top 200 Drugs" at www.rxlist.com.

This section covers pharmacology, dosage calculation, and child and adult immunizations.

<u>Pharmacology</u>

Pharmacology is the study of drugs and pharmaceuticals. The agencies that regulate drugs and drug administration are the Food and Drug Administration (FDA), which controls and regulates the drugs accepted for use in the U.S., and the Drug Enforcement Agency (DEA), which controls the administration and use specified drugs.

Drug Schedule

Schedule	*Use*	*Example*
I	Illegal or restricted to research; high abuse potential.	Marijuana and heroin
II	Medical use with limitations; high abuse potential.	Cocaine, Demerol, morphine, oxycodone, and Ritalin
III	Medical use with limitations; moderate abuse potential.	Codeine and barbiturates
IV	Medical use with limitations; low abuse potential.	Valium, Xanax, and Ativan
V	Medical use, over-the-counter, and low abuse potential.	Benadryl and Robitussin

Common Drug Routes

- Buccal - Placed between the cheek and gum via spray, gel, or tablet. Examples: nitroglycerine and glucose.
- Inhalation - Inhaled into the respiratory system via mists, sprays, and masks. Examples: oxygen and albuterol.
- Intradermal (ID) - Injected into the dermal skin layer at a 15 degree angle via a 25 - 27 gauge needle. Example: tuberculin skin test.
- Subcutaneous (SC) - Injected into the subcutaneous tissue at a 45 - 90 degree angle via a 22 to 25 gauge needle. Example: insulin.
- Intramuscular (IM) - Injected into the muscle at a 90 degree angle via an 18 to 23 gauge needle. Example: Rocephin. Common sites for IM injections include the deltoid (upper arm), gluteus medius (the dorsogluteal area), and the vastus lateralis (thigh).

- Z-track - A specific IM injection used when the medication could irritate the subcutaneous tissue. The skin at the injection site is pulled to one side before injection. After injection, the skin is released, and the medication cannot seep into the subcutaneous layers.
- Intravenous (IV) - Injected into a vein via an 18 to 22 gauge needle. Example: antibiotics and fluids.
- Ophthalmic - Placed into the eye via ointment or drops.
- Oral - Taken by mouth and swallowed via capsule, tablet, liquid, gel, or solution.
- Otic - Placed in the ear via drops.
- Parenteral - Any injected medication (SC, IM, ID, or IV).
- Sublingual - Placed under the tongue via gel or tablets.
- Topical - Placed on the skin via patch, ointment, cream, liquid, or spray.
- Transdermal - Placed on the skin via patch.
- Urethral - Placed into the urethra and bladder via a catheter.
- Vaginal - Placed into the vagina via applicator (cream or suppository).
- Rectal - Placed into the anus via applicator (cream or suppository).

The Six Rights of Drug Administration

- Right patient - Check the name on the physician's order and verify the patient's first and last name.
- Right drug - Check the drug label on three separate occasions: when taking the drug container out, check the drug expiration date and name, after placing the medication in the dispenser (syringe or medication cup), and before returning the container to the storage or trash.
- Right route - Check the physician's order for correct route.
- Right dose - Check the physician's order for the right dose.
- Right time - Check the physicians' order for the right time to give the medication.
- Right documentation - Record the medication administration in the medical record, noting date, time, drug, route, dose, site, results, tolerance, patient education, and signature of medical assistant with title.

Dosage Calculation

The body surface area (BSA) is used for administering pediatric medications. This value is determined by comparing body weight and height with averages on a nomogram graph. When dosage recommendations for children specify micrograms, milligrams, or units per square meter, the dosage is obtained by simple multiplication. Also, there is a special formula used to calculate a child's dosage from the adult dosage:

Child's BSA (in m^2) x Adult dose / $1.7 m^2$

Conversion of Body Weight

- Measurements – 1 pound (lb.) = 16 ounces (oz.) and 1 kilogram (kg) = 2.2 pounds (lb.)
- Pounds to kilograms – 1 kilogram (kg.) = Divide pounds by 2.2 where kilograms are expressed to the nearest tenth.
- Kilograms to pounds – Multiply kilograms by 2.2 where pounds are expressed to the nearest tenth

Infusion Rate Calculation Formula

Infusion therapy is the responsibility of the nurse. Certain calculation methods are commonly used. The nurse must consider certain patient populations (elderly and pediatric), as well as certain patient conditions and restrictions. Flow rate determination is used to calculate the amount of fluid to be given over a specific time period. Flow rates are ordered as milliliters per hour or minute, total volume over a set number of hours, or number of drops per minute. Also, the infusion rate calculation formula is:

$$\frac{\_\_\_ (mL/hr) \times \_\_\_ gtt\ factor}{60\ (time\ in\ minutes)} = \_\_\_ drops\ per\ minute$$

Childhood Immunizations

The childhood immunization schedule is the recommendation of public health officials for immunity against childhood diseases. Immunizations are only given to healthy infants and children, so the medical assistant should be sure that the patient does not have any active fever or illness. If this occurs, the patient should be rescheduled when he or she is well. Also, check the patient's health history and be sure that there is no past history of allergies or convulsions. The parent should be advised on the benefits and risks of all immunizations prior to administration.

Most immunizations are given in a "series." When more than one dose is required for immunity, the shot sequence is referred to as a primary series. The primary series requires a booster for the series to be complete and effective. Here are the most common immunizations:

- Diphtheria - This is an acute infectious disease caused by *Corynebacterium diphtheriae*, which is a gram-positive club-shaped bacillus. Symptoms of diphtheria include headache, fever, sore throat, and malaise. Immunization: DTaP.

- Pertussis - Also known as whooping cough, pertussis is an acute infectious disease caused by the gram-negative bacillus *Bordetella pertussis*. Symptoms include fever, dry cough, and sneezing. Immunization: DTaP.

- Tetanus – This immunization is used against *Clostridium tetani,* the bacteria that leads to tetanus. Symptoms include stiff jaw, fever, and weakness. Immunization: DTaP.

- Haemophilus influenza type B - This infectious disease is caused by a non-motile, gram-negative parasitic bacterium. Symptoms include sore throat, fever, cough, and muscle aches. Immunization: HIB.

- Measles - Also called rubeola, measles is spread by direct contact, indirect contact, or from droplet infection. Lasting around 10 days, it causes a red skin rash, runny nose, cough, and sore throat. Immunization: MMR.

- Mumps - Caused by an infectious organism that attacks the parotid and salivary glands, mumps is transmitted by direct contact or droplet infection. Immunization: MMR.

- Rubella - Also known as the German measles, rubella is caused by a virus that leads to an upper respiratory infection. Other symptoms are fever, arthralgia, and a fine, red rash. Immunization: MMR.

- Hepatitis B - This is a highly contagious form of viral hepatitis, caused by the hepatitis B virus (HBV). It is transmitted by contact with contaminated saliva, semen or blood. Symptoms include nausea, vomiting, fever, jaundice, and dark urine. Immunization: HBV.

- Varicella - This is a highly contagious viral illness that is better known as chickenpox. It is spread by direct contact and droplet infection. Symptoms include pruritic rash, fever, headache, and general malaise. Immunization: VZV.

- Polio - This is a serious disease that can lead to infantile paralysis (poliomyelitis). Symptoms include headache, nausea, vomiting, and rash. Immunization: IPV.

Adult Immunizations

Healthcare workers can prevent potential debilitating illnesses through the use of immunizations. Important adult immunizations and vaccines are:

- Influenza Vaccine – Influenza viruses are associated with approximately 36,000 deaths each year in the U.S. alone. The influenza vaccine contains three virus strains: two type A and one type B. Clinical researchers found that aging adults who receive this vaccine have less severe influenza illness, fewer complications from the pneumonia, and fewer deaths.

- Pneumococcal Vaccine – Pneumococcal infections cause around 40,000 deaths every year in the U.S. The pneumococcal vaccine gives that patient immunity to the *Streptococcus pneumoniae* organism. All adults over the age of 65 years should receive this vaccine, as well as those who are considered high risk. The injection is given intramuscularly in the deltoid muscle.

- Herpes Zoster Vaccine –The herpes zoster virus vaccine can prevent shingles for people over the age of 60 years. The vaccine contains live, attenuated varicella zoster virus that is 14 times greater than the varicella vaccine given to children. This injection reduces the occurrence of shingles, and for those who do develop shingles, it lessens illness severity.

- Tetanus Vaccine – Most aging adults are not aware that they need to be immunized against *Clostridium tetani*, the bacteria that lead to tetanus. The tetanus vaccine is given every 10 years for adults and is usually available as tetanus-diphtheria toxoid (Td), which is given intramuscularly.

EMERGENCIES

Medical emergencies are uncommon in the physician's office, but the medical assistant will encounter them from time to time. The office will have specific protocols, depending on the type of practice. The office will typically have a "crash cart" or a stocked emergency supply area. Supplies will include:

- Personal protective equipment
- CPR mask
- One-way breathing valve device
- Bag-valve-mask (BVM)
- Oxygen
- First aid supplies
- Necessary medications

Hemorrhage

Bleeding can be arterial, venous, or capillary. Arterial bleeding is more serious and life-threatening, but venous bleeding can lead to sever blood loss. Without control, bleeding can quickly lead to shock or death, so quick intervention is essential. To control bleeding:

- Apply direct pressure to the area.
- When the dressing is soaked with blood, apply another dressing and continue with pressure.
- Elevate the bleeding area above the level of the heart.

First-Degree Burns

First-degree burns involve superficial damage only, where the epidermis is slightly reddened and painful. Treatment involves the application of cool compress for pain relief and the prevention of infection with a dry sterile dressing.

Second-Degree Burns

Second-degree burns are called partial-thickness burns because they involve the epidermis, dermis, and some of the subcutaneous tissue. As with first-degree burns, the goal of treatment is to relieve pain and prevent infection. Cool the skin with cold water or a compress, and dress with a dry, sterile dressing.

Third-Degree Burns

Third-degree burns are called full-thickness burns, these injuries are the most serious of the three, involving all skin layers and some muscle and bone. If this occurs, cover the injured area with a sterile cloth and apply cool sterile water or normal saline. Keep the patient in a supine position with the head lower than the body. Remove any loose clothing or jewelry near the burn. the medical assistant should keep the patient calm and quiet while waiting for emergency assistance.

Chest Pain

Chest pain that is related to the heart can be of a serious nature, such as angina or myocardial infarction (MI). Also, chest pain related to the lungs could indicate a pulmonary embolism (PE) or other serious pulmonary condition. While waiting for assistance:

- Keep the patient calm, warm, and quiet.
- Monitor and record vital signs,
- Administer nitroglycerine per physician's order.
- Apply oxygen.
- Perform an ECG.
- Be prepared to do CPR if needed.

Choking

Choking occurs when there is partial or complete obstruction of the airway by a foreign body. If not dislodged, the foreign body can lead to patient's loss of consciousness or cardiac arrest. If the patient is conscious, perform the Heimlich maneuver (abdominal thrust) in order to dislodge the obstruction. Should the patient become unconscious, position him or her on the floor in the supine position, and attempt to remove the foreign object.

Diabetic Emergencies

Two types of diabetic emergencies are hyperglycemia (high blood sugar) and hypoglycemia (low blood sugar). Normal blood glucose is between 70 mg/dl and 150 mg/dl. When glucose drops below 60 mg/dl, it is considered an insulin reaction. When blood glucose is over 400 mg/dl, the patient could go into a diabetic coma.

Hypoglycemia

- For a conscious patient, give some form of simple sugar, such as hard candy, soda, orange juice, and crackers.
- Perform a finger-stick blood glucose check.
- If level persists to be low, give some form of protein, such as milk, peanut butter, or meat.
- For an unconscious patient, notify the physician and follow orders.

Hyperglycemia

- For a conscious patient, notify the physician and follow orders.
- Patients with severe hyperglycemia should be treated in the hospital setting.
- If you are unsure of high or low blood sugar, give sugar first, then, check the glucose level.

Indication	*Hypoglycemia (below 60)*	*Hyperglycemia (over 400)*
Breath	No change	Fruity or sweet odor
Skin	Cold and clammy	Warm and dry
Behavior	Irritable, tremors, and/or confused	Drowsiness, fatigue, and or lethargy
Level of consciousness	May become unresponsive	Disoriented or coma
GI system	Hunger and nausea	Nausea, vomiting, and thirst
Pulse	Normal or elevated	Weak and rapid
Onset of symptoms	Rapid	Slow

Seizures

A patient diagnosed with epilepsy or a seizure disorder will occasionally have a seizure. This occurs as the result of abnormal brain activity. The main goal for require treatment is to prevent injury to the patient.

- Move items from the area around the patient.
- Provide privacy to the patient.
- Assure that the patient's clothing is not affecting circulation.
- Monitor for excessive vomiting or saliva, and move the patient to his or her side if this occurs.
- Allow the patient to rest after the seizure is over.
- Transport the patient to the hospital per physician orders.

Shock

Shock is a serious condition that occurs due to cardiovascular system depression. The signs and symptoms of shock include low blood pressure, diaphoresis, a weak, rapid pulse, rapid respirations, weakness, pale skin, and possibly nausea and/or vomiting. Treatment depends on the type of shock, including:

- Assess ABCs and address problems.
- Administer supplemental oxygen.
- Position the patient so that lower extremities are above heart level.
- Keep the patient quiet, calm, and warm and provide support.
- Closely monitor the vital signs.
- Transfer to emergency services.

Hypovolemic Shock	Occurs from a decrease in circulating blood volume, either from hemorrhage, severe burns, or traumatic injury.
Cardiogenic Shock	Occurs from the heart failing to pump blood adequately, due to myocardial infarction, congestive heart failure, or electrical conduction issues.
Neurogenic Shock	Occurs when vasodilation causes injury to or dysfunction of the neurological system.
Septic Shock	Occurs due to massive bacterial infection where toxins are released into the bloodstream.
Anaphylactic Shock	Occurs from an allergic reaction to an allergen (Martin, 2009).

Syncope

Syncope (also known as a syncopal episode or fainting) is the partial or complete loss of consciousness due to decreased circulation to the brain. Simple fainting often occurs as a reaction to a blood draw or when a patient has not eaten. First aid measures include:

- Assist the patient to lie down before fainting occurs.
- Apply a cool cloth to the patient's face or use ammonia to stimulate consciousness.
- Assess the ABCs to assure adequate airway and circulation.
- Monitor the patient's vital signs.
- Elevate the patient's legs higher that the head.
- Keep the patient warm, quiet, and calm.
- Notify the physician if a prolonged period of unconsciousness continues.

Heat-Related Illnesses

Heat-related illnesses are preventable by limiting activities during the peak sun hours of 10 a.m. and 4 p.m., wearing loose-fitting clothes, and staying hydrated. Exertional heat occurs when running or exercising in hot climates which makes body temperature rise. First aid measures for heat stroke include placing ice on the neck, chest, axillae, and groin, removing clothes, and wetting the patient with tepid water. Older adults are at increased risk for heat-related illnesses.

Predisposing Factors of Heat Stroke

- High humidity
- Obesity Seizures
- Dehydration
- Beta-adrenergic blockers

Snake Bites

When a patient sustains a snake bite, the nurse must assess for the risk of envenomation. Signs of a poisonous snake are depressions between each eye of the snake, as well as curved fangs, swelling at the site, and secretions on the skin after the bite. If a patient sustains a snake bite from a poisonous snake, the first measure is to apply a constricting band proximal to the fang marks. Poisonous snakebites can cause hemoptysis, hematuria, petechiae, and extensive bruising from disseminated intravascular coagulation. A bite from a pit viper can cause tissue necrosis, massive tissue swelling, hypovolemic shock, and renal failure. A bite from a coral snake will cause mild, transient pain at the bite site, cranial and peripheral nerve defects, nausea, vomiting, and total flaccid paralysis.

Antivenin polyvalent is given with caution to patients who exhibit previous allergic reaction to anti-venom therapy. The medical assistant must closely monitor the patient for anaphylactic shock. Anti-venom can also cause serum sickness, which results in a skin rash with pruritus.

Bee Stings

If a patient is allergic to bee stings, he or she will experience swelling at the sting site, wheezing, laryngeal edema, deterioration in mental status, and labored rapid breathing. Treatment for an anaphylactic reaction involves administration of 1.5 mL of 1:1000 epinephrine intramuscular. The patient also needs an intravenous line and cardiac monitoring. The medical assistant should instruct the patient to wear a medical alert bracelet, carry an EpiPen, and be cautious of areas where bees are likely to live.

Fluid and Electrolyte Imbalances

Fluid compartments of the body include the intravascular, intracellular, and extracellular areas. The intravascular compartment is fluid inside a blood vessel, the intracellular compartment is the fluid inside the cell, and the extracellular compartment is the fluid outside the cell in the interstitial space or transcellular areas (peritoneal, pleural, cerebrospinal, and synovial). Third-spacing of fluid occurs when there is accumulation and trapped extracellular fluid in a body space, such as joint cavities, the pleural spaces, or within soft tissues. Edema is excess fluid in the interstitial spaces, from cardiac or liver failure, or localized, from burns or traumatic injury.

Electrolytes are substances that exist in the human body, dissolve in solution, and have electrically charge atoms or ions. When there is fluid loss, the body loses electrolytes. The kidneys play a major role in regulating fluid and electrolyte balance, with the quantity of fluid determined by the amount of water ingested and the amount of waste excreted.

Homeostasis is the medical term that indicates relative stability of the internal body fluid balance. Fluid volume deficit is dehydration, which occurs when the fluid intake is not sufficient for the body. Dehydration is caused by inadequate fluid intake, fluid shifts between compartments, increased fluid loss from perspiration, diarrhea, and ketoacidosis, renal failure, chronic illness, and chronic malnutrition. Fluid volume deficit is corrected by administration of IV fluids, use of antidiarrheal medications, and treatment of the electrolyte imbalance, if necessary.

Fluid volume excess occurs from over-hydration, where fluid intake and retention exceeds the body's requirements. The goal of treatment is to correct electrolyte imbalances if present, eliminate the underlying cause of the overload, and restore fluid balance. Care interventions include administering diuretics, assessing intake and output, and monitoring for complications.

Emergency Preparedness

Disaster Level

A disaster level involves the anticipated necessary response by Level I, Level II, and Level III.

- Level I – Local emergency response organizations and personnel can adequately manage and contain the disaster and its aftermath.

- Level II – Regional efforts and assistance from surrounding communities can effectively manage the disaster and its aftermath.

- Level III – Statewide and federal assistance is required to manage and control the disaster and its aftermath.

NUTRITION AND ORAL HYDRATION

Nutrition is a basic need of all people. Medical assistants should have the knowledge to educate and care for patients with various nutritional disorders and needs, as well as those who are healthy. Nutrients include carbohydrates, fats, proteins, sugars, vitamins, minerals, electrolytes, and water, all which are necessary for energy, growth, and development. Malnutrition is the concept of a deficiency of these nutrients. Enteral nutrition is the administration of nutrition via a tube.

Therapeutic Diets

- Clear liquid diet – This diet consists of fluids and some electrolytes for dehydration prevention. A clear liquid diet is often given to a malnourished patient who has not eaten for some time. Before many intestinal tests and surgeries, patients are often placed on a clear liquid diet. Food items include water, broth, clear beverages, gelatin, popsicles, hard candy, and diluted fruit juices.

- Full liquid diet – This diet is used as a transition diet when going from clear liquids to soft or altered foods. Patients are often placed on the full liquid diet following surgery, as well as when there is difficulty swallowing, chewing, or tolerating solid foods. Foods on this diet include ice cream, milk, pudding, custard, sherbet, strained soups, refined cooked cereals, juices, and breakfast drinks.

- Mechanically altered diet – This diet is used when a patient has difficulty chewing and swallowing. Foods include dried fruits, nuts, raw fruits, vegetables, fried foods, tough, salted, or smoked meats, and course-textured foods.

- Soft diet – This diet is used for patient s with swallowing or chewing problems, as well as those with ulcerations of the mouth, gums, or throat. Foods that contain nuts and seeds are not allowed, and raw fruits and vegetables and whole grains should be avoided.

- Low-residue, low-fiber diet – This diet is used when there is inflammation or scarring or the gastrointestinal tract and/or motility is decreased. Foods include refined cooked cereals, white bread, cooked potatoes, refined pasta, white rice, and dairy products.

- High-fiber diet – This diet is used for patients with constipation, obesity diabetes, diverticulosis, and hyperlipidemia. Foods include whole grain products, seeds, nuts, beans, leafy vegetables, and fruits.

Special Considerations

Patients experiencing renal failure who are on dialysis should eat a diet of controlled amounts of sodium, potassium, calcium, phosphorus, and fluids. A patient with hypertension should be advised of a low sodium diet. Highly processed and refined foods have large amounts of sodium, whereas fruits and vegetables do not. A patient with malabsorption syndrome must follow a low-fat diet. For patients with cirrhosis, a diet rich in thiamine is encouraged.

Vegans do not eat any animal products, and many vegetarians eat little or no dairy and animal products. These patients are at risk for deficiencies in vitamins B12, and D, zinc, iron, calcium, protein, and omega-3 fatty acids. Pesco-vegetarians eat seafood but no animal or dairy products. Lacto-vegetarians eat dairy products but no animal products or eggs. Finally, lacto-ovo-vegetarians eat dairy products and eggs, but no animal products or seafood

Notes
intentionally left blank

Notes
intentionally left blank

Notes
intentionally left blank

VII. PRACTICE QUESTIONS

1. The directional term that means "toward the upper body region" is:

A. Superior
B. Inferior
C. Anterior
D. Posterior

Answer: A. Superior

Superior is toward the head, or toward the upper body region. Inferior is toward the lower part of the body. Anterior (ventral) is on the belly or front side of the body. Posterior (dorsal) is on the buttocks or back side of the body.

2. In the word "hyperglycemia," which word part is the prefix?

A. hyper
B. glycem
C. emia
D. ia

Answer: A. hyper

A medical term often has three parts: the prefix, the root, and suffix. The prefix begins the word, modifies the root, and not a part of all medical terms, as in hyperglycemia and hyperactive; hyper- modifies the word parts "glycem" and "active." The root is the center part of the word, holds meaning, and is often referred to the body. A suffix ends the word, modifies the root, refers to a procedure, action, or condition, and is not part of all medical term.

3. Which body cavity contains the lungs, heart, and large blood vessels?

A. Cranial
B. Spinal
C. Thoracic
D. Abdominal

Answer: C. Thoracic

The cranial cavity contains the brain. The spinal cavity contains the spinal cord, and extends from the brainstem in the cranial cavity to the end of the spinal cord. The thoracic cavity contains the lungs, heart, and large blood vessels, and is separated from the abdomen by the diaphragm. The abdominal cavity contains the stomach, intestines, liver, gallbladder, pancreas, spleen, and kidneys, and is separated from the thoracic cavity by the diaphragm. The pelvic cavity contains the urinary bladder, urinary structures, and reproductive organs.

4. Regarding body cells, the nucleolus is:

A. The center of the cell that contains DNA.
B. A small structure inside the nucleus that contains RNA and ribosomes.
C. The thin outer layer of the cells, which regulates what leaves and/or enters.
D. The rod-shaped material in the cytoplasm.

Answer: B. A small structure inside the nucleus that contains RNA and ribosomes.

The cell membrane is the thin outer layer of the cells, which regulates what leaves and/or enters. The cytoplasm is a colloidal substance in the cell that holds structures in place. The nucleus is the center of the cell that contains DNA. The nucleolus is a small structure inside the nucleus that contains RNA and ribosomes. Centrioles are rod-shaped material in the cytoplasm.

5. The integument (skin) makes up how much of the body's total weight?

A. 10%
B. 15%
C. 18%
D. 20%

Answer: C. 18%

The integument is the skin, which makes up around 18% of the body's weight. The skin and accessory structures (glands, nails, and hair) make up the integumentary system.

6. When you see a word with the suffix "ia," what does this mean?

A. Condition
B. Under
C. Beside
D. Removal

Answer: A. Condition

Prefixes begin the word, as in "epi-" (on/upon), "hyper-" (over), "hypo-" (under), and "para-" (beside). Suffixes end the word, as in "-ia" (condition) or "-ectomy" (removal). An example would be "anemia," which is a condition of low blood count.

7. You are assisting the physician with a procedure. He tells you he is going to "incise" a lesion. You know that this means:

A. To remove
B. To cut into
C. To cauterize with a heated instrument.
D. To remove dead skin tissue.

Answer: B. To cut into.

A biopsy is removal of a small section of tissue. Debridement is removing dead skin tissue. Electrocautery is cauterization with a heated instrument. Incise is to cut into something.

8. Of the following skin lesions, which one is not elevated?

A. Papule
B. Nodule
C. Plaque
D. Pustule

Answer: C. Plaque

A papule is a solid, elevated 1.0 cm skin lesion, such as a wart, mole, or lichen planus. A nodule is a solid, elevated 1- 2 cm skin lesion, such as a lipoma, lymph node, erythema nodosum. A pustule is an elevated fluid-filled skin lesion, such as a pimple, impetigo, or abscess. A plaque is a flat, elevated 1.0 cm or greater skin lesion, such as psoriasis or seborrheic keratosis.

9. Which type of dermatitis is caused by hypersensitivity to drugs, allergens, microorganisms, latex, chemicals, metals, and plants?

A. Atopic dermatitis
B. Contact dermatitis
C. Stasis dermatitis
D. Seborrheic dermatitis

Answer: B. Contact dermatitis

Atopic dermatitis (eczema) is caused by irritants or allergens that activate mast cells, eosinophils, T lymphocytes, and monocytes. Stasis dermatitis is associated with phlebitis, varicosities, and vascular trauma. Contact dermatitis (allergic dermatitis) is caused by hypersensitivity to drugs, microorganisms, allergens, latex, chemicals, metals, and plants.

10. Which form of tinea occurs on the nails?

A. Tinea capitis
B. Tinea corporis
C. Tinea manis
D. Tinea unguium

Answer: D. Tinea unguium

Tinea: Capitis (scalp), corporis (ringworm), pedis (Feet), manis (hand), and unguium (nail).

11. The bones that are of varied shapes, such as the zygoma and vertebrae are called:

A. Long bones
B. Short bones
C. Sesamoid bones
D. Irregular bones

Answer: D. Irregular bones

Long bones are tubular (femur, tibia, fibula, humerus, ulna, and radius). Short bones are cuboidal (carpals and tarsals). Flat bones are thin and flat (scapula, sternum, and skull). Irregular Bones are of varied shapes (zygoma and vertebrae). Sesamoid bones are rounded (patella).

12. You are assisting with a cast application. The physician mentions that the patient has a fracture of the ulna. Which bone is this?

A. The kneecap
B. The smaller, lower leg bone
C. The smaller, lower arm bone
D. The larger, lower arm bone

Answer: C. The smaller, lower arm bone

The patella is the kneecap. The lower leg bones are the fibula (smaller one) and the tibia (larger one). The radius is the larger of the two lower arm bones, and the ulna is the smaller one.

13. Which muscle abducts the upper arm and is often used for intramuscular injections?

A. Biceps
B. Deltoid
C. Triceps
D. Rectus femoris

Answer: B. Deltoid

The biceps flexes the elbow. The triceps extends the elbow. The rectus femoris flexes the thigh. The deltoid abducts the upper arm and is often used for IM injections.

14. All of the following are true concerning osteoporosis EXCEPT:

A. It is an infection of the bone.
B. It is decreased bone mass.
C. It is decreased bone density.
D. It occurs from malabsorption of calcium.

Answer: A. It is an infection of the bone.

Osteomyelitis is a bone infection caused by bacteria. Osteoporosis is a condition of decreased bone mass and density, which occurs due to malabsorption of calcium and other substances.

15. Which form of arthritis is caused by excessive uric acid in the joints?

A. Osteoarthritis
B. Rheumatoid arthritis
C. Septic arthritis
D. Gouty arthritis

Answer: D. Gouty arthritis

Osteoarthritis is degeneration and inflammation of the joint. Rheumatoid arthritis is a progressive autoimmune disease that affects the connective tissues and joints. Septic arthritis is an infectious process that generally affects a single joint. Gouty arthritis is caused by excessive uric acid in the joints.

16. Which suffix means "inflammation?"

A. –algia
B. –itis
C. –emia
D. –ar

Answer: B. -itis

The suffix -algia means "pain." The suffix -ar means "pertaining to." The suffix -emia means "blood." The suffix -itis means "inflammation."

17. The physician asked you to assist with a patient who has "epitaxis." What is the body part involved with this condition, and what is draining from that body part?

A. Nose – Mucous
B. Nose – Blood
C. Mouth – Saliva
D. Eye – Tears

Answer: B. Nose – Blood

Epitaxis means "nose bleed."

18. Pneumonia is caused by which of the following?

A. Bacteria
B. Protozoa
C. Viruses
D. All of the above

Answer: D. All of the above

Pneumonia is inflammation of the lungs due to aspiration, bacteria, protozoa, viruses, fungi, or chlamydia.

19. Of the following, which is NOT a symptom of hypotension?

A. Chest pain
B. Blurred vision
C. Dizziness
D. Fainting

Answer: A. Chest pain.

Hypotension (also called low blood pressure) is caused by a drop in both systolic and diastolic arterial blood pressure and insufficient oxygen in blood. The symptoms include dizziness, blurred vision, and syncope (fainting).

20. The prefix that means "false" is:

A. Pseudo-
B. Nulli-
C. Extra-
D. Dys-

Answer: A. Pseudo-

Nulli- means "none." Extra- means "outside." Dys- means "painful." Pseudo- means "false."

21. When menstruation ceases for 3 cycles or 6 months, this is called:

A. Primary amenorrhea
B. Secondary amenorrhea
C. Primary Dysmenorrhea
D. Secondary Dysmenorrhea

Answer: B. Secondary amenorrhea

Primary amenorrhea is when menstruation has never occurred. Secondary amenorrhea is when menstruation ceases for 3 cycles or 6 months. Primary dysmenorrhea is painful menstruation at the beginning menstruation. Secondary dysmenorrhea is painful menstruation due to an underlying condition, such as endometriosis, tumors, or polyps.

22. Testicular torsion is caused by:

A. Congenital abnormal development of the tunica vaginalis and spermatic cord or trauma.
B. Obstruction or other processes.
C. Inflammation of the epididymis.
D. Inflammation of the testes.

Answer: A. Congenital abnormal development of the tunica vaginalis and spermatic cord or trauma.

Cryptorchidism is undescended testes, which is cause by obstruction or other processes. Epididymitis is inflammation of the epididymis, which is caused by trauma, injury, or infection. Orchitis is inflammation of the testes, which is caused by a virus, such as mumps. Testicular torsion is twisting of the testes, which is caused by congenital abnormal development of the tunica vaginalis and spermatic cord or trauma.
Symptoms include severe pain, nausea, vomiting, edema, and fever.

23. Which root word means "thirst"?

A. Dips/o
B. Meat/o
C. Glyc/o
D. Lith/o

Answer: A. Dips/o

Meat/o means "meatus." Glyc/o means "sugar." Lith/o means "stone." Dips/o means "thirst."

24. Which of the following is NOT a symptom of cystitis?

A. Low back pain
B. Urinary frequency
C. Dysuria
D. Hypertension

Answer: D. Hypertension

Cystitis is inflammation and infection of the urinary bladder, which is caused by bacteria. Symptoms include low back pain, dysuria, frequency, and urgency.

25. Which organ produces bile and breaks down wastes?

A. Gall bladder
B. Liver
C. Pancreas
D. Spleen

Answer: B. Liver

The liver is the organ that produces bile and breaks down wastes. The gallbladder is a small organ that stores bile. The pancreas is the organ that produces enzymes for digestion. The spleen is tiny organ located in the left upper abdomen area that filters blood.

26. What gastrointestinal condition, common among older people, causes diarrhea, gas, and abdominal pain?

A. Peptic ulcer
B. Pyloric stenosis
C. Appendicitis
D. Diverticulitis

Answer: D. Diverticulitis

Peptic ulcer is an erosive area on the gastric mucosa cause by smoking, alcohol, stress, aspirin, genetics, bacteria, and use of anti-inflammatory drugs. The symptoms are abdominal pain, dark tarry stools, and nausea. Pyloric stenosis is an infantile condition caused by pyloric sphincter narrowing, and the symptoms are failure to thrive and projectile vomiting. Appendicitis is inflammation of the vermiform appendix that projects from the cecum, which is caused by obstruction of the lumen results in infection. It is not common in older people, and the symptoms are abdominal pain and fever. Diverticulitis is inflammation of the diverticula in the colon, which is an aging condition caused by infection. The symptoms include diarrhea, gas, and abdominal pain.

27. What is the function of the lymph?

A. Sends leaked interstitial fluid into the venous system.
B. Assists with immunity.
C. Helps with filtering blood.
D. All of the above.

Answer: D. All of the above

Lymph sends leaked interstitial fluid into the venous system, assists in immune function, and helps with filtering blood. Lymph nodes are small structures of concentrated lymph tissue.

28. Which type of anemia occurs due to blood loss, low iron intake, and poor iron absorption?

A. Pernicious anemia
B. Hemolytic anemia
C. Iron deficiency anemia
D. Sickle cell anemia

Answer: C. Iron deficiency anemia

Iron deficiency anemia involves small erythrocytes and reduced hemoglobin. It is caused by blood loss, low iron intake, and poor iron absorption. Pernicious anemia involves large stem cells, and it is caused by inability to absorb vitamin B12. Hemolytic anemia involves short survival of mature erythrocytes, and it is caused by excessive destruction of RBCs. Sickle cell anemia involves abnormal sickle-shaped erythrocytes, and it is caused by an abnormal type of hemoglobin.

29. Which gland that is located on top of each kidney and secretes corticosteroids?

A. Thyroid gland
B. Adrenal gland
C. Pituitary gland
D. Parathyroid gland

Answer: B. Adrenal gland

The adrenal glands are two structures located on top of each kidney. They secrete corticosteroids (cortisone, aldosterone, and androgens). The thyroid gland is located over the trachea, and it secretes thyroxine and triiodothyronine. The pituitary gland (master gland or hypophysis) is located at the base of the brain near the sella turcica, and it releases numerous hormones. The parathyroid glands are located on the posterior region of the thyroid gland, and they secrete parathyroid hormone.

30. In the word "hemiparalysis," which word part is the prefix that means "half?"

A. hemi
B. para
C. lys
D. is

Answer: A. hemi

Hemi- is the prefix that means "half."

31. How many lumbar vertebrae are there?

A. 12
B. 7
C. 5
D. 4

Answer: C. 5

There are 7 cervical vertebrae, 12 thoracic vertebrae, 5 lumbar vertebrae, 5 sacrum vertebrae, and 4 coccyx vertebrae.

32. All of the following are true concerning a transient ischemic attack (TIA) EXCEPT:

A. It is a cerebrovascular disease.
B. It is caused by temporary reduction of blood flow to the brain.
C. It produces slurred speech, paresthesia of the face, and mental confusion.
D. It is an infarction of the brain due to lack of blood flow.

Answer: D. It is infarction of the brain due to lack of blood flow.

A transient ischemic attack (TIA) is temporary reduction of blood flow to the brain causes stroke-like symptoms, and a cerebrovascular disease. Symptoms include slurred speech, paresthesia of face, mental confusion. A cerebrovascular accident (CVA) is infarction of the brain due to lack of blood flow caused by atherosclerotic disease, thrombus, embolus, or hemorrhage.

33. Which of the following is NOT a common symptom of a seizure?

A. Loss of awareness
B. Aura
C. Facial paralysis
D. Incontinence

Answer: C. Facial paralysis

Epilepsy is a chronic seizure disorder, which is caused by history of head trauma or brain disease, tumor, hemorrhage, infection, high fever, and brain edema.
Symptoms include aura, loss of awareness, incontinence, alternate contraction and relaxation.

34. The inner layer of the eye that contains rods and cones is the:

A. Cornea
B. Sclera
C. Choroid
D. Retina

Answer: D. Retina

The cornea is the outer layer of the eye that refracts light to focus on the posterior eye. The sclera is the white of the eye that extends from the cornea to the optic nerve. The choroid is the middle layer of the eye that contains pigment. The retina is the inner layer of the eye that contains rods and cones.

35. You are assisting the physician with a tympanostomy. What will be done during the procedure?

A. Surgical repair of the cornea.
B. Insertion of tubes into the tympanum.
C. Removal of a portion of the temporal bone.
D. Creation of a small opening in the middle ear.

Answer: B. Insertion of tubes into the tympanum.

Keratoplasty is surgical repair of the cornea. Apicectomy is removal of a portion of the temporal bone. Fenestration is creation of a small opening in the middle ear.

36. What characteristic would you expect to find/see with a patient who has nystagmus?

A. Double vision
B. Cross-eyes
C. Rapid involuntary eye movements
D. Pink sclera

Answer: C. Rapid involuntary eye movements

Diplopia causes double vision. Conjunctivitis causes pink sclera. Nystagmus causes rapid, involuntary eye movements. Strabismus causes cross-eyed.

37. A patient with "swimmer's ear" will have which of the following symptoms?

A. Hearing loss
B. Ear pain
C. Vertigo
D. None of the above

Answer: B. Ear pain

Otitis externa (swimmer's ear) is infection and inflammation of the outer ear caused by bacteria or fungus. Symptoms include ear pain and discharge.

38. Which age in Erikson's theory of psychosocial development involves autonomy vs. shame and doubt, as well as the task of gaining basic control over self and the environment?

A. Birth to 18 months
B. 18 months to 3 years
C. 3 years to 6 years
D. 6 years to 12 years

Answer: B. 18 months to 3 years

With the autonomy vs. shame and doubt stage, the person tries to gain a sense of self-control and adequacy.

39. Bereavement is the time period of mourning. The amount of time varies from person to person, but typically is:

A. 3 to 5 months
B. 6 to 12 months
C. 24 to 36 months
D. 36 months or longer

Answer: B. 6 to 12 months

Bereavement typically lasts 6 to 12 months. Grief is a normal response to loss and mourning is the public expression of grief. The three types of grief are acute, chronic, and anticipatory. With chronic grief, the person is at risk for depression, which is characterized by feelings of sadness and changes in mood.

40. Which phase of a crisis is where the patient has physical symptoms, relationship problems, and increasing disorganization?

A. Phase 1 – External precipitating event
B. Phase 2 – The threat
C. Phase 3 – Failed coping
D. Phase 4 – Resolution

Answer:　　C. Phase 3 – Failed coping

With phase 1, external precipitating event, there is a situation that occurs or something happens. Phase 2, the threat is where there is a perceived or actual threat causes increased anxiety where the patient copes or fails to cope. With phase 3, failed coping, the patient fails to cope, which produces physical symptoms, relationship problems, and increasing disorganization. Phase 4, resolution involves mobilization of internal and external resources, and the patient is returned to the pre-crisis level of function.

41. Coping behaviors are:

A. Emotion-focused
B. Problem-focused
C. Both A and B
D. Neither A nor B

Answer:　　C. Both A and B

Coping mechanisms are learned external behaviors and internal thought processes that are used to decrease discomfort and pain. Coping behaviors can be emotion-focused or problem-focused. With emotion-focused behaviors, the patient alters a response to stress by thinking, saying or doing something that makes him or her feel happier or normal. Problem-focused behaviors are done to alter the stressor in some way.

42. A four year-old child who was previously potty trained now is experiencing incontinence. The mother tells you that she and her husband have recently separated. What self-defense mechanism could this child be experiencing?

A. Denial
B. Displacement
C. Projection
D. Regression

Answer: D. Regression

Denial is avoidance of a particular problem by refusing to recognize it or outright ignoring it. Displacement is the transfer of feelings for a threatening person, place, or thing to another neutral person, place, or thing. Projection is the assignment of feelings or motivation to another person, place, or thing. Regression is the demonstration of behavior characteristics that are from an earlier developmental stage.

43. All of the following are components of the medical assistant job description EXCEPT:

A. Title of the position
B. Summary of the position
C. Age and race of the employee
D. Qualifications for the job

Answer: C. Age and race of the employee

The job description is a document used in healthcare facilities to specify what is expected of employees. The job description should contain: title of the position, supervisor of the employee, summary of the position, primary duties of the job, expectations of the job, requirements of the position, qualifications for the job, and additional criteria relevant to the facility. Age, race, religion, and marital status are not relevant to employment.

44. A healthcare worker who works under the supervision of a pathologist or physician and performs chemical, microscopic, and/or bacteriologic testing on blood and body tissues is called a:

A. Certified nursing assistant
B. Laboratory technician
C. Phlebotomist
D. Physician's assistant

Answer: B. Laboratory technician

A certified nursing assistant (CNA) provides basic nursing skills and patient care to people in adult day care centers, nursing homes, office settings, and hospitals. This person is registered and/or licensed. A laboratory technician (often called a medical technologist) is someone who works under the supervision of a pathologist or physician and performs chemical, microscopic, and/or bacteriologic testing on blood and body tissues. A phlebotomist, also called an accessioning technician, is a person who is trained in drawing blood. A physician's assistant (PA) is a person trained to practice medicine under the supervision of a physician.

45. An example of a communication device is a/an:

A. Fax machine
B. Telephone
C. Personal digital assistant
D. All of the above

Answer: D. All of the above

Examples of communication devices include fax machine, telephone, and personal digital assistant (PDA).

46. What is the communication style used to encourage others to view ideas as beneficial to their needs and reassures the staff by creating an emotive and empathetic connection?

A. Persuasive
B. Assertive
C. Passive
D. Aggressive

Answer: A. Persuasive

Persuasive style encourages others to view ideas as beneficial to their needs, displays authority to build trust, and reassures staff by creating an emotive and empathetic connection. Assertive style involves standing up for personal rights and expressing feelings, beliefs, and thoughts in an honest, direct, and appropriate way that does not violate another individual's rights. Passive style involves violation of your own rights by failing to express feelings, beliefs, and thoughts and allowing others to violate your rights. Aggressive style involves violation of the rights of others by directly standing up for your personal rights in an inappropriate manner.

47. An 82 year-old American woman does not answer you when you ask her a question at the front desk. She has no history of cognitive or psychological impairment. The medical assistant understands that which of the following communication barriers is the problem:

A. Language barrier
B. Hearing impairment
C. Disinterest
D. Cerebrovascular accident

Answer: B. Hearing impairment

The most common communication barriers include hearing impairment, language barriers, and developmental, cognitive, and/or psychological impairment.

48. A medical assistant named Sue is answering the phone in the morning at the Family Medical Clinic where she works. When answering the telephone, what would be the best phrase for her to use?

A. Hello. I'm Sue. How can I help you?
B. Good morning. This is the Family Medical Clinic, Sue speaking, can I help you?
C. Hi there! Sue here. Do you want to make an appointment?
D. Good morning. I'm a medical assistant with Family Medical Clinic. What do you need?

Answer: B. Good morning. This is the Family Medical Clinic, Sue speaking, can I help you?

The proper steps to answering the office phone include: answer before the fourth ring, greet the caller with "Good morning" or "good afternoon," provide the name of the facility, as well as your name, use a standard closing, such as "thank you for calling," and allow the caller to hang up first.

49. What is the purpose of screening phone calls for the physician in the medical office?

A. To free up the medical assistant
B. To manage the physician's time
C. To only permit paying patients to speak to the physician
D. None of the above

Answer: B. To manage the physician's time

The purpose of screening calls is to manage the physician's time by referring necessary calls only and taking messages for other calls.

50. When giving patient information over the phone, the medical assistant must:

A. Verify that the caller is indeed the patient.
B. Give information only to the patient.
C. Be sure the conversation is not heard by other patients.
D. All of the above.

Answer: D. All of the above

According to HIPAA standards, certain guidelines apply to the telephone. These include verify that the caller is indeed the patient, give information only to the patient, be sure the conversation is not heard by other patients, avoid discussing telephone conversations around patients, and do not leave information on a patient's voice mail.

51. Which of the following is NOT one of the three types of civil law?

A. Tort law
B. Contract law
C. Administrative law
D. Criminal law

Answer: D. Criminal law

Law is a set of rules that govern actions, regulate conduct, punish offenders, and remedy wrongs. The two types of law are criminal law and civil law. These rules and regulations apply to crimes committed against an individual or property. The three types of civil law are tort law, contract law, and administrative law.

52. Nonfeasance is:

A. The failure to act, which results in or causes harm.
B. The performance of an improper act, which results in or causes harm.
C. The failure to act or improper action, which results in serious damage or death to an individual.
D. All of the above

Answer: A. Nonfeasance the failure to act, which results in or causes harm.

Nonfeasance is the failure to act, which results in or causes harm. Misfeasance is improper action, which results in or causes harm to a person. Malfeasance is the performance of an improper act that results in or causes harm. Malpractice is the failure to act or improper action that results in serious damage or death to an individual. For malpractice to occur, four things must occur: the patient-physician relationship was established (duty), the professional neglected to act or acted improperly (dereliction), a negative outcome occurred from an action or lack of an action (direct cause), and the patient sustained harm (damages).

53. People who can give consent for medical services and care are:

A. Patient
B. Legal competent adult in charge of patient's care
C. Emancipated minor
D. All of the above

Answer: D. All of the above

Only certain people can give consent for medical services and care: The patient, a legal competent adult in charge of patient's care, an emancipated minor, minors in the armed forces, minors seeking services for sexually transmitted infections (STIs), and minor parent with custody of his/her minor child.

54. The document that states who the patient designates necessary medical decisions regarding withholding medical treatment is:

A. Durable power of attorney
B. Document of attorney
C. Living will
D. Organ donation

Answer: A. Durable power of attorney

Document that states who the patient designates necessary medical decisions regarding withholding medical treatment. Living will a document that specified means to sustain the patient in case of terminal conditions. Durable power of attorney is document that states who the patient designates necessary medical decisions regarding withholding medical treatment.

55. What credential required to practice a profession is issued by an official state agency or department?

A. Licensure
B. Certification
C. Accreditation
D. Registration

Answer: A. Licensure

Licensure is this is the credential required to practice a profession, which is issued by an official state agency or department. Certification is various healthcare occupations are subject to certification or registration. Accreditation is this is a type of credentialing, which typically involves a healthcare facility, agency, or organization. This voluntary process involves standards that are specific to the person or facility.

56. Removing medical records that are beyond the time of the statute of limitations:

A. Assembling
B. Maintaining
C. Purging
D. Retrieving

Answer: C. Purging

Purging is removing medical records that are beyond the time of the statute of limitations.

57. Active files are:

A. Patients who have been seen within 3 - 5 years (depending on the practice's policy).
B. Patients who have not been seen within the past 3 - 5 years (depending on the practice's policy).
C. Patients who are deceased, have moved, or have reached legal age limit (pediatrics).
D. None of the above.

Answer: A. Patients who have been seen within 3 - 5 years (depending on the practice's policy).

Active patients have been seen within 3 - 5 years (depending on the practice's policy). Inactive patients have not been seen within the past 3 - 5 years (depending on the practice's policy). Closed files mean the patient is deceased, has moved, or has reached legal age limit (pediatrics).

58. All of the following are true concerning the Health Information Technology for Economic and Clinical Health (HITECH) Act EXCEPT:

A. It was enacted under a section of the American Recovery and Reinvestment act of 2009.
B. It promotes the adoption of health information technology and electronic medical records (EMR).
C. It mandates the protection of privacy using the EMR system.
D. It affects medical billing, patient records, and employee communication.

Answer: C. It mandates the protection of privacy using the EMR system.

The Health Information Technology for Economic and Clinical Health (HITECH) Act was enacted under a section of the American Recovery and Reinvestment act of 2009. The HITECH Act promotes the adoption of health information technology and electronic medical records (EMR). Areas affected include medical billing, patient records, and employee communication. The Patient Protection and Affordable Care Act (PPACA) of 2010 mandates the protection of privacy using the EMR system. With this legislation, insurance agencies are no longer able to drop patients due to pre-existing health conditions.

59. If the physician choses to dismiss a patient from the practice, he or she must:

A. Send a letter of dismissal by certified mail.
B. Give the patient a written notice.
C. Refuse to see the patient.
D. Notify the patient's spouse, parent, or significant other.

Answer:　　A. Send a letter of dismissal by certified mail.

The physician has the right to refuse to accept a patient into the practice, or to terminate the patient-physician relationship. If the physician choses to dismiss a patient from the practice, he or she must send a letter of dismissal by certified mail, and a copy should be retained for the medical record.

60. Software that produces information using pictures is called:

A. Word processing
B. Graphics
C. Database
D. Spreadsheet

Answer:　　B. Graphics

Software applications are programs on the computer that perform important functions for the medical office. Word processing is software used to write physician notes, reports, memos, transcripts, and letters. Graphics is software that produces information using pictures. Database is software that provides templates for office activities, such as progress notes, laboratory information medication lists, and health histories. Spreadsheet is software that produces a spreadsheet of numeric calculations from data entered, such as financial reports, invoices, and budgets.

61. The device that allows the information to be accessed from a compact disc (CD) is:

A. The central processing unit (CPU)
B. The hardware
C. The modem
D. The disk drive

Answer:　　D. The disk drive

Hardware is the central processing unit, hard drive, disk drive, motherboard, keyboard, and monitor. Central processing unit (CPU) is the circuit on a microchip that processes data. The modem is a device connecting the computer to the telephone line. The disk drive is the device that allows the information to be accessed from a compact disc (CD).

62. The determination of record organization and sequence is associated with:

A. Type of practice
B. Frequency of access
C. Physician preference
D. All of the above

Answer: D. All of the above

The determination of record organization and sequence is associated with type of practice, frequency of access, and physician preference.

63. Which type of file has the patient's problems listed on a form at the front of the chart, and when an encounter occurs, that number and problem is noted?

A. Problem-oriented medical record (POMR)
B. Source-oriented medical record (SOMR)
C. Subjective-oriented medical record (SOMR)
D. Subjective/Objective/Assessment/Plan (SOAP)

Answer: C. Source-oriented medical record (SOMR)

Source-oriented medical record (SOMR) files are divided into two sections, with one for progress notes, and one for diagnostic reports. Problem-oriented medical record (POMR) files have the patient's problems listed on a form at the front of the chart, and when an encounter occurs, that number and problem is noted. Subjective/Objective/Assessment/Plan (SOAP)'s format involves first documenting the chief complaint along with symptoms (subjective), followed by the physician's findings (objective), the diagnosis(es) (assessment), treatment, tests, education, and follow-up (plan).

64. What class is used for bulk mail, such as catalogs, books, and other printed material that weighs less than 16 ounces?

A. First-class
B. Second-class
C. Third-class
D. Fourth-class

Answer: C. Third-class

First-class mail must weight 13 ounces or less, and most mail will be sent in this manner. Second-class mail is used for mailing periodicals or newspapers. Third--class is used for bulk mail, such as catalogs, books, and other printed material that weighs less than 16 ounces. Fourth-class is used for third-class mail that weighs more than a pound.

65. Scheduling of two or more patients for the same appointment slot is called:

A. Double Booking
B. Cluster scheduling
C. Under Booking
D. None of the above

Answer: A. Double Booking

Scheduling of two or more patients for the same appointment slot is called double-booking. Cluster scheduling is the grouping of similar appointments together during the day or week, and advanced scheduling involves scheduling patients weeks or months in advance. Under Booking occurs when there are too many gaps between appointments, chic can be costly to the practice.

66. All laboratory equipment should contain labels regarding:

A. Chemicals
B. Biohazardous waste
C. Electrical shorts
D. All of the above

Answer: B. Biohazardous waste

In the reception area, file drawers should not remain open, and wall cupboards must be secure. All office equipment should operate correctly with no evidence of damage or electrical shorts. All laboratory equipment should contain labels regarding biohazardous waste. Also, chemicals that are volatile should not be kept beyond their expiration date and should be stored appropriately.

67. What should the medical assistant have listed on the inventory card for each supply item?

A. Name of supplier
B. Phone number of supplier
C. Cost of the item
D. All of the above

Answer: D. All of the above

The medical assistant may be required to maintain an inventory of administrative and clinical supplies. The best method of organizing supplies is to prepare a separate inventory card for each frequently used item. Keep the name, phone number and address of the supplier, as well as the cost of each item.

68. When should the physician list of fees be reviewed?

A. Every 3 months
B. Every 6 months
C. Every 8 months
D. Every 12 months

Answer: D. Every 12 months

The office will have a list of fees changed for various services and products used in the practice. This list is reviewed each year or when state or federal systems change. The list is based on overhead costs, such as rent, equipment, utilities, and supplies. The practice must set and maintain fees above actual cost of service to remain open and profitable.

69. What is the purpose of accurate record keeping?

A. It ensures financial management of the practice.
B. It ensures that the physician is paid for services
C. It ensures that patients are credited for payments.
D. All of the above

Answer: D. All of the above

Accurate record keeping is a crucial component of financial management as it ensures that the physician is paid for services that patients are credited for payments.

70. What information is on the encounter form?

A. The amount of the transaction, procedure codes, and diagnosis codes.
B. The patient's demographic information.
C. The practice or physician's name, address, and phone number.
D. All of the above

Answer: D. All of the above

The information on the encounter form includes the amount of the transaction, procedure codes, and diagnosis codes, all which is necessary to file an insurance claim. The form also has the patient's demographic information and the practice or physician's name, telephone number, and address.

71. Diagnosis codes are linked to service/procedure codes, which are derived using:

A. The Current Procedural Terminology (CPT)
B. The Healthcare Common Procedure Coding System (HCPCS)
C. Both A and B
D. Neither A nor B

Answer: C. Both A and B

Diagnosis codes are reported in filed location 21 on this form. These codes are linked to service/procedure codes, which are derived using the Current Procedural Terminology (CPT) and Healthcare Common Procedure Coding System (HCPCS).

72. Which statement is true concerning the Uniform Hospital Discharge Data Set (UHDDS)?

A. It is a standard data set adopted by the federal government for collection of data for Medicare and Medicaid.
B. It is a standard data set adopted by the state government for collection of data for Medicare and Medicaid.
C. It is a physician fee schedule implemented by Medicare in 1992.
D. It is used to reimburse inpatient rehabilitation facilities.

Answer: A. It is a standard data set adopted by the federal government for collection of data for Medicare and Medicaid.

The Uniform Hospital Discharge Data Set (UHDDS) is a standard data set adopted by the federal government for collection of data for Medicare and Medicaid. Coders sometimes need to report some of the elements of UHDDS when they code. The Resource-Based Relative Value Scale (RBRVS) physician fee schedule was implemented by Medicare in 1992. Inpatient rehabilitation facilities (IRFs) are reimbursed under the inpatient rehabilitation facility prospective payment system (IRF PPS).

73. Major medical insurance covers all of the following EXCEPT:

A. The costs of catastrophic expenses from injury, trauma, or serious illness.
B. Visits where there is an actual disease, illness, or condition.
C. Routine preventive care and physical examinations.
D. The costs of cosmetic procedures.

Answer: D. The costs of cosmetic procedures.

Major medical insurance covers the costs of catastrophic expenses from injury, trauma, or serious illness. Some policies only cover visits where there is an actual disease, illness, or condition, and not routine examinations. Other insurance plans cover routine preventive care and physical examinations.

74. What is a benefit for the patient who has managed care insurance?

A. Lower copays and premiums
B. Better choice of physicians
C. Covers cosmetic procedures
D. All of the above

Answer: A. Lower copays and premiums

Managed care is a popular method used to reimburse for healthcare services. Managed care organizations (MCOs) offer cost-effective services, lower copays, and lower premiums by using primary care providers who channel patients to the most affordable, quality care options. Also, they use specific treatment guidelines and utilize selective contracting with institutions and providers to achieve a discounted rate.

75. Which of the following is a true statement concerning Medicare insurance?

A. Medicare pays 90 percent and the patient pays the remaining 10 percent. The patient must meet a $100 deductible before Medicare begins to pay for services.
B. Medicare pays 80 percent and the patient pays the remaining 20 percent. The patient must meet a $200 deductible before Medicare begins to pay for services.
C. Medicare pays 80 percent and the patient pays the remaining 20 percent. The patient must meet a $100 deductible before Medicare begins to pay for services.
D. Medicare pays 75 percent and the patient pays the remaining 25 percent. The patient must meet a $150 deductible before Medicare begins to pay for services.

Answer: C. Medicare pays 80 percent and the patient pays the remaining 20 percent. The patient must meet a $100 deductible before Medicare begins to pay for services.

Answer C is the true statement.

76. Which part of Medicare pays for services and supplies, such as outpatient services, ambulatory surgical services, home health care, and medically necessary equipment and supplies?

A. Part A
B. Part B
C. Part C
D. Part D

Answer: B. Part B

Part A, Hospital and institutional Care Coverage, covers expenses such as semiprivate rooms, meals and special diets, and all medical necessary services, such as skilled nursing, home health, hospice, and rehabilitation. Part B, Supplemental and Nonhospital Care Coverage, pays for services and supplies that are not covered under Part A, such as outpatient services, ambulatory surgical services, home health care, and medically necessary equipment and supplies. Part C, Medicare Advantage Organization (MAO) Plans, includes Medicare Health Maintenance Organizations (HMOs), Medicare Preferred Provider Organizations (PPOs), Medicare Private Fee-for-Service Plans (PPFSs), and Medicare Medical Savings Account Plans (MSAs). Part D, Prescription Drug Plan (PDP), includes Medicare Advantage Plans (MA-PDs), Private Prescription Drug Plans (PDPs), and premiums paid by the beneficiary.

77. TRICARE military insurance covers all of the following EXCEPT:

A. Active-duty personnel stationed on or near a major military base
B. Active-duty personnel families
C. Retired service members
D. Dependents of retired service members

Answer: A. Active-duty personnel stationed on or near a major military base.

Military personnel are covered by healthcare workers employed by the military. Their spouses and children are covered under TRICARE, which covers active-duty personnel families, as well as retired members, dependents of retired members, and dependents of personnel who died during active duty.

78. Employers pay premiums to an insurance carrier for workers' compensation insurance. This workers' compensation premium is based on:

A. The degree of occupational risks for the employees.
B. The number of workers employed.
C. Both A and B
D. Neither A nor B

Answer: C. Both A and B

Workers' compensation insurance pays for medical care costs and a portion of lost wages when a worker is injured or becomes ill on the job. Employers are required to pay premiums to an insurance carrier for the entire worker's compensation insurance policy. The premium is based on the degree of occupational risks for the employees, as well as the number of workers employed.

79. What does ICD-9-CM stand for?

A. *International Classification of Diseases* (ICD) ninth revision (9) Clinical Modifications (CM)
B. *International Classification of Diseases* (ICD) ninth edition (9) Class Modulators (CM)
C. *International Clinical Diseases* (ICD) ninth revision (9) Class Modifications (CM)
D. Internal Classification of Diseases (ICD) ninth edition (9) Clinical Modifications (CM)

Answer: A. *International Classification of Diseases* (ICD) ninth revision (9) Clinical Modifications (CM)

Choice A is correct. The use of ICD-9-CM allow for tracking of patients and healthcare costs. A diagnosis establishes medical necessity and is reported on the CMS-1500 form in block 21 and 24E.

80. The Alphabetic Index of the ICD-9-CM lists:

A. Classification of diseases and injuries
B. Supplementary classification codes (V and E codes)
C. Both A and B
D. Neither A nor B

Answer: D. Neither A nor B

The Tabular List contains classification of diseases and injuries (codes 001.0 – 999.9) and supplementary classification (V and E codes). The Alphabetic Index of the ICD-9-CM manual lists main terms in body type, as well as sub-terms indented below the main terms.

81. The Uniform Hospital Discharge Data Set (UHDDS) definition of principal diagnosis applies to inpatients in:

A. A long-term care facility
B. A short-term care facility
C. An acute care facility
D. All of the above

Answer: D. All of the above

The Uniform Hospital Discharge Data Set (UHDDS) definition of principal diagnosis applies only to inpatients in acute, short-term, long-term care and psychiatric hospitals.

82. "History of" codes (V10 - V19) are used as:

A. Primary codes
B. Secondary codes
C. Both A and B
D. Neither A nor B

Answer: B. Secondary codes

"History of" codes (V10 - V19) are used as secondary codes, as long as they impact current treatment or care.

83. For a patient who is being seen for a routine prenatal visit with no complications, the coder should use:

A. Code V22.0, Supervision of normal first pregnancy
B. Code V22.1, Supervision of other normal pregnancy
C. Either A or B
D. Neither A nor B

Answer: C. Either A or B

For a patient who is being seen for a routine prenatal visit with no complications, the coder should use codes V22.0, Supervision of normal first pregnancy, or V22.1, Supervision of other normal pregnancy.

84. Regarding accounting principles, ensuring accuracy in totals by comparing them to set criteria is called:

A. Posting
B. Adjusting
C. Billing
D. Balancing

Answer: D. Balancing

Postings is transferring information from the journal (day sheet) to the accounts receivable ledger or to the individual patients' ledgers Adjustments are changes made to the amount of money owed for reasons other than additional payments or services. Billing is when records of charges are sent to the patient in the form of statements to show balance due and to request payment. Balancing is ensuring accuracy in totals by comparing them to set criteria.

85. The form given to the patient to indicate the charges for services is called:

A. The day sheet
B. The patient ledger
C. The charge slip
D. The receipt

Answer: C. The charge slip

The day sheet is a daily record of the services rendered and payments received. The patient ledger is a patient statement or itemized statement that is an individual for of each patient's accounts. The charge slip is a form given to the patient to indicate the charges for services. (This is often a copy of the superbill). The receipt is a numbered form that indicates the payments a patient has made.

86. What process is a means of verifying the information on the bank statement and tallying it with the information in the check?

A. Endorsement
B. Check registration
C. Statement development
D. Reconciliation

Answer: D. Reconciliation

Endorsement involves signing the back of the check as the payee for the amount represented on the front. The check register, also called the checkbook, is a computer program or book that has a chronologic listing of all checks written, deposits made, and balance. Bank statements are reports sent from the bank that list all account activities, including deposits, checks written and cashed, bank charges, and balances. Reconciliation, also called balancing, is a process is a means of verifying the information on the bank statement and tallying it with the information in the check register.

87. Employee's Withholding Allowance Certificates are also called:

A. W-2 forms
B. W-4 forms
C. I-4 forms
D. I-9 forms

Answer: B. W-4 forms

W-4 forms are called the Employee's Withholding Allowance Certificates, and they are federal tax forms for each employee that shows the number of tax exemptions claimed. A W-2 form is a federal tax form prepared for each office employee containing all income and deductions from the previous year.

88. Infections can be mild or severe, and the acuteness of an infection relies on the:

A. Pathogenicity
B. Parasiticy
C. Chain of infection
D. All of the above

Answer: A. Pathogenicity

When an organism establishes an opportunistic relationship with a host, the process is called infection. The process of infection starts with the transmission of organisms and ends with the development of infectious disease. Infections can be mild or severe, and the acuteness of an infection relies on the disease-causing potential (pathogenicity). The relationship between human and organism can be intricate and valuable or illness-producing when the parasite sustains life at the expense of the host.

89. Which stage of the infection process is when symptoms begin to appear?

A. Incubation period
B. Prodromal stage
C. Acute illness stage
D. Convalescent stage

Answer: B. Prodromal stage

The incubation period the organisms establish presence inside the susceptible host. With the prodromal stage, the symptoms of infection begin to appear. In the acute illness stage, the organisms are growing and spreading quickly inside the host. With the convalescent stage, the damaged tissue begins healing, and symptoms resolve.

90. Since many patients with HIV, hepatitis B, and hepatitis often have no visible symptoms, what set of principles is used by all healthcare workers who have direct or indirect contact with patients?

A. Transmission-based precautions
B. Contact precautions
C. Universal precautions
D. Droplet precautions

Answer: C. Universal precautions

Also called universal precautions, standard precautions hold that all patients are infected or colonized with microorganisms, whether or not there are symptoms and written diagnoses, and that a uniform level of caution should be used when caring for any given patient. There are three types of transmission-based precautions: contact precautions, droplet precautions, and airborne precautions. These precautions are devised for the care of patients with known infections or illness or those who are colonized with infective microorganisms.

91. You have assisted a physician with a procedure where blood and body fluids were handled. When should you remove your fluid-resistant gown?

A. Before leaving the patient's room and after doing hand hygiene.
B. Before leaving a patient's room and before doing hand hygiene.
C. After leaving a patient's room and before doing hand hygiene.
D. After leaving a patient's room and after doing hand hygiene.

Answer: B. Before leaving a patient's room and before doing hand hygiene

The CDC recommends healthcare workers remove fluid-resistant gowns before leaving a patient's room and before doing hand hygiene.

92. The absence of infectious organisms is called:

A. Asepsis
B. Sterilization
C. Surgical aseptic practice
D. Surgical field

Answer: A. Asepsis

Asepsis is the absence of infectious organisms. Asepsis principles involve sterilization processes to completely eliminate all microorganisms, as well as appropriate delivery of items. Surgical aseptic practice is based on the premise that most infections occur due to exogenous organisms or pathogens that are external from the body. Medical assistants can monitor the surgical field to decrease patient risk.

93. Radiation safety measures include:

A. Label potentially radioactive material.
B. Limit time spent near the source.
C. Use a shielding device to protect vital organs.
D. All of the above

Answer: D. All of the above

Radiation safety involves the use of various protocols and guidelines of the healthcare facility. Radiation exposure is monitored with a film badge. Safety measures include label potentially radioactive material, limit time spent near the source, use a shielding device to protect vital organs, and place the patient with radiation implants in private room.

94. A metal device used to test for auditory acuity and bone vibration is called a/an:

A. Otoscope
B. Nasal speculum
C. Tuning fork
D. Reflex hammer

Answer: C. Tuning fork

An otoscope is a device used to examine the inside of the ears, and it has disposable covers that should be changed after each patient. A nasal speculum is a device that dilates the nares for examination. It must be cleaned between patients. A reflex hammer is a small rubber head hammer used to test reflexes. A tuning fork is a metal device used to test for auditory acuity and bone vibration.

95. Which type of sterilization is also known as cold sterilization, and is used for heat-sensitive equipment, such as endoscopes?

A. Dry heat
B. Chemical sterilization
C. Steam heat
D. Steam sterilization

Answer: B. Chemical sterilization

Sterilization is the process of destroying living organisms. Dry heat is used for sterilizing instruments that corrode easily, and it requires one hour of heat at 320 degrees F. Chemical sterilization is also known as cold sterilization, and it is used for heat-sensitive equipment, such as endoscopes. Steam heat is also known as autoclaving, and it is the most common method used in the medical office.

96. Which type of cast is fairly waterproof and lighter than other types and is applied using warm water to moisten the casting material?

A. Air cast
B. Fiberglass cast
C. Plaster cast
D. Stockinet cast

Answer: B. Fiberglass cast

Plasters are rolls of casting material that are moistened with warm water before being applied in a rolling manner. The extremity will be covered first with a stockinet and cast padding. A fiberglass cast is applied just like the plaster type, but it is fairly waterproof and lighter. An air cast is a plastic envelope cast, which is inflated, easily applied, and removable.

97. Which of the following is NOT one of the types of cardiac polarity?

A. Polarization
B. Apolarization
C. Depolarization
D. Repolarization

Answer: B. Apolarization

The electrical activity of the heart follows a conductive pathway resulting in the cardiac cycle (heart pumping blood). There are three types of cardiac polarity: polarization, depolarization, and repolarization. Polarity is the electrical status of cardiac muscle cells in an attempt to maintain electronegativity inside the cells for distribution of ions, such as potassium, sodium, and chloride.

98. The Q, R, and S waves together represents contraction of the two ventricles, which is called:

A. The QRS interval
B. The QRS complex
C. The Q to S interval
D. The Q to S complex

Answer: B. The QRS complex

The QRS complex is where the Q, R, and S waves are together, which represents contraction of the two ventricles. The PR interval is where the P and R waves together represent the time the electrical impulse travels from the sinoatrial (SA) node to the atrioventricular (AV) node. The QT interval is where the QRST waves together represent a full cardiac cycle.

99. What does the ECG stylus do?

A. It receives impulses via electrodes
B. It moves across the ECG paper.
C. It records the heart electrical activity.
D. All of the above.

Answer: D. All of the above

The stylus is the pen-line device that receives impulses via electrodes, moves across the ECG paper, and records the heart electrical activity.

100. An ECG visible heart beat that originates outside of the heart's pacemaker (SA node) is known as:

A. Premature ventricular contraction (PVC)
B. Asystole
C. Ectopic beat
D. Premature atrial contraction (PAC)

Answer: C. Ectopic beat

A premature ventricular contraction (PVC) is a contraction of ventricles that occurs early. Asystole is the absence of a heart rate (flat line). An ectopic beat is a beat that originates outside of the heart's pacemaker (SA node). A premature atrial contraction (PAC) is an atrial contraction that occurs early.

101. Involuntary or voluntary muscle or other movement by the patient seen on the ECG is called:

A. Somatic tremors
B. Wondering baseline
C. Alternating current interference
D. All of the above

Answer: A. Somatic tremors

Artifacts are interruptions or disturbances in the ECG strip, which results from activity outside the heart. Somatic tremors are involuntary or voluntary muscle or other movement by the patient. A wandering baseline is movement of the stylus from the center of the paper in a "wandering" fashion, which results from electrodes that are too loose or too tight, dirty electrodes, or from oil on the patient's skin. Alternating current interference occurs from other sources of electricity in the room, such as improper grounding or equipment.

102. To ambulate with a walker, the patient must be able to:

A. Hold the handgrips
B. Come to a standing position
C. Support the body weight on the hands
D. All of the above

Answer: D. All of the above

To ambulate with a walker, the patient must hold the handgrips for stability, be able to come to a standing position, and support their body weight on their hands while balancing.

103. For Medicare to cover DME, it must be:

A. Approved by the insurance company
B. Ordered by one of the patient's physicians
C. Both A and B
D. Neither A nor B

Answer: C. Both A and B

For Medicare to cover DME, it must be approved by the insurance company and ordered by one of the patient's physicians. Medicare will only cover DME if the physician or supplier is enrolled in the Medicare program. When the supplier is not enrolled with federal Medicare services, Medicare cannot limit how much the supplier charges for the DME.

104. A patient has a body temperature of 97.9 degrees Fahrenheit. What is this considered?

A. Low
B. High
C. Normal
D. None of the above

Answer: C. Normal

Normal body temperature is 98.6 degrees Fahrenheit but the range is between 97.8 to 99.1 degrees. Normal body temperature is harder to control as a person gets older due to a decreased amount of subcutaneous fat below the skin.

105. The normal adult pulse rate at rest is:

A. From 55 to 95 beats per minute.
B. From 60 to 100 beats per minute.
C. From 70 to 90 beats per minute.
D. From 50 to 90 beats per minute.

Answer: B. From 60 to 100 beats per minute.

The heart beats a certain number of times each minute. This is considered the heart or pulse rate. The normal adult pulse rate at rest is from 60 to 100 beats per minute.

106. Which of the following will NOT lower the respiratory rate?

A. Narcotic use
B. Tuberculosis
C. Drug overdose
D. Diabetic coma

Answer: B. Tuberculosis

A person's respiratory rate is the number of breaths taken per minute. The normal respiratory rate is 12 to 20 breaths per minute. Conditions that can elevate the respiratory rate include acute respiratory distress, asthma, COPD, pneumonia, heart failure, bronchitis, and tuberculosis. Use of narcotic use, drug overdose, or a diabetic coma can lower the respiratory rate.

107. The physician asks you to assist the patient into a supine position. What would you do?

A. Have the patient lie on his or her back with knees bent and feet flat on the table.
B. Have the patient lie on his or her stomach.
C. Have the patient lie on his or her back with arms to the sides.
D. Have the patient lie face up with his or her body elevated at a 45 to 90 degree angle.

Answer: C. Have the patient lie on his or her back with arms to the sides.

With the supine position, the patient lies on his or her back with arms to the sides. The dorsal recumbent position is where the patient lies on his or her back with knees bent and feet flat on the table. With the prone position, the patient lies on his or her stomach. The Fowler's position is where the patient lies face up with his or her upper body elevated at 45 to 90 degrees.

108. Factors that affect patient learning include all of the following EXCEPT:

A. Motivation
B. Adaption to disease or illness
C. Age
D. Ability of the physician

Answer: D. Ability of the physician

Factors that affect patient learning include motivation, adaption to disease or illness, age, pain, language, socioeconomic barriers, cultural barriers, and ability of the educator.

109. How long should you wash hands before a surgical procedure?

A. 5 minutes
B. 10 minutes
C. 15 minutes
D. 20 minutes

Answer: B. 10 minutes

With surgical hand washing, healthcare workers need to wash their hands for 10 minutes.

110. Knives of varying blades and sizes used to cut, dissect, and incise skin are called:

A. Scalpels
B. Hemostats
C. Forceps
D. Scissors

Answer: A. Scalpels

Forceps are two-handled tools used to grasp, crimp, and move tissue. Hemostats are straight or curved tools used to compress vessels or tissue. Scissors are two-bladed tools used to cut tissue, skin, and materials. Scalpels are knives of varying blades and sizes used to cut, dissect, and incise skin.

111. Which method of surgery involves destroying tissue by cryogenics (freezing), which employs liquid nitrogen applied to the surgical site?

A. Electrosurgery
B. Cryosurgery
C. Endoscopy
D. Laser surgery

Answer: B. Cryosurgery

The cryosurgery method involves destroying tissue by cryogenics (freezing), which employs liquid nitrogen applied to the surgical site for the purpose of lesion removal or tissue destruction. The electrosurgery method involves cutting and cauterization of the skin and tissues using an electric current directed to a specific anatomic region. The laser method of surgery uses electromagnetic radiation in narrow beams for diagnostic and treatment applications. Endoscopy is the use of a special instrument to examine the inside of the body, such as the respiratory or gastrointestinal tract.

112. A patient in the clinic has a wound where the outer layers of the skin are removed due to scraping. What type of wound is this?

A. Laceration
B. Puncture
C. Contusion
D. Abrasion

Answer: D. Abrasion

With an abrasion, the outer layers of the skin are removed from scraping, which causes a small amount of clear or thin, blood-tinged drainage. A laceration is a traumatic, jagged cut that results in irregular wound edges. With a contusion, the top layers of skin are bruised, and bleeding occurs below unbroken skin from blunt trauma. A puncture is a small, round hole in the skin and tissues from a sharp, pointed object.

113. What is the longest amount of time to leave a tourniquet on during a blood draw?

A. 30 seconds
B. 60 seconds
C. 90 seconds
D. 120 seconds

Answer: B. 60 seconds

When drawing blood, ask the patient if he or she has latex or tape allergies, assess the antecubital region of both arms, place the tourniquet three to four inches above the site of puncture, and do NOT leave the tourniquet on for longer than one minute.

114. Which blood collection tube contains the anticoagulant sodium citrate and is used for coagulation studies?

A. Yellow top
B. Red/gray top
C. Blue top
D. Lavender top

Answer: C. Blue top

Yellow top contains sodium polyanethole sulfonate and is used for blood cultures. Red/gray (tiger) top contains a silicone serum separator and is used for tests requiring blood serum. Blue top contains anticoagulant sodium citrate and is for coagulation studies. Lavender top contains ethylenediaminetraacetic acid (EDTA) and is used for hematology studies.

115. When collecting a capillary blood specimen from an infant, which site is best to use?

A. The heel
B. The big toe
C. Either A or B
D. Neither A nor B

Answer: C. Either A or B

Capillary puncture for adults and children is best when obtained from the third or fourth finger, and for infants, use the heel or big toe.

116. Chemicals that react in specific ways when exposed to known substances are called:

A. Control samples
B. Calibration
C. Reagents
D. Quality measures

Answer: C. Reagents

Quality control measures allow for testing accuracy through careful monitoring of various procedures. Calibration involves testing procedures where the equipment generates a result set by a known value. Control samples are specimens with known values, used to check for testing accuracy. Reagents are chemicals that react in specific ways when exposed to known substances.

117. Of the following laboratory tests, which one is *not* CLIA-waived?

A. Fecal occult blood
B. Hemoglobin
C. Ovulation testing
D. Blood cross matching

Answer: D. Blood cross matching

CLIA-waived tests include urinalysis, dipstick, urinalysis, tablet reagent, fecal occult blood (guiac), urine pregnancy test, blood glucose, erythrocyte sedimentation rate (ESR), hemoglobin (Hgb), hematocrit (Hct), strep A test, and ovulation testing. Blood cross matching is a high-complexity test that is not CLIA-waived.

118. You are obtaining a urine specimen for urinalysis. The patient only provides a 10 ml specimen. The medical assistant understands that this is:

A. Too little urine for the test
B. Too much urine for the test
C. An adequate specimen amount
D. None of the above

Answer: A. Too little urine for the test

Urine is assessed for various reasons in the medical office. The medical assistant should collect 30 to 50 ml of urine for specimens.

119. An adult female patient has a hemoglobin value of 12.2 g/dL. The medical assistant knows that this is:

A. Low
B. High
C. Normal
D. Invalid

Answer: C. Normal

The hemoglobin test determines the level of hemoglobin in the blood. Normal values include 14 to 16.5 g/dL (adult male) and 12 to 15 g/dL (adult female).

120. Of the following, which is not considered a coagulation study?

A. Prothrombin time (PT)
B. Activated partial thromboplastin time (aPTT)
C. Platelet count
D. White blood cell count

Answer: D. White blood cell count

Prothrombin time (PT) with international normalized ration (INR) measures the amount of time it takes in seconds for a clot to form. Activated partial thromboplastin time (aPTT) evaluates the coagulation sequence function by measuring the amount of time it takes in seconds for plasma to clot after partial thromboplastin is added to it. Platelet count measures platelets, which assist with the coagulation process. White blood cell count is a hematology test.

121. This electrolyte is responsible for regulating the pH of body fluids, and normal values are between 22 and 29:

A. Sodium
B. Potassium
C. Chloride
D. Bicarbonate

Answer: D. Bicarbonate

Serum sodium is an electrolyte that maintains osmotic pressure and acid-base balance, assists in the transmission of nerve impulses, is absorbed from the small intestine, and is excreted in the urine, and normal adult sodium values are between 135 and 145 mEq/L. Serum potassium is an electrolyte that regulates the cellular water balance, acid-base balance, and electrical conduction in muscle cells, and normal adult potassium values are between 3.5 and 5.1 mEq/L. Serum chloride is an electrolyte that functions to balance cations, acts as a buffer during oxygen-carbon dioxide exchange, and aids in maintenance of osmotic pressure, and normal adult chloride values are between 98 and 107 mEq/L. Serum bicarbonate is an electrolyte responsible for regulating the pH of body fluids, and normal adult sodium bicarbonate values are between 22 and 29 mEq/L.

122. A culture involves collecting a specimen with an applicator swab for the purpose of:

A. Growing pathogens from the inoculated.
B. Determining if a pathogen is susceptible to antibiotics.
C. Both A and B
D. Neither A nor B

Answer: A. Growing pathogens from the inoculated.

Sensitivity testing is used to determine if a pathogen is susceptible to antibiotics. A culture involves collecting a specimen with an applicator swab for the purpose of growing pathogens form the inoculated substance. The transport media is in a tube structure.

123. A patient who had a tuberculosis test returns 2 days later with a raised, hardening of the skin around the injection site. The medical assistant understands that this means the test is:

A. Negative
B. Positive
C. Inconclusive
D. None of the above

Answer: B. Positive

The Mantoux tuberculin test (also called purified protein derivative or PPD) is a type of intradermal skin test. To perform this test, the healthcare worker injects a small amount of tubercle bacillus into the patient's skin and reads the result in 48 to 72 hours. A "positive" result involves induration, which is a raised, hardening of the skin around the injection site.

124. When assessing visual acuity in a four year old child, which chart is used?

A. Snellen chart
B. E chart
C. Either A or B
D. Neither A nor B

Answer   B. E chart

Visual acuity is the measurement of eyesight and vision. The Snellen chart is used for adults, and the E chart is used for children.

125. What is the difference between an audiometry test and an impedance audiometry test?

A. Audiometry is a hearing test that measures the patient's response to various tones, which are recorded in decibels (db.) and frequencies, whereas impedance audiometry is a hearing test using an ear probe to measure the ossicle and tympanic membrane mobility.
B. Impedance audiometry is a hearing test that measures the patient's response to various tones, which are recorded in decibels (db.) and frequencies, whereas audiometry is a hearing test using an ear probe to measure the ossicle and tympanic membrane mobility.
C. Audiometry is gross measurement of hearing done when the healthcare worker whispers behind the patient and asks what was said, whereas impedance audiometry is a gross hearing measurement for infants is done by eliciting a loud clap or bang and assessing the infant for a cry or jerk reaction.
D. None of the above

Answer: A. Audiometry is a hearing test that measures the patient's response to various tones, which are recorded in decibels (db.) and frequencies, whereas impedance audiometry is a hearing test using an ear probe to measure the ossicle and tympanic membrane mobility.

Choice A is the right answer.

126. Which of the following is NOT true concerning pulse oximetry?

A. This test measures the volume and flow of air.
B. This test assesses blood oxygen concentration.
C. This test is a measurement of the percentage of oxygen in the blood.
D. This test is noninvasive.

Answer: A. This test measures the volume and flow of air.

A pulse oximeter (pulse ox) is a small device used to assess blood oxygen concentration. Pulse oximetry is the measurement of the percentage of oxygen in the blood. This is a simple, noninvasive test. A pulmonary function test (PFT) is a means of respiratory testing where volume and the flow of air are measured by using a spirometer.

127. Which diagnostic test uses high-frequency inaudible sound waves to produce images based on echoes?

A. X-ray
B. Ultrasound
C. Computed tomography
D. Magnetic resonance imaging

Answer: B. Ultrasound

An X-ray is a basic radiograph performed in many physician's offices. Computed tomography (CT) is a detailed radiograph that permits cross-sectional views of a body region, acquired as a camera rotates around the patient. Magnetic resonance imaging (MRI) uses a combination of nonionizing radiation and a magnetic field that permits examination of the internal body structures. Ultrasound (US) uses high-frequency inaudible sound waves to produce images based on echoes.

128. Valium, Xanax, and Ativan are considered:

A. Schedule I drugs
B. Schedule II drugs
C. Schedule III drugs
D. Schedule IV drugs

Answer: D. Schedule IV drugs

Schedule I drugs include marijuana and heroin. Schedule II drugs are cocaine, Demerol, morphine, oxycodone, and Ritalin. Schedule III drugs are codeine and barbiturates. Schedule IV drugs have medical use with limitations, are of low abuse potential, and include Xanax, Ativan, and Valium.

129. Which of the following is NOT a common site for intramuscular (IM) injections?

A. Vastus lateralis
B. Gluteus medius
C. Triceps
D. Deltoid

Answer: C. Triceps

Common sites for IM injections include the deltoid (upper arm), gluteus medius (the dorsogluteal area), and the vastus lateralis (thigh).

130. When administering an interdermal injection, what angle should you use and what gauge needle should be used?

A. 10 degree angle/20 - 22 gauge needle
B. 15 degree angle/22 - 24 gauge needle
C. 15 degree angle/25 – 27 gauge needle
D. 25 degree angle/25 – 27 gauge needle

Answer: C. 15 degree angle/25 – 27 gauge needle

Intradermal (ID) injection is deposited into the dermal skin layer at a 15 degree angle via a 25 - 27 gauge needle, such as with a tuberculin skin test.

131. The physician asks you to give a medication by "sublingual" route. Where would you give the medication?

A. In the muscle.
B. In the subcutaneous tissue
C. Placed on the skin
D. Placed under the tongue

Answer: D. Placed under the tongue

The intramuscular route involves medication injected into the muscle. The subcutaneous route involves medication injected into the subcutaneous tissue. The topical route involves medication placed onto the skin. The sublingual route involves medication placed under the tongue via gel or tablets.

132. The order is for 50 mg/m² of the medication. The child's body surface area is 0.5 m². What would the correct dosage be for this child?

A. 12.5 mg
B. 25 mg
C. 35 mg
D. 50 mg

Answer: B. 25 mg

Child's BSA (in m²) x Adult dose / 1.7 m²
Child's dosage = 0.50 m² x 50 mg / m²
= (0.50 x 50) mg

133. A female patient weighs 176 pounds (lbs.). What would this patient's weight be in kilograms?

A. 60 kg
B. 70 kg
C. 80 kg
D. 90 kg

Answer: C. 80 kg

1 kg = 2.2 lbs
x kg = 176 lbs

x kg = 176 lbs x 1 kg/2.2 lbs
x kg = 80 kg

134. With the MMR immunization, what three diseases are covered?

A. Measles, mumps, and rubella
B. Measles, mumps, and rubeola
C. Meningitis, German measles, and rubeola
D. None of the above

Answer: A. Measles, mumps, and rubella

MMR covers measles, mumps, and rubella. Measles, also called rubeola, is spread by direct contact, indirect contact, or from droplet infection. Mumps is caused by an infectious organism that attacks the parotid and salivary glands, mumps are transmitted by direct contact or droplet infection. Rubella, also known as the German measles, is caused by a virus that leads to an upper respiratory infection. Other symptoms are fever, arthralgia, and a fine, red rash.

135. Of the following adult patients, which one is NOT a candidate for the pneumococcal vaccine?

A. A 72 year old man with hypertension.
B. A 22 year old woman with asthma.
C. A 62 year old man with COPD
D. A 64 year old woman with osteoarthritis.

Answer: D. A 64 year old woman with osteoarthritis.

The pneumococcal vaccine protects against pneumococcal infections, which cause around 40,000 deaths every year in the U.S. The pneumococcal vaccine gives that patient immunity to the *Streptococcus pneumoniae* organism. All adults over the age of 65 years should receive this vaccine, as well as those who are considered high risk (those with lung diseases).

136. The tetanus vaccine is given every __ years for adults.

A. 5
B. 10
C. 15
D. 20

Answer: B. 10

Most aging adults are not aware that they need to be immunized against *Clostridium tetani*, the bacteria that lead to tetanus. The tetanus vaccine is given every 10 years for adults and is usually available as tetanus-diphtheria toxoid (Td), which is given intramuscularly.

137. Normal blood glucose is:

A. Between 50 mg/dl and 100 mg/dl
B. Between 60 mg/dl and 125 mg/dl
C. Between 70 mg/dl and 150 mg/dl
D. Between 90 mg/dl and 200 mg/dl

Answer: C. Between 70 mg/dl and 150 mg/dl

Two types of diabetic emergencies are hyperglycemia (high blood sugar) and hypoglycemia (low blood sugar). Normal blood glucose is between 70 mg/dl and 150 mg/dl. When glucose drops below 60 mg/dl, it is considered an insulin reaction. When blood glucose is over 400 mg/dl, the patient could go into a diabetic coma.

138. Which type of bleeding is the most serious and life-threatening?

A. Arterial bleeding
B. Venous bleeding
C. Capillary bleeding
D. Lymph bleeding

Answer: A. Arterial bleeding

Bleeding can be arterial, venous, or capillary. Arterial bleeding is more serious and life-threatening, but venous bleeding can lead to sever blood loss. Without control, bleeding can quickly lead to shock or death, so quick intervention is essential.

139. A patient is in the office after suffering a burn to her left hand. The epidermis is slightly reddened and painful, but the dermis and other tissues are not involved. What type of burn is this?

A. First-degree burn
B. Second-degree burn
C. Third-degree burn
D. Fourth-degree burn

Answer: A. First-degree burn

First-degree burns involve superficial damage only, where the epidermis is slightly reddened and painful. Second-degree burns are called partial-thickness burns because they involve the epidermis, dermis, and some of the subcutaneous tissue. Third-degree burns are called full-thickness burns, these injuries are the most serious of the three, involving all skin layers and some muscle and bone.

140. When treating hypoglycemia in the office, what should the medical assistant give the conscious patient?

A. Orange juice
B. Crackers
C. Soda
D. Any of the above

Answer: D. Any of the above

For a conscious patient, give some form of simple sugar, such as hard candy, soda, orange juice, and crackers, and perform a finger-stick blood glucose check. If level persists to be low, give some form of protein, such as milk, peanut butter, or meat. For an unconscious patient, notify the physician and follow orders.

141. Which of the following is NOT a symptom of hyperglycemia, where the blood sugar is above 400 mg/dl?

A. Cold, clammy skin
B. Fruity or sweet odor to breath
C. Drowsiness and fatigue
D. Weak and rapid pulse

Answer: A. Cold, clammy skin

The symptoms of hyperglycemia with a blood sugar above 400 mg/dl include fruity or sweet odor to breath, drowsiness, fatigue, lethargy, disorientation, nausea, vomiting, thirst, and weak and rapid pulse.

142. A patient is having a seizure in the medical office waiting room. After a few seconds, he begins to vomit. What should the medical assistant do?

A. Provide privacy for the patient.
B. Move items from the area around the patient.
C. Move the patient to his side.
D. Assure that the patient's clothing is not affecting circulation.

Answer: D. Move the patient to his side.

The main goal for treatment is to prevent injury to the patient. If a seizure occurs, the medical assistant should move items from the area around the patient, provide privacy to the patient, assure that the patient's clothing is not affecting circulation, monitor for excessive vomiting or saliva, and move the patient to his or her side if this occurs, allow the patient to rest after the seizure is over, and transport the patient to the hospital per physician orders.

143. Which type of shock occurs when vasodilation causes injury to or dysfunction of the neurological system?

A. Hypovolemic shock
B. Anaphylactic shock
C. Neurogenic shock
D. Cardiogenic shock

Answer: C. Neurogenic shock

Hypovolemic shock occurs from a decrease in circulating blood volume, either from hemorrhage, severe burns, or traumatic injury. Anaphylactic shock occurs from an allergic reaction to an allergen. Cardiogenic shock occurs from the heart failing to pump blood adequately, due to myocardial infarction, congestive heart failure, or electrical conduction issues. Neurogenic shock occurs when vasodilation causes injury to or dysfunction of the neurological system.

144. A patient has her blood drawn, gets nauseated, and reports that she feels faint. What is the first thing the medical assistant should do?

A. Apply a cool cloth to the patient's face.
B. Use ammonia to stimulate consciousness.
C. Assist the patient to lie down.
D. Elevate the patient's legs.

Answer: C. Assist the patient to lie down.

First aid measures for syncope include: assist the patient to lie down before fainting occurs, apply a cool cloth to the patient's face or use ammonia to stimulate consciousness, assess the ABCs to assure adequate airway and circulation, monitor the patient's vital signs, elevate the patient's legs higher that the head, keep the patient warm, quiet, and calm, and notify the physician if a prolonged period of unconsciousness continues.

145. Of the following, which is NOT a predisposing factor of heat stroke?

A. Alpha-adrenergic blocker use
B. Obesity
C. High humidity
D. Dehydration

Answer: A. Alpha-adrenergic blocker use

Predisposing factors for heat stroke include beta-adrenergic blockers, obesity, seizures, dehydration, and high humidity.

146. If a patient is allergic to bee stings, he or she will experience:

A. Nausea, vomiting, and loss of consciousness
B. Swelling at the sting site, wheezing, laryngeal edema, deterioration in mental status, and labored rapid breathing
C. Itching, rash, and redness at the sting site
D. All of the above

Answer: B. Swelling at the sting site, wheezing, laryngeal edema, deterioration in mental status, and labored rapid breathing.

147. Which of the following will correct fluid volume deficit?

A. Administration of IV fluids
B. Use of antidiarrheal medications
C. Treatment of electrolyte imbalance
D. All of the above

Answer: D. All of the above

Dehydration is caused by inadequate fluid intake, fluid shifts between compartments, increased fluid loss from perspiration, diarrhea, and ketoacidosis, renal failure, chronic illness, and chronic malnutrition. Fluid volume deficit is corrected by administration of IV fluids, use of antidiarrheal medications, and treatment of the electrolyte imbalance.

148. When over-hydration occurs, the goal of treatment is to:

A. Correct electrolyte imbalances
B. Eliminate the underlying cause of the overload
C. Restore fluid balance
D. All of the above

Answer: D. All of the above

Fluid volume excess occurs from over-hydration, where fluid intake and retention exceeds the body's requirements. The goal of treatment is to correct electrolyte imbalances if present, eliminate the underlying cause of the overload, and restore fluid balance.

149. Which diet is used for patients following surgery when there is difficulty swallowing or chewing solid foods?

A. Clear liquid diet
B. Full liquid diet
C. Mechanically altered diet
D. Soft diet

Answer: B. Full liquid diet

The full liquid diet is used as a transition diet when going from clear liquids to soft or altered foods. Patients are often placed on the full liquid diet following surgery, as well as when there is difficulty swallowing, chewing, or tolerating solid foods. The clear liquid diet consists of fluids and some electrolytes for dehydration prevention. A clear liquid diet is often given to a malnourished patient who has not eaten for some time, but it is not appropriate for patients with swallowing problems. The mechanically altered diet is used when a patient has difficulty chewing and swallowing, but is not used following surgery. The soft diet is used for patients with swallowing or chewing problems, as well as those with ulcerations of the mouth, gums, or throat, but is not used following surgery.

150. People who eat dairy products and eggs, but not animal products and seafood are called:

A. Pesco-vegetarians
B. Lacto-vegetarians
C. Lacto-ovo-vegetarians
D. Vegans

Answer: C. Lacto-ovo-vegetarians

Vegans do not eat any animal products, and many vegetarians eat little or no dairy and animal products. These patients are at risk for deficiencies in vitamins B12, and D, zinc, iron, calcium, protein, and omega-3 fatty acids. Pesco-vegetarians eat seafood but no animal or dairy products. Lacto-vegetarians eat dairy products but no animal products or eggs. Lacto-ovo-vegetarians eat dairy products and eggs, but no animal products or seafood

NOTES
(INTENTIONALLY LEFT BLANK)

NOTES
(INTENTIONALLY LEFT BLANK)

CMA Essential Test Tips DVD from Trivium Test Prep!

Dear Customer,

Thank you for purchasing from Trivium Test Prep! We're honored to help you prepare for your CMA exam.

To show our appreciation, we're offering a **FREE *CMA Essential Test Tips* DVD by Trivium Test Prep**. Our DVD includes 35 test preparation strategies that will make you successful on the CMA. All we ask is that you email us your feedback and describe your experience with our product. Amazing, awful, or just so-so: we want to hear what you have to say!

To receive your **FREE *CMA Essential Test Tips* DVD**, please email us at 5star@triviumtestprep.com. Include "Free 5 Star" in the subject line and the following information in your email:

1. The title of the product you purchased.
2. Your rating from 1 – 5 (with 5 being the best).
3. Your feedback about the product, including how our materials helped you meet your goals and ways in which we can improve our products.
4. Your full name and shipping address so we can send your FREE *CMA Essential Test Tips* DVD.

If you have any questions or concerns please feel free to contact us directly at 5star@triviumtestprep.com.

Thank you!

0585483712